FEAR ITSELF

ALSO BY TAMMY BRUCE

The New Thought Police: Inside the Left's Assault on Free Speech and Free Minds

The Death of Right and Wrong: Exposing the Left's Assault on Our Culture and Values

The New American Revolution: Using the Power of the Individual to Save Our Nation from Extremists

FEAR ITSELF

Exposing the Left's Mind-Killing Agenda

TAMMY BRUCE

BROADSIDE BOOKS

HarperCollins books may be purchased for educational, business, or sales promotional use. For information, please email the Special Markets Department at SPsales@harpercollins.com.

Dedication photograph by Xanthe Elbrick

FIRST EDITION

Designed by Michele Cameron

Library of Congress Cataloging-in-Publication Data
Names: Bruce, Tammy, author.

Title: Fear itself : exposing the left's mind-killing agenda / Tammy Bruce.

Identifiers: LCCN 2024001365 (print) | LCCN 2024001366 (ebook) | ISBN 9780063228528 (hardcover) | ISBN 9780063228535 (ebook)

Subjects: LCSH: Fear—Political aspects—United States. | Political psychology—United States. | Communication in politics—United States. | Right and left (Political science)—United States. | Individualism—United States. | United States—Politics and government—Psychological aspects.

Classification: LCC JA74.5 .B78 2024 (print) | LCC JA74.5 (ebook) | DDC 320.97301/4—dc23/eng/20240207

LC record available at https://lccn.loc.gov/2024001365

LC ebook record available at https://lccn.loc.gov/2024001366

24 25 26 27 28 LBC 5 4 3 2 1

FOR SYDNEY

who taught me about unconditional love
and the power of fearlessness

I must not fear. Fear is the mind-killer. Fear is the little-death that brings total obliteration. I will face my fear. I will permit it to pass over me and through me. And when it has gone past I will turn the inner eye to see its path. Where the fear has gone there will be nothing. Only I will remain.

—FRANK HERBERT, *DUNE*

CONTENTS

INTRODUCTION

Something's Not Right

"Something's not right." I've said that to myself many times in the last few troubling and tumultuous years. I bet you have as well.

It's a plaintive remark, made as we connect the dots between the abnormal cultural and political dumpster fires erupting all around us. It's also an acknowledgment that left-wing bullies who fancy themselves social and political Masters of the Universe have weaponized fear in a sinister effort to control us. They want to frighten us into cowering in the corner, so we let them restructure our society and dictate a new set of core beliefs they demand we embrace, confirming their imagined superiority in all things. They even demand we change how we speak and write language so they can change the way we think.

The frenetic manipulation of communication, language, media, education, and politics by leftists in this country has gone on for so long and is now so embedded in the socioeconomic machine that no matter when you read this, I know you will be in the midst of an orchestrated effort to control your sense of reality. Whether it be war, a crime epidemic, a plague, civil strife, economic chaos, mental health crises, drug abuse, food and energy scarcity, or the always reliable "climate change emergency," the system of government, media, big business, and education will be constantly at work keeping you afraid, unsure, exhausted, and living paycheck to paycheck.

With the book's title, at first blush you might understandably think it's about a large political and cultural issue—the impact of fear on society. And you're right, but it's also a very personal issue. Fear is a psychological tactic discussed, contemplated, and implemented for thousands of years by grifters, sophists, politicians, tyrants, and other unsavory characters bent on control and power. This book is about all that, but only in part. What my research and experience reveal, and what I share with you in the pages that follow, is that for Marxists and their leftist wingmen, inducing fear is the tactic with which to achieve their ultimate *personal* goal—**killing your mind**. Fear is supposed to be transitory. Killing your mind is forever.

Our main epigraph perfectly illustrates this understanding. Frank Herbert's classic 1965 American science fiction novel *Dune*, like many of the novels you'll see referenced in the following chapters, presents some of humanity's most pressing philosophical and political issues using the immensely powerful literary mechanism of science fiction or fantasy. The use and impact of fear was not a new concern appearing in mid-twentieth century literature, but an ancient and primordial tool used against those who threaten the status quo by those who pathologically guard their power and control. For writers who experienced the scourge of World War II and the advance of fascism, exposing the weaponizing of fear became urgent. As it now is for us as we approach the end of the first quarter of the twenty-first century.

If they can keep you in an unthinking fear loop, they can stop you from questioning or confronting them about the damage they heap onto society. There is one necessary component for the left's agenda to be successful—the annihilation of the ordinary person's personal courage—the trait required to withstand danger and fear. When courage is lost, with it goes the willingness to confront the powerful and malevolent.

It is this conjuring of ancient, mindless fear that tyrants have perfected through millennia, propelling us into actions and decision-making based on emotion, absent the mediators of logic and reason. It is not about distracting us with frightening event after frightening event but indoctrinating us into a perpetual fear-based "new normal." It's an exhausting state, creating anxiety, paranoia, and with it a retreat from social and political life. The goal of killing our minds, turning us into fear-driven automatons lacking confidence and courage, willing to bow and conform, is the putrid soup served up by the Marxists, tyrants, bullies, and bureaucracies, preferring that all of us stay out of their way.

The deliberate strategy of using fear as a weapon of control dates back to ancient times, but modern communications and other technological tools give the fearmongers power unimaginable in years past. Marxists, bullies, and malignant narcissists occupying positions of power throughout our governmental and cultural infrastructure are using fear to distract, depress, isolate, and mentally disarm us. And sadly, they're succeeding.

But I have a secret for you, and this book will reveal it in great detail—the left is weak, and they know it. Their only hope for success is keeping you distracted and too afraid to look up. Having once been on the left, I can tell you that every ounce of so-called progressive energy is spent on keeping us manipulated, brainwashed, and afraid. Every day, every project, every action is required to maintain the fraud of this leftist fearmongering. Killing our minds is the singular goal for the left, and it's a 24/7 effort.

You may read this and think: That's not me. I'm not afraid. However, you have friends or family who are like this. They are probably longtime Democrats, and you have watched them move from classically liberal to seeing everything through a haze of hysterical, apocalyptic talking points.

Progressives are desperate for us to believe that we are the problem, that America is the problem, and most of all, that any and all dissent from their orthodoxy must be quashed. Why? Because leftist ideology is a house of cards; the only way to maintain it is to either imprison their opposition, or, at the very least, imprison the minds of those who object.

The answer to our dilemma starts with understanding that fear itself is natural, but *weaponizing fear* is an unnatural construct; that fear is a constantly used tool to specifically keep us from inquiring or questioning. It is a method that is so refined and has been used for so long that being constantly afraid in various degrees feels natural and normal—but it's not. Killing our minds—creating such despair through fear that we abandon any sense of hope, passion, or drive to be involved in the course of our lives—is not an easy thing to do. The plan is weakened the moment we become aware of the agenda and the tactics involved, making us immediately less vulnerable to the fearmongering meant to start our spiral into anxiety and confusion.

We are seen by the bureaucratic state as pawns to be kept poor, ignorant, and afraid. Our overcoming this assault starts with information, and it starts now. By the end of this book, it will be clear to you how we can and will overcome this modern catastrophe of the Marxist state in America.

The catastrophic reaction by our government and the left-wing media in response to the COVID-19 pandemic illustrates my central argument. Excited and self-obsessed, the progressive establishment demanded we sacrifice our freedom, our decency, and sometimes even our lives to validate their sense of self-importance. The bureaucratic excitement was palpable. A global "emergency" would be their ticket to speed along the quelling of populations who, in their rotted worldview, were too ignorant to know what was good for them. These tiny tyrants were wrong, as they often are.

Then their masks came off, and many of them partied, traveled, and dined out as they mandated masks and lockdowns for everyone else. Any semblance of reasoned governing evaporated as the suit-wearing malignant narcissists running our country and many other nations decided this was the turning point to implement fear using every available method possible. How far could they push us? What idiotic rules could they impose? By drowning us in fear and turning us against each other, how many minds could they kill, how much power could they grab?

The catastrophe of the pandemic was not just the virus itself that claimed millions of lives around the world, but also the orgy of fear, abuse, punishment, and deadly decisions the establishment class inflicted on the rest of us. The economy was shredded, the education of children suffered with the closure of schools, small businesses closed forever, and loved ones died alone in hospitals. Thousands of infirm Americans were killed[1,2,3] when some governors shockingly ordered people infected with

COVID to be moved into the most vulnerable environment of them all—nursing homes.[4,5]

Some politicians and bureaucrats are now, ironically, telling us they lost *their* minds during the height of the pandemic because they were too concerned and simply made mistakes. Some are suggesting we should forgive and forget.[6] Their excuses sound much like the sentiment former football star O. J. Simpson expressed as he leaned over his murdered ex-wife's casket at her funeral and whispered: "I loved you too much . . . that was my problem . . . I loved you too much."[7] Simpson was eventually found responsible by a civil jury for killing both Nicole Brown Simpson and her friend Ron Goldman in 1994, in an all-too-familiar domestic abuse outcome. The disgraced former football star died of cancer in 2024.

Much like a person being targeted every day by a violent, irrational, and pathological spouse, we are in the midst of a wholly unnatural and calculated circus of fear, anxiety, and control. In our case, it is implemented not just by one person who desires to control our lives but by a cadre of politicians, bureaucrats, journalists, and establishment lackeys appointing themselves experts, champions, leaders, leftist social justice warriors, and even, as Dr. Anthony Fauci once claimed, the human embodiment of science itself.[8] With Marxism needing a makeover, they've even given themselves the positive-sounding name "progressives," as if anyone opposed to their malevolent ideology is opposed to progress and wants to drag society backward into a less enlightened and less compassionate time.

The tactics of abusive government and the techniques unleashed in domestic violence are almost identical. *Psychology Today* details the means batterers use as they target their partners. See if any of this strikes you as familiar:

> Abusers make their victims doubt what they know and establish the terms of reality to make their behavior seem acceptable or normal. Some tactics that abusers employ include isolating victims socially, restricting access to information, and enforcing rules with punishments. An abuser's mind control is powerful and grounded in social forces, making it challenging for victims to leave an abusive relationship.[9]

Domestic abusers use mind control, gaslighting, language shifts, and threats to personal economic and social safety to gain complete and unchallenged control of the lives of their victims. Abusers in control of government and other dominant institutions in our society do the same thing on a massive scale as they seek to dominate us all. They isolate us socially, lecture us about how we are irredeemably racist or bigoted, and tell us we are destroying the environment and threatening the extinction of all life on Earth. They criminalize thoughts and speech, censoring information and media outlets that dare to expose the truth or allow us to have a voice. They fire people for having the wrong opinion, and socially shun those who don't accept their "politically correct" ideological diktats.

As the rules dictated by progressives become more absurd, and the dangers associated with challenging the status quo become existential, the left anticipates the average person will naturally retreat. We are to surrender not just from public life, but from caring about the country and what our survival means for the world. Killing our minds is the only way their backward and deadly progressivism can survive.

The October 7, 2023, massacre of Israelis by the Hamas terrorist group, when over 1,400 civilians were murdered in horrific ways, thousands wounded, and hundreds taken hostage, all videotaped to be shared around the world,[10] was meant to frighten all of humanity, and to inspire psychopaths.

Like a well-oiled machine that had been switched on, immediately after the carnage thousands of people were demonstrating and marching at universities and in the streets in the centers of Western civilization—including New York; Washington, DC; London; Paris; Madrid; Rome; Sydney, in support of . . . Hamas terrorists. These displays included openly chanting "gas the Jews,"[11] to assaulting, harassing, threatening, and chasing Jewish bystanders, students, and anyone else who displayed or voiced support for Israel or the Jewish people.[12, 13, 14]

These obscene spectacles were spawned by the left's success at dividing Americans against each other by race, and the brainwashing of their acolytes (conveniently through universities), implementing the cancer of Marxism's Critical Race Theory (CRT) to poison our society with a zero-sum game of oppressed versus oppressors. This dynamic was made-to-order for Jew-hating Islamists who were likely thrilled with how easy it was to fold the Jews in with everyone else condemned as "colonists" and "oppressors." Suddenly, terrorizing Jews throughout the United States and worldwide became freedom fighting within the progressive infrastructure.

Brainwashing people into believing that millions of other human beings—their neighbors, friends, family, coworkers—are a stain on humanity because of an immutable characteristic requires mind-killing. Logic, reason, and rationality have to be abandoned in order to operate on such a medieval level. It is the instilling of this degree of fear and envy that unlocks the door to loathing.

History is full of genocides made possible because one group was brainwashed into believing another group was "irredeemable" and dangerous. Once "whiteness,"[15] a deliberately malleable term, is demonized and condemned, the next trick is declaring all critics and political opponents as "white" (regardless of their race or ethnicity) because they have the same conceptual "privilege" or are in league with people who happen to be white.[16] It's madness, of course, but the twentieth century is a showcase of that barbarity, with the twenty-first century beginning to give it a run for its money.

After decades of professors inculcating students with the Marxist theory that, as a matter of social justice principle, white people can and should be hated, what has followed is not surprising. The fruit of that poisonous tree has obscenely manifested as open marches declaring solidarity and support for a psychopathic terrorist group's savage attack on Jewish people—including babies, women, the disabled, and the elderly.

Whether it is terrorism, war, crime, or civil strife, political rhetoric is meant to frighten everyone into compliance with whatever the latest emergency decree might be, or to be foot soldiers of envy and hate spreading more suffering, oppression, and fear. Either way, the social derangement continues, as the lives of average people are destroyed, individual freedom is quashed, and politicians become even more wealthy and powerful.

In the past, we have been able to rely on American values to keep our country from falling into that disgusting and nihilistic Old World inclination toward fascism and genocide. But alarmingly, surveys do indicate an unusual and dangerous recent retreat by the American people from the values that have made our country the greatest on Earth.

According to a 2023 *Wall Street Journal*/National Opinion Research Center survey, dwindling numbers of Americans are embracing the values of patriotism, religion, and community involvement. The *New York Post* reports that the survey found that only "38% of Americans say patriotism is 'very important' to them, down from 70% who said the same in 1998. Slightly more Americans (39%) placed the same importance on religion, down from 62% who said faith was 'very important' to them 25 years ago. The percentage of Americans who said raising children was 'very important' fell to 30% in the new poll, down from 59% in 1998. Meanwhile, the share of Americans who valued involvement in their community as 'very important' fell to 27%—down from a high of 62% in 2019, the last time the question was polled."[17]

"Social justice" activists must love this poll. The goal is to convince people all institutions and systems are corrupt. Only wholesale social engineering by a government rebuilt from the ground up can fix problems this big, they insist. As people lose hope they retreat. That's the impact of a generation of Americans emerging from schools that have become Marxist indoctrination camps. Children are being taught that the traditional values of their parents and grandparents are bigoted and as outdated as horse-drawn carriages and the telegraph. The brave souls who dare stand up to progressive dogma are being denounced, canceled, and demonized by the left.

Our situation is so dire that even the *New York Times,* choosing to ignore its own role as the Democratic Party's woke stenographer-in-chief dutifully debasing the American potential, published an editorial in 2022 headlined "America Has a Free Speech Problem." They lamented:

> For all the tolerance and enlightenment that modern society claims, Americans are losing hold of a fundamental right as

> citizens of a free country: the right to speak their minds and voice their opinions in public without fear of being shamed or shunned. This social silencing, this depluralizing of America, has been evident for years, but dealing with it stirs yet more fear. It feels like a third rail, dangerous. For a strong nation and open society, that *is* dangerous.[18]

You don't say!

Moreover, in 2020—as we were enduring the Black Lives Matter/Antifa summer of riots—the Cato Institute found only members of the far left felt free to express their political opinions without fear of repercussions. In a national survey of two thousand Americans, Cato found that "62 percent of Americans say the political climate these days prevents them from saying what they believe because others might find it offensive." Further, the fear of what will happen if you speak up is nonpartisan, as "majorities of Democrats (52 percent), Independents (59 percent), and Republicans (77 percent) all agree they have political views they are afraid to share . . . large majorities or near majorities of people across race, sex, and income all feel like they can't say what they believe. That means this effect is not simply concentrated in one identity group, but pervasive across all."[19]

Most Americans, including Democrats, don't want what progressives are selling. The left has been able to capture control of the Democratic Party because the classical liberals in that party are conditioned by the environment of fear as much as everyone else. And perhaps they were taken by surprise. That's what gaslighting will do to you. Being afraid to speak up allows bullies and thugs to prevail. Self-censorship is not necessarily due to the fear of offending, per se; our history is one of great debate and new ideas. But being canceled—losing one's job or becoming a target of threats and violence—is a steep new price to pay.

We are inundated with slogans and indoctrinated with the Marxist doublespeak of the new woke ideology, as illustrated by the cancerous spread of Diversity, Equity, and Inclusion (DEI) in schools, government, and the private sector. Propaganda in schools and the left-wing media targets us and our children, weaponizing social issues involving sex and race to deliberately cause a cleaving of children from their parents.

The left's deception is designed to inculcate all of us with lies meant to destroy our trust in ourselves, our families, and communities. The goal of all this is to further social divisions, paranoia, and ultimately a retreat from social and political life. The worst case has already been glimpsed, as riots, mob violence, arson, racist hate crimes, and open support of terrorism against the Jewish people are a few examples of the destruction of our social fabric.

Make no mistake—what we are all experiencing isn't a "new normal" or the result of some natural process that mysteriously creates this chaos. We are experiencing the Marxist agenda in full swing. For the past several years, the average American has been fed a pack of leftist lies, including false claims that:

- All white people, our system of government, schools, capitalism, and all other aspects of American society are—and always will be—systemically and irredeemably racist.
- Concerned and politically active parents who support conservative values and causes are "threats to democracy" and domestic terrorists. Agents of the state are better able than parents to raise children.
- The Russian government was so desperate for Trump to be president that they tried to fix the 2016 election and planted a fake Hunter Biden laptop in 2020.
- Rioting, looting, and burning down businesses, homes, and government offices in American cities by social justice warriors qualifies as "mostly peaceful protests."
- Looting is reparations for the oppressed.
- Speech that contradicts the leftist narrative is violence and must be punished.
- Academic meritocracy and standardized academic tests are racist and unfair.
- Those who challenge or question the leftist narrative must be excised from public life.

One of the most disturbing aspects of the leftist worldview is the demand that we be judged not as individuals, but by our various group identities—skin color, gender, sexual orientation, religion (or lack thereof), ethnicity, political beliefs, and on and on. You are not you. You have a share of group rights, but no individual rights. Hence the obsession with "equity"—proportional representation of every group in every area of endeavor.

Dr. Martin Luther King Jr. had a very different, and powerful, message calling for the celebration of the individual transcending what we now know as the scourge of identity politics, in his transformative 1963 "I Have a Dream" speech: "I have a dream that my four little children will one day live in a nation where they will not be judged by the color of their skin but by the content of their character."[20] Woke and identity politics, and the racism on which they rely, are also the antithesis of the ideals that animated America's founders when they approved our Constitution.

Considered discretely, each of the fear tactics being employed by the progressive establishment and its handmaidens in the media, business, and academia might be considered an irritation that can be overcome. But taken collectively and dished out day after day against an unsuspecting population, the result is the slow cooking of the minds and souls of the American people.

The victory of the radical left and the triumph of fear over reason, group entitlements over individual rights, and lies over truth are not inevitable. We can fight and win the battle for the American soul and America's future if we understand the challenges we face and how to overcome them. I wrote this book to help guide you, my fellow Americans, in this vital task.

I said earlier I have a secret for you. Actually, I have two, both of which are revealed in this book. Our way to victory over the heinous forces working to destroy our nation starts with us but is different than what you have been told in the past. This book provides you with *knowledge* that is kryptonite for the left. The first step—knowing the history, strategy, and details fueling the left's assault on our country and our futures—sweeps aside the carefully constructed but false curtain of lies and fear. The first step in getting a loved one out of an abusive relationship is letting them know that you know they are in crisis. Admitting what is happening is empowering, and knowing you are not alone is vital as it unlocks the desire and ability to confront what's happening.

Your second step, I discuss at the end. It is personal and powerful, and it is the thing that most terrifies the left here at home and around the world. It is an inspirational and transformative act we each have in our toolbox for life—*courage*. This is the thing the left and their disciples work to crush in each of us every single day. We can find safety in numbers, but for those of us who have been overcome by it, what I also know is that fear is a weak state, weak enough that it is a constant occupation of the left to maintain its influence on us.

For us, or those in our lives who seem lost and think turning to extremes is the answer, our influence can make the difference. The good news is that it takes very little to crush fear's control over us; something as simple as looking up, noticing, being aware of our environment. Choosing to take control of how we perceive and interact with events, situations, and even the rhetoric of others can change everything.

In the aftermath of World War II and the development of the nuclear bomb, C. S. Lewis addressed the concern of many in the public about the new threats to life, peace, and safety human beings face. Like most of what Lewis wrote, it is prescient and serves us as well in the twenty-first century as it did his readers in 1948:

> What the wars and the weather (are we in for another of those periodic ice ages?) and the atomic bomb have really done is to remind us forcibly of the sort of world we are living in and which, during the prosperous period before 1914, we were beginning to forget. And this reminder is, so far as it goes, a good thing. We have been waked from a pretty dream, and now we can begin to talk about realities.[21]

So let us awaken, turn the page, talk about reality, influence and encourage our friends, and make a difference for ourselves and others by looking up and regaining our minds!

FEAR ITSELF

CHAPTER 1

The Terrible, Obscure Bioweapon

To make anything very terrible, obscurity seems in general to be necessary. When we know the full extent of any danger, when we can accustom our eyes to it, a great deal of the apprehension vanishes. . . . Those despotic governments, which are founded on the passions of men, and principally upon the passion of fear, keep their chief as much as may be from the public eye.

—EDMUND BURKE[1]

The eighteenth-century Irish statesman and philosopher Edmund Burke reminds us that tyrants know they can't control us completely by themselves; they rely on invisible hazards allowing the dirty work to be accomplished by our own imaginations, expanding on the fear of the threat exponentially.

We've all experienced fear, the emotion of self-preservation that keeps us alive but that can also scare us into irrationality and inaction. Fear sits at the core of our instinctual mind and at the forefront of our everyday lives. It is as familiar to us as love, just as confusing, and just as important. It can be both a gift and a curse.

This book is about fear and how it has been weaponized by today's unrecognizable Democratic Party, the left, and their sycophants in the self-obsessed progressive media to crush your spirit, fill you with self-doubt, and convince you to give up control of your life. It's time to expose, explain, and debunk this foundational strategy driving the reprobate "progressive" agenda. Read on, and you will see how we can conquer what President Franklin D. Roosevelt called "nameless, unreasoning, unjustified terror which paralyzes needed efforts to convert retreat into advance."[2] Roosevelt spoke in his first inaugural address as America was gripped by fear in the depths of the Great Depression. Today, we are gripped by fear of a different sort, a depression of the soul amplified by a Democratic Party that is very different from the one Roosevelt led. While fear can be a natural ally, we have seen it manipulated as a bioweapon designed by the progressive bureaucratic establishment. It is now everywhere, serving as a controlling foot soldier for a political machine contemptible of the citizen and incapable of empathy or functional leadership.

For generations, we have all been targeted by the political and attendant cultural establishments to ensure that fear controls our minds. The schemes and agendas put forth by the entrenched political establishment are designed to keep us ignorant, anxious, and feeling unable to control the present and future. The leftist elite want us to feel helpless and hopeless and dependent on Big Government to tell us what to do and how to do it to solve our problems. I am determined to help us smash that plan.

Make no mistake: there are legitimate and frightening crises and events deserving of our attention, concern, and action. This book exposes how the powerful exploit our natural and beneficial emotional reactions for the political benefit of the ruling class.

The manufactured climate change hysteria is a perfect example. It encompasses an issue we all care about—a healthy environment—and weaponizes it as a vague, changeable, and frighteningly massive threat requiring us, through intimidation and government edict, to dramatically alter the way society operates and how we live our lives. It can be molded into whatever the powers that be want it to be at any given moment. Most ominously, its framing as an issue relies on injecting into each one of us the lie that our very existence—*your* existence—is the problem.

Dissent from progressive "truth" is deemed heresy. With climate change, the left tells us that "settled science" dictates that we must end the use of fossil fuels and throw everyone in the oil, gas, and coal industries out of work; stop eating meat and devastate the agricultural economy; destroy tens of thousands of acres of land to generate unreliable and costly solar and wind energy; and raise taxes sky-high to fund a *multitrillion-dollar* transformation of our entire economy.

In the children's story, Chicken Little screams out, "The sky is falling, the sky is falling!" when an acorn lands on her head. In today's world, progressives scream just as hysterically that life on Earth is ending. If you disagree, in the view of the left, that makes you an evil and ignorant corporate stooge who denies reality and wants to see life on Earth destroyed.

Much to the frustration of the left, neither failed Democratic presidential candidates Al Gore and John Kerry, nor Climate Kid Greta Thunberg, compelled us to surrender.

The use of fear is designed to make us afraid to speak our minds about the political issues of the day and about changing cultural standards because we might lose our jobs or be shunned by leftists controlling Big Tech, academia, and business. Like Russian nesting dolls, these civil institutions are also captive within the larger schema with another brand of fear meant just for them and controlling those mechanisms of power.

The Few Gaslighting the Many

The key here is that few people are managing this effort—and it is a managed effort—using a form of psychological warfare to degrade our confidence, pride, and optimism about America, its history, and its future. That, you see, is the only way the left can win, by tearing down our people and customs because America's greatness depends on the greatness and confidence of our people. The majority of us don't agree with the far left agenda.[3, 4, 5] And the farther left the agenda goes, the more Americans see the scheme for the fraud it is. "Progressives" (a laughably absurd euphemism) have not persuaded and cannot persuade the American people to accept a suicidal level of social engineering, so all they have is smoke, mirrors, and a few people strategically placed throughout our institutions implementing the most complex gaslighting in human history.

You hear many references to "gaslighting" these days. It is an apt colloquialism brought to us by the classic film, 1944's *Gaslight*.[6, 7] In the movie, Ingrid Bergman's character is victimized by her husband, who manipulates her environment to make her think she is losing her mind so he can control her and her inheritance. In our case, gaslighting is a form of abuse and manipulation being used by the left as part of its effort to convince you you're something you're not—subconsciously racist, for example—while making you question your confidence, sense of self, and reality to the point where your denial is said to be proof you're guilty of the accusation du jour. Manipulating us in this way relies, in part, on our fear of abandonment, fear of loss, fear of not pleasing others, or fear of not fitting in. This book will discuss the gaslighting technique in detail and tell you how to protect yourself against it by recognizing the signs, being consciously aware as it is happening, and immunizing yourself from its intended effects.

Gaslighting allows bureaucrats to dictate everything from the smallest details of our lives to massive government spending that facilitates the associated development of an even more controlling bureaucracy. All the while, we are told such government excesses and erosions of our freedom are really designed to save us from our poor, unsure, gaslit selves.

Their argument is always that they know better. They understand what's happening. The rest of us don't have the capacity, education, or basic ability to function in the manner required by these gaslighters of government and society. Contempt for us is a necessary part of this malevolent agenda. In the following pages, this repulsive tactic, and those who implement it, will be exposed in detail and debunked entirely.

I'm here to tell you that our progressive would-be overlords will fail. By exposing their methods and intentions, this book will give you the information and power you need to crush the fraud of the forces determined to punk you into retreat, convinced that they can scare you into surrender. They're wrong, and my goal is to make sure you'll know exactly how to stop this charade of wokesters, fraudsters, the disturbed, and the craven.

A Tantrum of the Disturbed

Part of this book's mission is to expose the contrived and deliberate nature of the "social disturbances" we have suffered from for years, such as the riots following the George Floyd murder, not as organic but rather as calculated efforts by the American left, and its handmaiden, the Democratic Party. It's understandable to mistake what's happening in general to the country as a side effect of the woke agenda. But it is much larger than that, with "wokeness" being but one thread focused on making millions of Americans afraid to speak candidly about politics and culture. It is the cancerous result of what started as "political correctness," the first step in an indoctrination strategy meant to make nonconforming speech a crime.

Wokeness is just one front in the war against American culture, society, free markets, classic liberalism, and personal freedom. As those on the left are exposed as frauds and abusers, the last weapon they have available is to crush the country through psychological warfare and direct violence—a tantrum of the disturbed.

In the following pages, I will show you how all the leftist absurdity we see consuming American campuses, which we mistakenly thought was a phase and would at least be contained in the academy, was vomited out into society. With the election of Donald Trump, an axis of the academies, Big Business (including Big Tech and media), and government realized the American people had not been neutered. The overclass has not yet rendered the "little people" helpless. Since we had not succumbed to the left's earlier attempts to break us, a new, unforgiving blitz of punishment would have to begin.

In the eyes of the left, the biggest "crime" of all was committed by the American people when we handed the White House to Donald Trump and the whole of Congress to the GOP in 2016.

The progressive, enlightened class failed to convince Americans to hate themselves as racists, sexists, homophobes, and deplorables through fear and intimidation. As a result, they falsely indicted the nation as irredeemably evil by condemning law enforcement, unleashing direct violence in the name of "racial justice," and attacking cultural icons. The goal was to gaslight Americans into hating each other through fear and suspicion, and to see each other as members of Balkanized groups rather than as individuals. Americans were also condemned for "microaggressions" that were invisible to all but the most woke among us.

On top of this, woke and whiny college students would demand "safe spaces" to protect their oh-so-delicate sensibilities from the marketplace of ideas, and colleges would cave to their absurd and infantile demands by barring speakers from campus and books from courses that dared challenge the progressive dogma, while firing professors who dare to challenge the leftist status quo or simply do not comply with absurd woke rules.[8] In the process, schools and colleges have been transformed from places of learning into leftist indoctrination camps.

Meanwhile, the Black Lives Matter group advances its Marxist and anti-American agenda by hectoring us with accusations of racism that have become a staple in their fear-porn theater. We are told that if you are not black, you must be a racist, that our nation is "systemically racist" and irredeemable, and that America's founders were racists who fought the Revolutionary War to preserve slavery. We are also told we must atone for the genuinely evil institution of slavery that ended before most of our great-grandparents were born, and before the ancestors of some of us had even come to America. And Black Lives Matter and other leftist agitators tell us our government must pay trillions of dollars in reparations to the descendants of slaves.[9] Raise objections to any of this and you'll be asked why you haven't dealt with your own internalized racism.

If that's not enough to make you concerned about the future, we've seen marches protesting racism turn into riots in America's great cities, burning businesses and homes and leaving some people injured and dead. Many of the victims of this rioting were black, but somehow, their lives and livelihoods did not matter. Antifa, the fascist gang absurdly insisting they're not the fascists, joined in with the rioting, along with physical attacks on police, members of the media, and innocent bystanders. Weapons of choice included balloons filled with urine, and "milk shakes" of wet cement thrown into people's faces. How progressive!

Next up in the fear porn parade—the Democrats' "Defund the Police" movement. With riots and groups of disturbed and violent anarchists wandering through American cities and neighborhoods like something out of a horror movie, demonizing law enforcement is the next logical way to throw more gasoline on the fire of the contrived civil unrest.

This is a strategy we will see repeated: teach people to fear the problem *and* the solution. Then, there is nowhere to run to but unparalleled change. It removes any sense of security for the millions of law-abiding citizens of all races and ethnicities in lawless Democratic cities, and spreads fear throughout the nation watching the mayhem on TV.

The academy also retched onto society "Critical Race Theory." Initially started as a "movement" at ultraprogressive Harvard in the 1980s and then spreading among law schools around the country as an academic discipline,[10] the scourge is now one of the left's favorite weapons. It targets everyone from children in elementary schools to our military to Fortune 500 companies with race guilt, judgment, and condemnation.[11] Serving the core of the left's fear agenda, Critical Race Theory encourages and conditions people to judge and rank others by the color of their skin. Those on the left apparently do not know the definition of irony, so they believe combatting racism with more racism makes absolute sense. I don't know about you, but every now and then I expect to see Rod Serling walk around the corner, confirming we've crossed over into the Twilight Zone.

To those of us in the real world, none of this makes sense. But it does make us afraid, as it strikes at the core of foundational values and principles a free nation relies upon—free speech, law and order, due process, safety, comity, goodwill, and fairness. This and so much more is bearing down on the American polity like a punishment. And that's because it is.

This book's mission is to make it clear, on all these issues and more facing you, your family, and your friends, that you have not lost your minds. The threat of a crumbling civilized society you are witnessing is not normal or inevitable. There is, indeed, a method to the very serious madness consuming the people running our government, our schools and colleges, the left-wing media, and Big Tech. And it's a madness we can expose and defeat.

Fear in the Minds of Men, Then and Now

Progressives seem strangely but deliberately determined to frighten us into submission by using whatever "good crisis" presents itself. And if they can't find a crisis, they'll manufacture it.

Consider Democrat Rahm Emanuel, the former senior adviser to President Bill Clinton, congressman, chief of staff for President Barack Obama, and mayor of Chicago. In November 2008, just after the presidential election, Emanuel said the quiet thing out loud when he spoke at a business conference, just as the severity of the nation's financial collapse was becoming clear. The *Wall Street Journal* reported on his comments at the time:

> "The thing about a crisis—and crisis doesn't seem too strong a word for the economic mess right now—is that it creates a sense of urgency. . . ." This opportunity isn't lost on the new president and his team. "You never want a serious crisis to go to waste," Rahm Emanuel, Mr. Obama's new chief of staff, told a *Wall Street Journal* conference of top corporate chief executives this week. He elaborated: "Things that we had postponed for too long, that were long-term, are now immediate and must be dealt with. This crisis provides the opportunity for us to do things that you could not do before."[12]

Why would a crisis destroying people's lives be considered an opportunity by cynical politicians? Citizens are rightly skeptical of the government trying things they haven't tried before, especially on an enormous, disruptive scale. However, a crisis fosters fear, and enough fear will overcome that skepticism about huge social engineering projects. In other words, fear short-circuits your brain.[13]

Fear is an extensively studied emotion—not just the psychological aspect, but also the physiological changes it causes to the brain itself.[14] Discussing how fear and terror "hijack" the brain, Dr. Bruce Perry of the ChildTrauma Academy explains, "When people are terrorized, the smartest parts of our brain tend to shut down," directly changing the way we think.[15]

Moreover, Dr. Eric Hollander, professor of psychiatry at Montefiore/Albert Einstein College of Medicine in New York City, tells us that normally we "evaluate situations in a logical and conscious fashion and [consider] the risks and benefits of different behaviors—that gets short-circuited"[16] when faced with a frightening situation. When the brain is trying to process information while also dealing with an emotional state like fear, "problem solving becomes more categorical, concrete and emotional [and] we become more vulnerable to reactive and short-sighted solutions."[17] You've probably heard the expression "scared out of my wits." It's an accurate description of how fear can overpower our intelligence.

No wonder politicians never want to "let a good crisis go to waste." They know their disastrous policies only have a chance when Americans have had their brains short-circuited. The progressive establishment needs people to be psychologically vulnerable and illogical. If terrifying you gets them what they want, then so be it. Whatever it takes.

The circumstances of this hijacking of our minds are not normal, organic, or new. Philosophers from the ancients to the modern age have contemplated the power of fear, many with a focus on how humanity can overcome fear's nefarious impact on our thinking. Others saw opportunities to use fear as a psychological bioweapon with which to gain and wield power.[18]

From the ancient to the modern world—from Plato and Aristotle, to Marcus Aurelius, Niccolò Machiavelli, Thomas Hobbes, John Locke, and Edmund Burke—fear has fascinated philosophers trying to understand the human condition.

In 1532, Machiavelli "elevated fear to a fundamental principle of politics. In his treatise, *The Prince,* he advised that a political leader should learn how to inspire fear in his subjects. Fear allows political authorities to consolidate their power. . . ."[19] Moreover, "Machiavelli steadfastly insists that violence and cruelty are necessary means of effective political action."[20]

Yet it is Hobbes's view that seems most germane for our investigation, as his most influential work, *Leviathan*, in 1651 describes the establishment of a modern secular state, led by an all-powerful sovereign using fear as the legitimate option to "prevent social unrest."[21] He "recognized fear as a cornerstone of an inherently artificial political order. Such order helped transform individual fears into collective ones. Presented with a choice between fear [as delivered by the uncontrolled and terrorizing state of nature] and subjugation [fear chosen by and controlled by the state], Hobbes was sure people would prefer the second."[22]

In the past, governments created fear *of the government* in order to get the population to obey. Modern governments have figured out how to create fear over everything else to get the population to obey.

This can also be done by creating fear from "outside" the government. Today's political elite rely on academics and their assorted musings when considering policy and how to implement their agendas. However, there is a revolving door of people moving from government to media to universities and back again, resulting in a hellish merry-go-round that makes collusion and groupthink easier and even natural. It also allows a philosophy meant for debate and contemplation in a university seminar to be mistaken as a prescriptive to be implemented upon actual human beings.

The problem for modern politicians, and their Marxist sycophants who are inspired by Hobbes's philosophy, is that his premise relies on a contrived "state of nature" as the catalyst for the legitimacy of a state ruled by managed fear. "Life in the state of nature is characterized by insecurity where human behavior is dominated by the instinct of self-preservation . . . when individuals need to defend themselves against others, there is no pleasure in life. . . . Life is short, there is no society that can protect the individual, and violent death is frequent as crime is rife."[23]

Hobbes's seventeenth-century philosophic view of social and civil chaos very well might be mistaken by today's self-important malcontents as an actual prescription for the method with which to convince human beings to willingly submit to totalitarian terror. Setting cities on fire, condemning people for their rational and reasonable ideas and speech, defunding the police, and allowing violent criminals to roam free—while placing citizens in a position of having to constantly defend themselves literally and figuratively—presents an all-encompassing disorder that true believers relish as a necessary step to progress.

Fortunately for us, Hobbes was not a historian but a philosopher. The American people have the benefit of history to know the failure of revolutions emerging from the academy, and the rot of ideas like Marxism that is the foundation of communism and socialism.

Fear Itself

There is no single concept of fear all disciplines agree on.[24] This book focuses on the common sense understanding of the emotion, since that is what public and private tyrants of the past and the present have relied on to control people and gain power over them.

The *Oxford English Dictionary* defines fear as: "The emotion of pain or uneasiness caused by the sense of impending danger, or by the prospect of some possible evil. Now the general term for all degrees of the emotion; in early use applied to its more violent extremes, now denoted by *alarm, terror, fright, dread*. In 14th cent. sometimes pleonastically dread and fear."[25]

Edmund Burke, who is considered the father of classical conservatism, described fear as "the strongest emotion which the mind is capable of feeling."[26] On the issue of tyranny and despotic governments, his definition of fear explains why political establishments have always been enthusiastic about its use. He explains: "No passion so effectually robs the mind of all its powers of acting and reasoning as fear. For fear being an apprehension of pain or death, it operates in a manner that resembles actual pain."[27]

In *Fear,* Corey Robin's seminal book exploring how fear is used to shape our politics and culture, he notes: "Though most modern writers and politicians oppose political fear as the enemy of liberty, reason, and other Enlightenment values, they often embrace it, in spite of themselves, as a source of political vitality."[28] Moreover, "Whether condemning Jacobin terror, Soviet despotism, Balkan genocide, or September 11 terrorism, they [writers and politicians] see opportunities for collective renewal in the fear of these evils."[29]

This is what the media, politicians, and the omnipresent establishment apparatchiks likely tell themselves when opting to exploit horrific human tragedies to gain a political edge over the citizenry. There is always an excuse, always an explanation, to soothe even the subconscious when abusing one person or millions of people.

The problem is, if one actually cares about the polity and its people, the inclination would not be to exploit the "strongest emotion," but to explain, persuade, and engage. Imagine a relationship where a person's first instinct is to threaten or frighten you into doing something or intimidate you into behaving in a certain way. It might be the quickest way to push you into compliance, but it is certainly not a relationship based on respect and dignity. It is a bully's answer to life. This helps us understand the extent of the problem with our establishment being awash in bullies, grifters, and frauds who do damage to the country as they obsessively focus on frightening us into silence and surrender.

As a left-wing community organizer for many years focusing on violence against women in general and domestic violence in particular, I've been stunned by the undeniable similarities between the crime of domestic violence at the personal level and our ruling establishment's behavior toward citizens. And yet, I shouldn't have been so surprised by these similarities. It was my own recent encounter that helped me recognize the connection between the personal and political use of fear to control and manipulate.

Personal Fear Is Political Fear

Those who work to frighten us for political ends and those doing it on a personal level have this in common: they rely on our imaginations giving life to a sometimes vague, or whispered, or even obscure threat. No one can create a fear larger than what our imaginations allow. The tyrants and bullies among us know that. But often, all it takes is clarity and information to burst the controlling bubble of fear and dread.

An event in my own life provided me with this invaluable knowledge. It was an epiphany I had one night years ago in New York City in, of all places, the middle of Times Square. When I was younger, I was involved in a relationship that was emotionally and sometimes physically abusive. I finally extricated myself from that situation and I eventually understood—after years of therapy—that it had conditioned me into a state of generalized fear and anxiety.

Many of you may be able to relate to this. When you live in an unnatural and negative emotional state day after day, it becomes your normal. Through the benefit of psychotherapy and the support of friends, I was able to confidently overcome and manage the more deleterious effects of that experience and move on from the abusive conditioning to which I was subjected. Or at least, that's what I thought.

Fast-forward thirty years to New York City, where I was spending a great deal of my time working. For most of the previous fifteen years, this woman was not on my mind, never interrupting my thoughts or life. That changed a few years ago when she again began pursuing and harassing me.

One night, she ended up lying in wait outside of a studio where I was working. When I left the studio that evening to walk home, she stalked me to Times Square, where she accosted me, grabbing my arm. There was a look on her face I recognized from the past abuse, and it frightened me. She had threatened me at various times in the past, so this situation immediately raised many red flags for me about the danger I was facing. Looking back, it was as though a different region of my brain engaged and was guiding my actions. I now know what the fight-or-flight experience genuinely feels like. My frantic flight commenced.

Pulling away from her grip, I ignored her screaming pleas for my attention and ran as fast as I could in the chaos and crush of Times Square during a busy evening. She chased me, and I felt her repeatedly grab the back of my coat. I glanced back and observed her completely unhinged, her face twisted and her mouth open. In a blur, I saw other pedestrians noticing the frenzy, appearing concerned, but I ignored everything and had no idea what to do or where I was going.

At one point feeling I would not be able to get away, sure in my mind I was in physical danger, I remember the instant I actually considered running into traffic to escape her. Then, remarkably, at that moment, I noticed something you never see on a busy night in that area of midtown Manhattan—an available taxi, but it was several streets away. Simultaneously, I saw a traffic enforcement agent in the middle of the busy intersection.

In New York, those who control or direct traffic are not police officers, but city employees assigned exclusively to manage traffic. I made my way to him as the one person who could stop the sea of cars and get me to that taxi. Desperate and out of breath, I explained I was being chased and implored him to help me.

That young man then said something quite simple to me that changed everything. "Why don't you go to the police, right over there?" pointing to one of the NYPD teams assigned to Times Square standing nearby.

What was so remarkable was that in the midst of this episode, and even in the past, during my relationship with this person, I had *never* considered going to the police. It simply had never occurred to me, because this woman's behavior and the fear I lived with had become "normal," a familiar experience and emotion. It was just how things were. You don't go to the police when things are "normal." As I write these words, I realize how illogical and strange this must sound

I will never forget what happened next for as long as I live. It felt as though someone had flipped a switch in my mind as I thought to myself: "Wait a minute, this guy thinks I should go to the police. None of this is normal! None of this is okay. *Of course,* I should go to the police!" My God, I was going to run into traffic and risk my life to get away from her, but it didn't occur to me to approach the police?! The years of threats and mistreatment I had endured had conditioned me to respond irrationally to my fear of being harmed by simply running away instead of reaching out to law enforcement even when they were *steps away from me.* This wasn't normal or acceptable, but fear had short-circuited my rational thinking.

The traffic agent grabbed my shoulders and slightly shook me. I looked up and saw him staring over my shoulder with an intense look of concern on his face. I've always presumed he saw her at that point, waiting and watching. He said, "Wait, I understand. I'm getting you into that taxi. I'm going to take your hand. Stay with me," at which point the taxi, miraculously still available, had inched closer to us. He stopped cars in all lanes across Times Square and got me in that cab. "Call the police," he said, in what sounded like a gentle order. I did.

To make a long story somewhat shorter, my shift in awareness and against fear culminated in a restraining order against the woman, I increased my personal security, and I jumped through multiple hoops in New York City to get a handgun permit.

This experience was important to me, and I'm sharing it with you because it demonstrates the power of being conditioned by fear. I had never considered the solution my traffic hero suggested because the feeling of fear provoked by this woman had become normalized. The abused start to see the punishments and attacks as something they should be clever enough to avoid and possibly even their own fault.

This epiphany shook me out of an automatic and robotic response to a frightening situation. It was a life-changing reminder of the vital importance of maintaining logic and reason and the concomitant clarity of mind that helps our innate decision-making—*especially* during a frightening and disturbing event, when we need it the most.

None of us can eliminate all fear, and we shouldn't want to. Fear is a needed response to danger and can keep us out of harm's way. But we need to learn the right way to respond to fear—at least being guided by logic and clear thinking, rather than irrationality and unadulterated instinct. This strategy also helps us distinguish fear from cultivated anxiety and exploited fear responses. Look at it as your modern brain managing your ancient brain.

Problems Must Never Be Solved

Theorists studying political fear make a valuable point in differentiating personal fears from political fears. This is important because these different types of fear arise from different dynamics. Corey Robin posits this: "Private fears like my fear of flying or your fear of spiders are artifacts of our own psychologies and experiences and have little impact beyond ourselves. Political fear, by contrast, arises from conflicts within and between societies. . . . It may dictate public policy, bring new groups to power and keep others out, create laws and overturn them."[30]

While private and political fears are indeed different, it's valuable to consider how some people are particularly vulnerable to both. Those living with anxiety, which encompasses symptoms of fear, worry, and apprehension, are particularly vulnerable to political messages that exploit serious national events. While the first half of the twentieth century is often referred to as the "Age of Anxiety," the twenty-first century is giving it a run for its money. Throughout history, humanity has been susceptible to fear-based manipulation, which has been evident in how governments and societies have responded to threats such as terrorism, the COVID-19 pandemic, and savage Middle Eastern conflicts.

I look back with more understanding about how fearful events in my personal life made me more vulnerable to "fear messaging" because I had already acclimated to fear as a familiar feeling. It is no coincidence, for example, that it was after the emotionally shocking suicide of my first girlfriend when I was only nineteen that I became a left-wing activist.[31] My primary interests included, not surprisingly, feminism, violence, and protecting women from malign social and political influences.

It was the fear and anxiety impressed upon me by that experience that shaped my initial political and psychological view of society. The reality of a woman feeling so desperate and disturbed to think the only way out of the emotional predicament she was facing was self-annihilation also provoked my interest in psychology and faith. The violent shock of losing someone I loved stirred passions and interests that shape my life to this day.

In their effort to collect lost souls, the left's common declaration to society is that they are the defenders and saviors of the downtrodden, abused, and yes, frightened. Consequently, I was attracted to an environment that I was told existed to confront and change the unfair, bigoted, and misogynistic system leading too many people to despair and misery.

My emotional injury made me a perfect target for the left. I arrived looking for salvation from fear and the brutal unknown future, and my affliction was then exploited by the people who declared themselves the saviors and activists who would confront the bigots and bad guys. They claimed to want to change a system that existed to take advantage of the vulnerable. But in reality, they were exploiting vulnerable people like me and so many others.

My first three books, using my experience as a left-wing activist, exposed the leftists, feminists, and other grifters for the frauds they are. Over time, I realized that liberal social justice groups were not helping people in need or solving any of society's problems. They were, in fact, relying on *perpetuating* the unfairness and suffering of women, people of color, and others in need of real advocacy in order to maintain power, influence, and fundraise.

What I did not comprehend at the time was that there was an even more destructive and deliberate reasoning to the methods of the left. Leftists weren't just malignant narcissists who were callously making things worse because they didn't care. They were making things worse by design. They were *deliberately* exploiting our fears not just to crush the rest of us, but to maintain their own base and support.

The motive of activists on the left is an insatiable greed for power and political influence, based on their belief that they're worthier and better than everyone else. But it is also about owning issues surrounding victimhood and fear in order to control people who are likely damaged and more easily exploitable. The targets the left seeks to recruit as foot soldiers are young people looking to become activists, to right wrongs, and to save people—perhaps even themselves, as I was doing—and who have very few or no one else to rely on for guidance and support.

In my first book, *The New Thought Police*, I describe an incident that began to reveal for me how the fear-based tactics of liberal social justice activism were not just a fraud, but a mechanism with which to maintain political control and even to protect politically powerful people from exposure as frauds themselves.

I had been complaining to my feminist mentor at the time that some actions by liberal organizations were actually making certain situations worse. Perpetuating divisions and fear on the issues instead of trying to find solutions or common ground with conservatives on issues like violence against women, access to health care, and economic fairness perplexed me. We were supposed to make the world better, right? I was disabused of that romantic notion quickly and was stunned as she explained that "every now and then we need to rub salt into the wound" to maintain our position and influence. "Rubbing salt into the wound" means maintaining the feeling of perpetual victimhood and pain in your constituency so that you don't advocate yourself out of business.[32]

I was told that if we (the organized feminist movement) ever did become so successful that we weren't needed—something that was my goal as a feminist activist—it would be a problem because we would eventually be needed again. And what a disaster that would be, because we wouldn't be there! To avoid that catastrophe, we needed to make sure the wounds of our constituents would never quite heal, meaning we (the advocates) would always be needed, allowing us to continue to exist.

Only a leftist could deliver up this reasoning to explain why maintaining the misery of those who are suffering was actually a good thing in the long run. It was as ethical as a doctor withholding a cure for a chronic disease in order to keep patients coming in for a lifetime of treatments. Make no mistake: it also mirrors the loathsome reasoning guiding today's progressive grifters and the political establishment that this book is dedicated to unmasking.

I had these experiences thirty years ago, but they are evidence of a craven fraud still operating to this day. This is a hallmark of the left and its addiction to using and maintaining fear not just to control the population at large, but to control its own constituencies. The kings and queens of the left look on the rest of us as pawns, to be used and sacrificed as necessary to protect the royals.

The Left Rots from Within

As a government becomes more corrupt, its efforts to silence and control the people become ever more urgent. Over the past twenty-plus years, we have seen further expansion of bureaucracy and the rapid degradation of personal freedom. For much of this time, the overlords have used the guise of terrorism as an excuse to ignore, and lie about, the abuse of our constitutional protections.

In the aftermath of Donald Trump's election as president in 2016, members of an even more panicked and frantic American establishment revealed themselves to be the tiny tyrants they are. They stoked fear among the public that the new president was a "Russian spy," and that he and his team were fascists who were going to destroy the country. Setting the country on fire with constant and idiotic fearmongering about Trump being a "danger to democracy," some eventually resorted to labeling the president's supporters as actual terrorists.

In the pages that follow, I will pull back the curtain on this alliance of government, the academy, and business working in concert to control society through fear. This includes Big Tech censoring and silencing us either directly or through self-censorship by intimidation. It is the left's "social justice" groups perpetuating and cultivating "wokeism," not because it improves anyone's lives, but because it allows the left to control us in the name of racial and social justice. This is a war against all of us, our families, friends, and communities, and includes the nefarious plan to separate children from their families by demanding and facilitating indoctrination in our schools.

The good news is that Americans do not want the radical social and cultural shifts promoted by wokeism, a movement controlled by a small, but influential, number of people. Our self-appointed progressive saviors know the power of fear and are experts at using it, but they continue to underestimate the American people. We are not pawns. We are free men and women who can, and will, determine our own futures.

It's time we turn on the light, put our would-be leftist overlords smack-dab in the public eye, and take this country back.

CHAPTER 2

Hiding Your Wrongthink

Nothing in life is to be feared, it is only to be understood. Now is the time to understand more, so that we may fear less.

—MARIE CURIE[1]

None of the political and cultural assaults on our society in the last ten years are natural or organic. What's unfolding in front of us now is promulgated by a small number of well-entrenched leftists determined to revive a failed and deadly political theory at the expense of us, our families, and our country. They will fail, because when we expose what the left is up to, challenging and defeating them becomes much easier and more decisive.

If you told me I'd be writing again about political correctness in the twenty-first century, I would have laughed. PC was criticized aggressively in the 1980s and '90s; eventually, it was widely treated as a joke. Many considered it a fad growing out of the intellectual and emotional meltdown liberals were suffering after eight successful years of conservative Republican president Ronald Reagan.

Even now, the term *PC* can bring up cringing memories of increasingly desperate and insecure liberal and feminist activists who felt entitled to silence anyone who disagreed with them. These same whining fools then felt empowered to demand we change how *we* speak and write to accommodate *them*, labeling any expression they found offensive a "microaggression."

Published in the anxious post–World War II world of 1949, George Orwell's dystopian novel *1984*[2] dramatically warned of how control of language opens the door to totalitarianism and domination of our very thoughts. In the novel, the dictatorship Oceania invented the new form of expression called "Newspeak" as a weapon of mind control. Professor Steven Blakemore remarks on Orwell's conveyance in *1984* of the vital importance of language and speech to physical and psychological freedom:

> The Party is aware that language is potentially political, that even newspeak is potentially subversive to its ideology. Consequently, the Party's ultimate goal is to destroy language itself, and this is implicit in "the Principles of Newspeak" . . . [providing] a "world view," but it makes all other world views impossible because reality is only grounded in the Party's semantic vocabulary. Hence the citizens of Oceania cannot think in any terms other than what the Party invents or legitimizes. . . . As the Party violently breaks the delicate nexus between language and reality, it attempts to "break" the very nature of language as we know it.[3]

As we now know, political correctness was no passing fancy. The genuine history and origins of PC make clear its significant danger to the freedoms Western civilization gives us. PC was another of the many shots throughout the twentieth century to inject Cultural Marxism throughout the world, like a cancer seeking to metastasize through the entire body.[4]

Political correctness has now matured into a twenty-first-century version of a political *Rosemary's Baby*[5]—an idea cloaked as an unusual but benign situation, only to reveal itself as something terrible. Over time, it has birthed the monsters of wokeism, cancel culture, and "Critical Theory" academic indoctrinations, which is the umbrella ideology responsible for the racism and destructive scourge of Critical Race Theory (CRT).

As Christopher Rufo, the director of the Initiative on Critical Race Theory at the Manhattan Institute, puts it, CRT is "America's new institutional orthodoxy."[6] Moreover, he notes:

> Its supporters deploy a series of euphemisms to describe critical race theory, including "equity," "social justice," "diversity and inclusion" and "culturally responsive teaching." Critical race theorists, masters of language construction, realize that "neo-Marxism" would be a hard sell. Equity, on the other hand, sounds nonthreatening and is easily confused with the American principle of equality. But the distinction is vast and important.[7]

Over twenty years ago, in my first two books—*The New Thought Police*[8] and *The Death of Right and Wrong*[9]—I wrote of my time as a liberal "community organizer" and the troubling developments I witnessed as radical leftists were eclipsing classical liberals in both political and cultural activism. PC culture was part of this shift, and I, along with other classical liberals in the trenches, recognized that something more disturbing, consequential, and organized was happening. Censorship is always a control mechanism, and the politics of personal destruction soon emerged for those who do not comply or who dare to critique the agenda.

By the 1990s, it became clear that Marxists were also targeting our education system, from school boards to elementary schools to colleges and universities, in an organized effort to propagandize and shape the minds of impressionable students.

Writing about the Marxist origins of political correctness, professor and author Frank Ellis discusses official Soviet sources indicating the term and concept of political correctness were in use as early as 1921.

> The suddenness with which political correctness entered the public domain in the period between 1989–1991, and the ensuing arguments about the legitimacy of Western culture which lasted until well into the mid-1990s, implies

> that the concept of political correctness is a very recent phenomenon . . . but . . . New Left and postmodernist writers were required reading on the campus, we find political correctness established as an ideological criterion of Marxism-Leninism. Official Soviet sources clearly show that the term was in use as early as 1921.[10]

Moreover, Ellis notes:

> A review of a diverse and large body of Soviet and Western literature, written and published throughout the twentieth century, which was conducted in preparation for this article, repeatedly identifies the theme of correctness—ideological, political or theoretical—as a concern of exceptional importance for Marxist-Leninism and Maoism.[11]

For thousands of years, philosophers, writers, grifters, academics, politicians, and government officials (from kings to presidents and their underlings) contemplated how the lowly peasants and workers should be controlled and governed. In the twenty-first century, it's clear not much has changed as the use of fear remains a favorite of ruling regimes.

While political philosophers Machiavelli and Hobbes wrote hundreds of years ago that fear must be a tool in a leader's governing arsenal, for the modern left, and the Marxists in particular, *fear itself* is the endgame. Fear is the necessary element providing them the key to wealth and social, cultural, and political controversy.

The revolutionary left knows they can't persuade most Americans to embrace social engineering, not after the infamously deadly and failed socialist and communist experiment of the twentieth century. They have never been able to maintain their grasp of power with the natural will of the people anywhere on Earth once they were exposed for what they are. So rather than overtly proposing their agenda to the American people, they instead use pressure to box Americans into a frightened, acquiescent silence on all things political and cultural so that they can implement their agenda without obstacles.

The Sinister Strategy of Political Correctness

It's one thing to know that the bureaucratic elite and their triad of corporate, academic, and Big Tech enablers have decided that frightening us into submission is their best plan, but exactly how did they imagine implementing this? All we need to do is look around. Every cultural issue we're battling relies on one thing to be established, to continue, and to prevail: the citizen being too afraid consciously—and even more importantly, subconsciously—to freely engage in social and political life.

The left is turning speech and, ultimately, thoughts into acts that can result in public shaming and expulsion from our modern tribes. A politically incorrect comment—or, more often, a benign comment purposely misread—can get any of us labeled a terrorist or bigot or hatemonger, or any one of the innumerable "phobes." We've seen many cases where it gets someone fired or even arrested. The goal is to get us to censor ourselves and cower in fear, prompting our social and political retreat. Self-censorship is more powerful and effective than censorship imposed by government.

American intellectual historian L. D. Burnett examines the origin of political correctness at the Society for U.S. Intellectual History blog:

> This history—at least as I have been able to piece it together so far—begins not in the 1980s nor even in the 1960s. The use of the term "politically correct" as first an ideal and then an insult, first an aspiration and then an accusation, goes at least as far back as the 1930s. The double-edged connotation of the term was forged and sharpened in internal debates on the Left.[12]

Now undeniable, the power of speech is becoming increasingly seen as dangerous, and Orwell's nightmare of *1984* is becoming more of a reality in the twenty-first century. Academic researchers in Atlanta and St. Louis report, "Over the period from the heyday of McCarthyism to the present, the percentage of the American people not feeling free to express their views has tripled. In 2020, more than four in ten people engaged in self-censorship."[13]

The reality of this retreat from public discourse is so apparent even for the liberal bastion of the *New York Times*. Noticing the growing fear surrounding speech and thought, the newspaper commissioned a poll[14] to assess what has been wrought by cancel culture. "For all the tolerance and enlightenment that modern society claims, Americans are losing hold of a fundamental right as citizens of a free country: the right to speak their minds and voice their opinions in public without fear of being shamed or shunned," noted the newspaper. Their poll found, in part, "only 34 percent of Americans said they believed that all Americans enjoyed freedom of speech completely. . . . 84 percent of adults said it is a 'very serious' or 'somewhat serious' problem that some Americans do not speak freely in everyday situations because of fear of retaliation or harsh criticism."[15]

Moreover, a Cato Institute poll[16] documented the same development, with an even more significant majority of Americans confirming that we have a self-censorship problem, noting "nearly two-thirds of Americans say the political climate these days prevents them from saying things they believe because others might find them offensive." As an indicator of for whom the cancel culture bell tolls, "strong liberals," at 58 percent, are the only political group that feels perfectly safe saying what they believe, while 77 percent of conservatives feel they cannot.

The number of Americans retreating from public discourse and speaking their mind is not entirely surprising, as young people are increasingly authoritarian and vocal on the issue. In a fall 2023 survey that shocked many, the Foundation for Individual Rights and Expression (FIRE) found[17] that a quarter of college students felt using violence to stop someone from speaking on campus was acceptable.[18]

Political correctness, marketed by the left as humanitarian, has allowed a sinister and corrupt theory to invade every aspect of American society. Political correctness has metastasized into cancel culture and into the diseased CRT, becoming the left's key to unlocking a door to a new social and political order, threatening the freedom of thought and expression, values at the core of the American way of life.

Many of the problems and divisions we face today are the result of the left having waged a battle for the minds of our children. Young people emerge from indoctrination-center campuses to take leading roles in the media, education (at every grade level), law, business, and politics. We see the alarming results with freshly indoctrinated leftist acolytes from the academies flowing into government, business, law, media, and journalism. It is a course we must confront and reverse.

The Leftist Stairway to Hell

The Reverend Martin Luther King Jr. inspired Americans with a familiar faith-based metaphor to dismiss fear and encourage trust. "Take the first step in faith," the civil rights leader said. "You don't have to see the whole staircase, just take the first step."[19]

When it comes to earthly matters such as our family's security, the content of education, law and justice, crime, the economy, national security, the intention and goals of government, and personal freedom, it matters if that staircase leads to an optimistic future embodied by the American way of life or to a Marxist dystopian hellscape.

The dangerous staircase the left has constructed inevitably leads to a chaotic, lawless, and deadly human catastrophe. We are in the early stages of this now. We need to turn back before it becomes impossible to do so.

The purpose of political correctness was marketed by the left as a way to police the speech of the ostensibly powerful to keep them from offending the powerless. Accepting it means accepting that some discrimination must occur in order for equality to come about. The debate then becomes about segregating the American people into collectives based on immutable characteristics such as race, ethnicity, gender, and sexual orientation, and then assigning each to be among the powerful or the powerless (or as the oppressed versus the oppressor). Multiculturalism creates group, or collective, rights and entitlements, rejecting the concepts of individual rights and equality enshrined in the Declaration of Independence.

In 2016, Mike Gonzalez of the Heritage Foundation explained multiculturalism within its proper context as a deliberate leftist strategy designed to strike at the heart of unity in the United States:

> Multiculturalism as a social model is concerned with one culture and one culture only, the West, especially America and its heritage, because it wants to destroy or at least alter it and replace it with something else. The multiculturalism I am concerned with is the blueprint for replacing the American narrative with a counter-narrative that is animated by values of the left such as state control over our lives, dependence on government to apportion participation in society, and thinking of people as groups rather than as individuals and their families.[20]

Gonzalez continues on to note the importance of this Marxist strategy to infiltrate existing institutions like schools and media, helping to facilitate more rapid revolutions. Essentially, this is the strategy of "capturing the culture" and "delegitimizing" American norms. We are now seeing the success of that strategy every day.

This is the foundation of identity politics, a key part of the goal of annihilating the individual to achieve the new social order of collectivism.

Disrupt, Polarize, Politicize, Dismantle

The preparations by the left leading up to unleashing political correctness are clear. Disrupt the unity uniquely established by the United States as a nation of immigrants based on liberty and individual determination as opposed to a people's historical, collective geographical origins. They start by balkanizing the citizenry through multiculturalism. The next step is to politicize those divisions with identity politics, inviting the next imperative step—political correctness, the "humanitarian" scheme to use the strain of carefully drawn divisions to introduce the cancer that speech and thought are now dangerous.

Growing up, we were taught in school that America was a great melting pot, where people from around the world came together and forged a common bond and national identity. While no one expected us to relinquish our group attachments and identities, it was vital that we maintain a shared identity as Americans.

That is the key that has made the great American experiment a success. Political and social coherence is of primary importance for our nation to continue to be the beacon it is for people around the world. Identity politics rejects that notion, telling us instead that we are members of separate subgroups. Instead of emphasizing our commonalities, political correctness today emphasizes our differences, and dictates that we be divided rather than united.

As we will discuss in the chapters ahead, political correctness is the first step to every major political, social, and cultural catastrophe unfolding in the twenty-first century. The Marxist stairway's next steps grow increasingly bold and obvious in the left's attempt to submerge American society into a Marxist crisis: racial separatism, social credit scores, censorship via Big Tech, open borders, decriminalization, defunding the police, organized urban violence, outlawing political opposition, arresting political opponents, indoctrination centers, politicizing public education, targeting parents who dissent, and weaponizing health emergencies and environmentalism to limit individual freedom while expanding the reach and control of government.

There is absolutely nothing redeeming or valuable in any of these agendas. They are squarely aimed at destroying the fabric of the American Dream, which has made our country the envy of the world and a magnet for immigrants seeking freedom and better lives. It's as if we are seeing the Statue of Liberty blown to smithereens in New York Harbor, replaced with one of Karl Marx raising his fist in triumph.

It is now obvious why the left is desperate to keep us ignorant about the destination of their staircase into hell. Trickery is the only way to entrap Americans to take that first step of acquiescing to political correctness and submission to Big Government.

For a relatively small movement of radical leftists in America to have such an outsize impact, it's important to recognize that being in influential positions in key institutions is of paramount importance in the left's effort to deconstruct objective truth and reality. Unlike Senator Bernie Sanders of Vermont and Representative Alexandria Ocasio-Cortez of New York, who openly admit they are socialists, the overwhelming majority of socialists in the US vehemently deny their embrace of Marxism. Like the Big Bad Wolf who pretends to be Little Red Riding Hood's grandma in the fairy tale, most American socialists disguise themselves and their true intentions to swallow our freedoms.

Marxists do their handwringing, like most academics, in journals and books they expect will not be read by anyone other than their fellow travelers. But they're wrong. Consider this confession in a 2001 essay called "The (Un)defining of Postmodern Marxism," lamenting the growing irrelevance of Marxism and what the American left was doing in the last quarter of the twentieth century.[21] Noting the initial importance of co-opting other social movements, like feminism and environmentalism, the cure for their failure to persuade Americans about the utopia of Marxism is to co-opt, or invent, even more social movements:

> They have incorporated feminist and environmental issues into their platforms and debates as well as an awareness of the importance of ethnicity. But this has not been sufficient to alter the thrust of the historic socialist project. A real rupture is needed. . . . A postmodern Marxist approach with its emphasis on social and identity movements is most capable of making this break.[22]

Infiltrating social and identity movements was the ticket for the failed Marxists and other leftists in the twenty-first century. The foundation had been laid, especially in the academy. As the left gained controlling influence in media, education, and politics, the promotion of political correctness as a legitimate force in American life surged. While PC was defined and applied by Marxism early in the twentieth century, the reality of its tactics and goals that emerged after World War II became a cause for alarm among intellectuals.

The Unspeakable Becomes the Unthinkable

Ernst Cassirer (1874–1945) was a German philosopher known for his defense of moral idealism and liberal democracy at a time when fascism and the crushing of the individual coalesced in Nazi Germany. During World War II, Cassirer wrote about the danger of leftist extremists changing language. His classic *Myth of the State* was published posthumously in 1946:

> If we study our modern political myths and the use that has been made of them we find in them, to our great surprise, not only a transvaluation of all our ethical values but also a transformation of human speech. . . . New words have been coined, and even the old ones are used in a new sense; they have undergone a deep change of meaning. This change of meaning depends upon the fact that these words which formerly were used in a descriptive, logical, or semantic sense are now used as magic words that are destined to produce certain effects and to stir up certain emotions. Our ordinary words are charged with meanings; but these new-fangled words are charged with feelings and violent passions.[23]

Published in 1949, just three years after Cassirer's *Myth of the State*, Orwell's *1984* warning about the possibility of a very real totalitarian future has become our present. The left manipulates language to come up with new labels, new words, changed meanings, and misrepresentations to deceive the public. And not obscure words with which academics wrap themselves, but the most basic and fundamental of terms like what is a "woman." They also need to keep constantly changing language and meaning to keep the populace guessing what words are acceptable in society and what words are not. This is at the heart of nudging people toward self-censorship and, more alarmingly, toward an intellectual retreat from even thinking about the issues. After all, if it's too dangerous to speak of certain things, then self-protection suggests not even contemplating them.

How serious is the left at making speech an inherently dangerous exercise? Serious enough for Stanford University to establish the "Elimination of Harmful Language Initiative" (EHLI), wherein they would present problem words and phrases that should be eliminated from our lexicon due to their harmful effects, and the likelihood of offending people due to their racist and bigoted histories. In the "language guide" they offer up ten categories of prohibited words.[24]

The *New York Post* reported the list of more than one hundred banned words was thirteen pages long and included the word *American*, with the guide explaining that it "often refers to people from the United States only, thereby insinuating that the US is the most important country in the Americas," and advised *US citizen* should be used instead. Also, the word *immigrant* is a no-no and should be replaced with *person who has immigrated*. Under their listing addressing "ableist" slurs, the phrase *walk-in hours* must be jettisoned for the more inclusive *open hours*, so as to not insult the wheelchair-bound.[25]

It didn't end there. *Forbes* shared a number of other word crimes presented by Stanford's exclusion project, including *master* (and extended terms like *master list*) because "historically, masters enslaved people, didn't consider them human and didn't allow them to express free will, so this term should generally be avoided." *You guys* is no good because it "lumps a group of people using masculine language and/or into gender binary groups."[26]

Mentally ill and *insane* are to be jettisoned, we're told, because they are "ableist." Or, perhaps the researchers were anticipating the reaction to the report.

Guru? Yeah, no. It would insult the Buddhists. And whatever you do, don't call what you write a *white paper*. Because it implies white equals good. My favorite? The leftist political fringe, which had been lecturing us for years to use the term *trigger warning* if something potentially disturbing for the faint of heart might be mentioned, are now telling us to stop using the phrase—you guessed it—*trigger warning* because of the anxiety the warning itself can cause.[27]

When exposed, the project came under such sustained criticism and mockery that our betters at Stanford University, considered one of the more important education institutions in the world, panicked. Within two weeks of their release of the language guide, they killed the project, removed its website, and in its place coughed up an awkward attempt to explain and apologize. The Stanford chief information officer insisted the project "was created to address racist terms historically used in IT, such as 'master' and 'slave' to describe aspects of systems."[28] How that morphed into a thirteen-page booklet with more than 150 words wasn't fully explained.

Moreover, he noted, "The feedback that this work was broadly viewed as counter to inclusivity means we missed the intended mark. It is for this reason that we have taken down the EHLI site."[29] The university's president also issued a statement saying, in part, "at no point did the website represent university policy," that those involved meant well, and that "Stanford's 'efforts to advance inclusion must remain consistent with our commitment to academic freedom and free expression.'"[30]

Michael T. Nietzel, a former university president, wrote this about the absurd premise of the soon-to-be debacle: "Many of the words and phrases on the list are now normal forms of speech completely divorced from whatever offensive connotations can be imparted to them by invoking a history that reasonable people are not referencing when they talk. No one who uses the term *seminal* (yes, it's on the list) is doing so to 'reinforce male-dominated language.' Likewise, when faculty say that their research is undergoing *blind review*, they are not insulting people who cannot see."[31]

Stanford's "internal" goose-stepping into the censorship realm was not unique, but part of a widespread leftist agenda. Remember, nothing is a coincidence with the left. Having come from and escaped from that realm, I assure you, they are organizers and planners. On the left, nothing is left to chance. About a year prior to Stanford's public relations faceplant, the woke at Canada's CBC network in Ottawa decided it would be a great idea to create their own list of "words and phrases you might want to think twice about using."[32] Their list of forbidden words was as preposterous as Stanford's, confirming the obsession with training us to accept the absurd. Their list of the forbidden included *blackmail*, *black list*, and yes, *black sheep* (racist), *grandfathered in* (racist and patriarchal), *spirit animal* (racist), *savage* (racist colonizers), and even *brainstorm* (hurtful to those with brain injuries), among other problematic words like *dumb* and *lame*. That's one way to keep your critics quiet.

Twenty years ago we saw an iteration of this crazy-sauce agenda presented to the public when the woke mob tried to cancel *picnic*—yes, *picnic*—as a racist word allegedly stemming from people gathering to watch black people being lynched. This allegation was so preposterous, the website Snopes did a fact-check at the time and, lo and behold, found it completely false. The outlet noted, "Specious etymologies seem to be all the rage of late, and a dubious claim about 'picnic' fits that trend . . . neither the concept nor the word 'picnic' has anything to do with crowds gathering to witness the lynching of blacks (or anyone else, for that matter) in America."[33]

Nineteen years later, Reuters stepped up and performed their own fact-check when the *picnic* word hoax returned for a second act. They come right to the point: "Fact check: The word picnic does not originate from racist lynchings. . . . Images circulating on social media make the claim that the word 'picnic' originates from the racist, extrajudicial killings of African Americans. This claim is false."[34]

None of this is about protecting people from words. It's all about training people to believe that the language itself is systemically racist, and frightening people into not even knowing what is safe to say.

This is a perfect example of the left's commitment to changing the rules of normal life in such a haphazard and illogical way that people will opt to retreat from public life out of fear of what might come if an unknown rule is broken. It also trains us to accept (or else!) the illogical and idiotic changing of the most benign of words into warped racist attacks as an exploitation of our desire to be fair and unbiased. For the proposed victims of all these menacing, bigoted, and violent words, it instills a belief that danger is embedded in the language itself.

Political correctness was never about empathy and fairness, or even about vague and ubiquitous matters of "sensitivity." It has one goal—to control. To achieve this, PC begins to train us to distrust—or even fear—the intentions of others, and even our minds, our intentions, and our values. This mental conditioning manipulates the target—us—by exploiting our empathy and desire to do no harm to others.

With all this in play, the PC arguments and rules ultimately create a fear not just of speaking freely, but of even thinking freely. It's difficult to know the rules of what speech and thoughts are politically correct at any given time because the rules keep changing, are often contradictory, or make no sense. A phrase or term that's considered perfectly proper in one year can be labeled a slur or a microaggression the next. As with victims of domestic violence, this gaslighting causes us to question our perception of reality and lose trust in our sense of self.

And that's the point.

As political correctness has grown more extreme and absurd through the years, there has always been a price to pay for violating the PC codes. At first, you are accused of being a racist, sexist, ageist, xenophobe, homophobe, transphobe, or some other kind of bigot if you didn't conform to the Newspeak du jour. Next, you are called "problematic," or "dangerous," and your right to free speech disappears.

Any hint of rebellion in your speech is now seen as evidence of a fully compromised mind. Use the phrase "brown bag" or refer to a "picnic" and it is assumed that is just the tip of a racist iceberg.

Prescient Warnings

In 2006, when it was still possible to somewhat challenge leftist orthodoxy without facing the guillotine, the *Harvard Business Review* challenged political correctness as a "double-edged sword," causing problems in communication, trust, and relationships in the workplace. In "Rethinking Political Correctness," the publication stated:

> We are troubled, however, by the barriers that political correctness can pose to developing constructive, engaged relationships at work. In cultures regulated by political correctness, people feel judged and fear being blamed. They worry about how others view them as representatives of their

> social identity groups. They feel inhibited and afraid to address even the most banal issues directly. People draw private conclusions; untested, their conclusions become immutable. Resentments build, relationships fray, and performance suffers. . . . These dynamics breed misunderstanding, conflict, and mistrust, corroding both managerial and team effectiveness.[35]

The left's success with manipulating the public through political correctness ultimately led to government picking up the mantle by enacting hate crime laws and policy.

Make no mistake—hate crime laws serve the imperative leftist agenda goal of normalizing the concept that the federal government has a right to punish you for a thought crime in addition to the physical crime you are accused of committing.

As I discuss at length in *The New Thought Police,* prosecuting hate crimes is the act of criminalizing what people are feeling (hate isn't even a thought, it's a feeling) when they commit an act that is already a crime, such as murder, assault, rape, or robbery, etc. The secret Marxist sauce is the hate crime charge applies only to feelings that leftist bureaucrats have determined to be politically incorrect. As an example, if someone murders a woman (who happens to be gay) because he hates women, that's *not* a hate crime. But if a killer murders a woman who's gay and he hates gay people, that *is* a hate crime. Both murders involve hate. In both cases, the victim is homosexual. But the hate crime enhancement applies only to a specific type of hate felt by the murderer. It wasn't who was killed, per se, that matters to the state. It was what the perpetrator was *feeling*, and in this case, against a class promised protection by the leftist establishment.

The hate crimes concept was accepted by Americans in part because we were convinced that we needed to make a special statement (beyond regular criminal justice) against bigotry-inspired crimes. But for the left, the real goal is enshrining into society and then into law the notion that thoughts and feelings alone *can* be criminalized, making the argument for *thought crimes* possible. If we allow them, it's only a matter of time before leftist totalitarians focus on that ultimate end goal, reinforcing a deeply ingrained personal fear meant to impact each of us.

This is the beginning of the legal enshrinement of the idea that some people must be discriminated against for us all to become equal.

There is another factor here for minorities to consider who believe we benefit from hate crime laws. As a gay woman myself, I refuse to accept a crime committed against me to be considered more serious than the same crime committed against a woman simply because she does not fit into a politically designed protected class and I do. To justify this discriminatory cruelty, liberals argue that the murder of the gay woman must be considered more serious because it's meant to send a message of hate to the whole gay community, creating fear throughout that community. But the fact is, every murder sends a message and creates fear throughout the community in which it takes place, and often beyond. We are *all* impacted, emotionally and otherwise, by all crimes, regardless of the personal attributes of the victim or the feelings of the perpetrators.

If we truly want a system that is based on fairness and equality, we must reject the notion that some people matter more than others. This is one of the foundational elements of civil rights in this country and was the basis of every civil rights movement. Judicial punishments for murder, rape, assault, robbery, or any other crime must be applied equally, and victims must be treated equally.

Here Mr. Orwell makes another helpful appearance. Again warning about the dangers of emerging fascism, one of the most remembered lines in his 1945 political allegory *Animal Farm* comes when the animals overtake a farm from cruel and unfair humans, with the intention that all creatures will finally be treated fairly and equally. Yet pig leaders emerge, unfairness and inequality return, and the sign declaring the farm's commandments is painted over. The main commandment itself remains "All Animals Are Equal," but is changed to "All Animals Are Equal, but Some Are More Equal Than Others."

We know what's been happening in this country, the same disgraceful leftism that has condemned hundreds of millions of people the world over. Orwell watched it unfold in Soviet Russia and Nazi Germany. It destroyed those two countries and almost condemned the world. It was predictable and predicted. Many have warned us, perhaps none as brilliantly as Orwell.

Criminals and victims of crime are being treated differently in our country right now based on what demographic categories they fall into. This is already happening with "no bail" and even "no jail" rules being implemented in Democratic-controlled cities throughout the country. "Progressive" district attorneys are refusing to apply the law and setting violent criminals free as a direct result of embracing a political theory that codifies using different standards for different groups of people in the judicial system in a scheme to achieve Marxist "equity." That, of course, is wrong and unjust. It foments division, crime, more victims, and chaos in our communities. And it is exactly what the left thrives on.

All this is part of the left's effort to reinforce "otherness" through division and societal rules and laws, attempting to normalize the obscenity that some people are more important than others and are entitled to preferential treatment. If you don't agree with hate crime legislation or so-called equity rules, you are falsely attacked as a bigot.

The goal is to have your friends and neighbors attack you for your speech, your beliefs, and your values. Trust and camaraderie are abandoned. The left reinforces fear, shame, and confusion against those it targets, but it wants citizens to fear everyone except, ironically, the omnipotent bureaucratic state responsible for the divided and desperate state of nature to which we are subjected.

In Orwell's *1984,* the citizens of Oceania fear the Thought Police, who arrest and punish people for unapproved personal and political thoughts that pose a threat to the totalitarian government. The Thought Police keep track of what Newspeak labels "thoughtcrime" with the help of omnipresent cameras, microphones, and informers. Today, social media, website cookies that track our online activity, cell phones, computers with powerful programs, tracking devices, facial recognition software, surveillance drones, communications satellites, tiny hidden cameras and microphones, and other monitoring devices are ubiquitous and track us constantly. When writing *1984*, Orwell warned us about the totalitarian agenda, but modern technology has provided governments with far more powerful ways to keep track of us and our thoughts than anything available to the novelist's fascist antagonists.

In 2018, thought crime was again ready for its close-up and served as the subject of a *Yale Law Review* article. The "two sides" rhetorical argument is titled "Why Is It Wrong to Punish Thought?" We're fortunate the author concludes that punishing people for their thoughts would be a bad idea. He writes:

> It's a venerable maxim of criminal jurisprudence that the state must never punish people for their mere thoughts—for their beliefs, desires, fantasies, and unexecuted intentions. This maxim is all but unquestioned, yet its true justification is something of a mystery.[36]

A "mystery." Oh, brother. The fact that there is even a debate about whether or not thoughts should be punished in the United States is concerning. A small group of radicals who hold influential positions in education, media, legislation, and policy-making have leveraged their influence. Unfortunately, we must marshal strong arguments to explain why prosecuting people for their thoughts is not a good idea. This is going to be a battle, but we can win it.

Hard as it may be for some people to accept, Marxism and racism are being taught to children and young adults from kindergarten through graduate schools across the US today. It appears that far less instruction is taking place on the founding principles of our nation.

Freedom of thought has always been a fundamental problem for totalitarian regimes because it is the key to communication, inquiry, independent judgment and action, and dissent—things despots recognize as existential threats. Thought itself is the key to self-awareness, desires, understanding, and comprehension of the environment and circumstances we face as individuals.

Freedom of thought is inextricably linked to freedom of speech, and the two are intertwined as necessary components of personal and political freedom. America's founders knew this and enshrined freedom of speech as the first item in the Bill of Rights. They also knew that tyrants would necessarily need to censor speech to strike at the freedom of the mind itself. Freedom of thought, in other words, is the most basic of liberties. Professor Lucas Swaine of Dartmouth College reminds us:

> The American founders laud the importance of freedom of thought: Benjamin Franklin endorses it in a notable aphorism, contending that without freedom of thought there can be "no such thing as wisdom." More emphatic still is Thomas Jefferson's sweeping declaration that he has "sworn upon the altar of god, eternal hostility against every form of tyranny over the mind of man." The statement reflects Jefferson's antagonism towards illegitimate coercion and fear of reprisal, both of which powerful rulers have deployed to control populations and to silence dissent.[37]

America's founders boldly rejected the autocratic form of government that prevailed around the world in their day—rule by kings, queens, emperors, or military dictators. Instead of bowing down to powerful rulers who often considered themselves to be gods or divinely appointed leaders, Americans stood tall and embraced self-government. US citizens are their own sovereign rulers, electing public servants to carry out the will of the people. Our founders said Americans would be in charge of our own lives. The preamble to the Constitution makes crystal clear who is in charge in its first three words:

> **We the People** of the United States, in Order to form a more perfect Union . . .

Elevation of the individual through a representative democracy keeps a nation free. Yet the left focuses on smashing the individual. They've pushed repeatedly for rule by technocrat. Who else would presume to tell us what words are unsayable each year? It all comes down to replacing the free mind of the individual with collective reliance on the bureaucratic system for every need.

Dr. Carl Jung (1875–1961), revered as a great mind and one of the founders of modern psychiatry, understood the importance of the individual in society resisting the forces of the "dictator state." Ideological forces, he argued, will destroy Western civilization but can be defeated as long as the individual understands what's at stake.

In his 1957 treatise on the subject, *The Undiscovered Self: The Dilemma of the Individual in Society,* Jung issues a warning to the individual about the danger of despotic regimes:

> The moral responsibility of the individual is then inevitably replaced by the policy of the State (raison d'état). Instead of moral and mental differentiation of the individual, you have public welfare and the raising of the living standard. The goal and meaning of individual life (which is the only real life) no longer lie in individual development but in the policy of the State, which is thrust upon the individual from outside and consists in the execution of an abstract idea which ultimately tends to attract all life to itself. The individual is increasingly deprived of the moral decision as to how he should live his own life, and instead is ruled, fed, clothed and educated as a social unit, accommodated in the appropriate housing unit, and amused in accordance with the standards that give pleasure and satisfaction to the masses.[38]

The first half of the twentieth century was marked by mass death and destruction, caused by communist and fascist forces that had no regard for the individual and subjected their own citizens and enemy states to the iron fist of authoritarianism. The communists who rose to power in the Bolshevik Revolution as World War I raged; the fascists who fought and won the Spanish Civil War; the Axis powers of Nazi Germany, Italy, and Japan that sought to conquer much of the planet during World War II; the Nazis, who murdered six million Jews in the Holocaust; and the communist regimes that rose to power in China and Eastern Europe after World War II had many differences. But all shared a contempt for the rights and freedoms like those proclaimed in the Declaration of Independence and guaranteed to the American people by our Constitution.

Jung's prescription for not acceding to the mass despotic states of communism and fascism is to embrace and understand our power as individuals in a dynamic and personal way that will help us resist the overpowering nature of the despotic state.

Only when we understand what's truly happening, that we're not alone, and that none of this is natural or organic, can we be sure of ourselves and stand up to those working to gaslight and threaten us into their mindless mass. Only by being informed about the intentions, the failures, and the misery and destruction behind the left's worldview can we defend against it.

CHAPTER 3

The Fear Industrial Complex

Socialism is a philosophy of failure, the creed of ignorance, and the gospel of envy.

—WINSTON CHURCHILL[1]

We are now all targeted by what I call the Fear Industrial Complex, an insidious dynamic relying on the direct and indirect collusion between various societal, cultural, and political entities using fear to control and suppress the American public's willingness and ability to engage in social, cultural, and political life.

We know the bureaucratic establishment wants Americans on perpetual high alert, filled with anxiety, blaming themselves, surrendering control, and taking action to keep themselves out of the spotlight. It's time to look at how they do it.

Fundamentally changing the American system requires government, education, and business all being compromised by small groups and individuals moving from the Marxist rat nests of academia into human resource departments, corporate boardrooms, marketing, and executive suites. There they work to expel all conservatives by accusing them of whatever rights violations seem most administratively effective. If there are no conservatives, they expel all the moderates. Once the moderates are gone, the Marxist left will turn on their former allies in the non-Marxist left.

The power grabs include government, businesses, and schools (from K–12 to university and graduate schools) mandating woke policies through DEI rules and trainings; mainstreaming the scourge of identity politics, including public ad campaigns normalizing discrimination; the vandalism of language and changing definitions; and bullying and harassment through "cancellation," including the loss of employment, expulsion from school, and being spied on and debanked by financial institutions at the behest of the federal government.[2]

It is important to note that all the rules and policies moving through our culture promoting "social justice" are not solving problems or making life better. Most were never designed to do so. On the contrary, this assault on our culture and politics is frequently meant to make things worse. Its goal is to permeate American life with a chronic fear born of not knowing from one moment to the next what is safe to think, say, or do. It is a chaos meant to divide us and embed fear in the simplest acts of everyday life. Progressives imagine that frightened and exhausted Americans will have only one option—turning to government to manage and control the new Hobbesian world order. In reality, this is the equivalent of sending the *Hindenburg* to rescue the people of the *Titanic*.

We saw the real-time catastrophic impact of DEI unfold before our eyes here at home in the aftermath of the October 7, 2023, massacre of Israelis by the terrorist group Hamas. Three Ivy League university presidents were called before Congress to explain what they were doing to address antisemitic demonstrations on their campuses. A shocked nation watched as the three women refused to unequivocally denounce the Jew-hatred illustrated by some students, staff, and professors, and instead demurred, saying calling for the genocide of Jews would only be against their code of conduct depending on the "context."

The fallout was immediate, but their equivocation confirmed the institutionalizing of DEI policies in hiring, training, and curriculum has codifying discrimination as an acceptable answer to past discrimination. But even beyond that, this theory not only prescribes excluding people for immutable characteristics (race, gender, and ethnicity); it weaves in the noxious reasoning that demonizing certain types of people is reasonable, even necessary, as they are deemed irredeemably bigoted, "deplorable," if you will.

This shocking strategy of denouncing tens of millions of Americans is not new. It started with someone quite mainstream—Hillary Clinton. During her 2016 run for the presidency, she made quite the splash during interviews and public events where she introduced the strategy of smearing tens of millions of American voters as "deplorable," "irredeemable," and even "not American."[3] The people she smeared were committing the crime of supporting her opponent for the presidency, Donald Trump. This provided permission from a national leader to view and condemn a vast group of people simply because of who they were. This must be considered as one of the keys that unlocked the door allowing mob action against business owners, local police, Republicans, conservatives, white people, and ultimately, Jews.

Jon Miltimore and Dan Sanchez at the Foundation for Economic Education (FEE) expand on how Marxists embedded at American colleges not only did not abandon their failed ideology with the fall of the Soviet Union and communism but instead "mutated" with a focus on cultural Marxism. Indoctrinated college students were then churned out into society. Miltimore and Sanchez discuss how the original Marxist "class war doctrine" has shifted into an oppressed-versus-oppressor structure:[4]

> But instead of capital versus labor, it was the patriarchy versus women, the racially privileged versus the marginalized, etc. Students were taught to see every social relation through the lens of oppression and conflict. After absorbing Marxist ideas (even when those ideas weren't called "Marxist"), generations of university graduates carried those ideas into other important American institutions: the arts, media, government, public schools, even eventually into human resources departments and corporate boardrooms.[5]

Miltimore and Sanchez remind us that our current culture of fear—from cancel culture to crime to riots to perpetual victimhood—stems from Marxist indoctrination at American universities. The seeding of American institutions with indoctrinated Marxist foot soldiers creates a machine for finding oppression, and when they cannot find it, they will create it. The Fear Industrial Complex is an institutional demolition team masquerading as builders.

Weaponizing Envy

Interestingly, an important point rarely discussed or acknowledged is envy being at the core of the left's strategy. Great minds have been warning humanity about the dangers of envy for millennia. This emotion sparks hatred and resentment, which can be used to inflict fear into others.

Wholly different from jealousy, which emerges when a threat is perceived to affect a valued relationship, the *Oxford English Dictionary* defines envy as "Malignant or hostile feeling; ill-will, malice, enmity" that includes "The feeling of mortification and ill-will occasioned by the contemplation of superior advantages possessed by another."[6]

Many domestic abuse cases start with an abuser who is deeply jealous of their partner. The abuser surveils them, accuses them, denigrates them, and eventually decides, "If I can't have you, no one can." With envy, the comparable sentiment would be, "If I can't have that, no one can."

We're lectured, gaslit, bullied, and encouraged to believe that success is unfair and that it's a bigoted act to do well, and you may be punished in the end for the affront. With resentment and envy inculcated by the left targeting American society, the toxic brew of emotional and mental abuse can ultimately manifest itself in society as mass anxiety inhibiting action, causing depression, and ultimately allowing a relinquishing of control of one's life to others. And that's exactly what the left's malign forces intend.

The repercussions are increasingly dangerous.

From ancient history to our modern age, envy has fueled civil uprisings, war, and family violence. Today, it also fuels the demands of so-called progressives clamoring for "equity"—tilting the playing field until *outcomes* are equal—leading to insatiable demands, tensions between different groups of people, and condemnations of our country, values, and way of life.

The manipulators and grifters haven't changed much, but the mode and techniques used to indoctrinate and condition us have become more refined, detailed, and dangerous. Fear, envy, and mass anxiety are harnessed today against people from the smallest towns to the largest metropolises. Mass media, social media, and other technological advances allow abusive manipulation by the liberal establishment to target all of us everywhere, in ways inconceivable just a few decades ago.

Envy, while as old as the first humans, has now been embraced and weaponized by the left to gain control, money, and power to advance a radical and destructive cultural and economic agenda. The left and the increasingly corrupt and frenzied establishment it dominates have found the fruits of envy too exciting to ignore.

Envy is at the root of their denunciation of free markets, demonization of successful people, embrace of cancel culture, pursuit of woke religiosity, and promotion of all things doomsday. By design, envy is the fuel, deranged punishment is the result.

Envy is the missing link explaining how a small group of people can convince so many others to participate in organized actions that will destroy people's lives, and perhaps even their own. Envy can be encouraged, normalized, organized, and weaponized. And the left is doing just that.

The left's use of envy relies on messaging that does even further damage to the self-esteem of the individuals groomed and encouraged to be street activists. What leftists do to their own people in this process is as horrible as what they're doing to everyone else.

Consider this: Envy is based on a belief that what we desire is unfairly difficult or even impossible to achieve. This is a conviction that no matter our talent, passion, or commitment, we will never enjoy full access to what we desire. The left relies on convincing their constituents that they have no agency. They're useless, and will never accomplish anything on their own accord. So, the left tells us that Big Government must become bigger, and create suffocating new regulations, with a massive redistribution of wealth through exorbitant taxation of the wealthy and middle class.

The only action every American must take, in this worldview, is allowing the government to control everything. It is, they tell us, the only way we can be protected from the mob.

How does the left implant this feeling of doomed hopelessness, helplessness, and victimhood into its targets? By indoctrinating them into the belief that racism, sexism, homophobia, and other forms of prejudice have a stranglehold on society; that it is all "systemic."

We're told that "systemic racism," as an example, controls American society, that every white person is racist, and that the only way to eliminate prejudice is to eliminate free markets by destroying the system itself.

This works as an electoral strategy because perhaps no more than a quarter of America are straight, white males.

Overthrowing free markets, of course, is the fundamental doctrine of communism, as advanced by Karl Marx and Friedrich Engels in *The Communist Manifesto* in 1848. But in reality, the utopian vision of communism painted by Marx and Engels is a cloaked tale of revenge. Marxism has turned every nation that has embraced it into a hellish nightmare. The last thing we need would be to adopt this poisonous and destructive philosophy in the United States.

A more recent incarnation of this philosophy of victimhood is known as Critical Race Theory and so-called anti-racism. Make no mistake—this cultural and academic agitprop is nothing new; it is regurgitated Marxism. I address these issues in detail later in this book, but I mention them now to spotlight the necessary and deliberate effort by the left to brainwash millions of people, beginning in childhood, with the lie that nothing they do in life will matter because everything and everyone is bigoted and arrayed against them, or they themselves are condemned to being genetically racist and irredeemable.

This was once a fringe view, and the complaint of people suffering from paranoia—"Everyone is against me!" But now the Democratic Party perpetuates this ideology of victimhood and self-pity, and how victimizers are everyone and everywhere. This is how envy is seeded in the individual and weaponized.

We are confronting in our country a political and economic philosophy based on a doctrine of despair instills fear into people to make them believe they have no future and that everyone is their enemy. Their struggle will never end, they are told. This is a modern-day version of the ancient Greek myth of Sisyphus, a king condemned after his death to eternally roll a heavy rock up a steep hill in Hades, only to have it roll down before reaching the top so he can begin the painful labor again.

Indoctrinating people with the view that everything they do is hopeless uses fear to cultivate envy, resentment, and a turn to violence, just as neo-Marxists hope they will. This is what communists and socialists have done in every country they have parasitically taken over and then destroyed.

We all understand there are problems in every society, including our own, and there always will be. What's important is that America is a nation always working to become better. It's a constant effort, like practicing medicine—we're never finished. We must always refine and improve our nation while remaining true to the divine template of governance left to us by the Founding Fathers. That's why the world continues to try to reach our shores. Setting this nation on fire by embracing a dead and cancerous political theory of envy is not our best option.

Most of us work to achieve our dreams, understanding that in a free society not everything is fair, and we work to improve what's *possible*. Most of us strive to achieve our version of the American Dream (which is unique for everyone), earning enough to have a middle-class lifestyle, raise a family, and have fulfilling and enjoyable times. The American middle class enjoys a quality of life better than anyone else in the history of humanity.

This outlook requires rational optimism and some level of basic self-confidence. But like demons invading dreams, those on the left work to destroy the individual's self-esteem and spirit, instilling the false belief that individuals have no agency, and that there is no hope.

To this point, the American philosopher John Rawls wrote in his book *A Theory of Justice*: "Envy is collectively disadvantageous; the individual who envies another is prepared to do things that make them both worse off, if only the discrepancy between them is sufficiently reduced."[7] The left relies upon this as a solution imagined by people who have been convinced they have no agency and will never amount to anything of their own volition.

Passionate political differences are not new for Americans. Even before we were an independent nation, Americans were hotly divided on whether to wage war against Britain to seek independence. Our country is the product of, and provides a platform for, unique ideas put forth by dynamic men and women. Over three centuries of our nation's history, we have become well acquainted with social activism and advocacy. But most Americans believe in and strive for a political discourse based on persuasion and debate, respectfully viewing fellow Americans who disagree with them as adversaries rather than enemies.

This is a posture requiring enough human decency to not call for erasing individuals from the public square, destroying their ability to make a living, or encouraging violence against them simply because they have an opinion that differs from our own. That's not a very high bar, but it's an exceedingly important one.

Indoctrinated Rage

For the past ten years, and really over the past thirty years, it's safe to say we've seen civilized mutual respect not just disappear but be replaced with a level of personal rage and hate, allowing no quarter for disagreement. Gone are the days when a Republican president, Reagan, could be seen at dinner together with a Democratic House Speaker, Tip O'Neill. It is now a brutal and ugly environment that makes it particularly dangerous for conservatives to speak their minds or for nonconformists of any stripe (especially classic liberals) to challenge progressive orthodoxy.

The behavior of leftists and their goals never change. Why is this? Because Marxist theory is actually just envy normalized, organized, and weaponized. It is predictable and constant in those afflicted or conditioned. Like malignant narcissism, there is no resolution for envy, other than the arbitrary and totalitarian redistribution of wealth and political power. And in countries where that was implemented, the result was not a utopia of fairness and bliss, but instead chaos and collapse. It is a mindset and psychology that is never satisfied or resolved and only assuaged through revenge and destruction.

For leftists, and Marxists in particular, what they say and do is never solely about the issues. Their real aim is to promulgate their cancerous radical agenda using the pretext of social issues. They usually claim to be paragons of virtue motivated by some larger ideal (equity, justice, morality) to attack things they have declared to be unfair or wrong. They characterize their struggle as a battle between good and evil, blasting anyone who disagrees with them in the harshest terms.

This is why AOC famously wore a custom Brother Vellies "Tax the Rich" ivory wool jacket dress to the $35,000-per-ticket Met Gala. No matter how much she has, it's not enough.

Within the larger political weaponization of envy by the left, the only thing that matters is their point of view, and the money and power that come with it. The implanting of malignant fear into society is a tool developed within their distorted and traumatic worldview, which is a product of their envy.

Sociologist Anne Hendershott observes: "Marxism, the pernicious theory that still motivates many within academia and beyond, is based entirely on envy. The Marxist promise of 'fairness' to the proletariat was a promise of a utopian world in which all conditions that produce envy will disappear. The Marxist assures us that an egalitarian world would remove all targets of envy so that the envious will have nothing to envy."[8]

Envy has been understood and considered one of the more dangerous moral failings of humanity for millennia. Aristotle precisely observed in *Rhetoric* that envy is pain at the good fortune of others.[9] In *Nicomachean Ethics*, he wrote: "Jealousy is both reasonable and belongs to reasonable men, while envy is base and belongs to the base, for the one makes himself get good things by jealousy while the other does not allow his neighbor to have them through envy."[10]

In his contribution to the Oxford University Press series *The Seven Deadly Sins*, Joseph Epstein penned the volume "Envy," wherein he notes: "Envy, to qualify as envy, has to have a strong touch—sometimes more than a touch—of malice behind it. Malice that cannot speak its name, cold-blooded but secret hostility, impotent desire, hidden rancor, and spite all cluster at the center of envy."[11]

Moreover, on envy being the driving force in Marxism, Epstein is blunt: "The great class struggle is about nothing less than the enviable advantages that the upper classes have over the lower—advantages that, even at the cost of bloody revolution, must be eliminated. For this reason, Marxism has even been described as a blood cult, with envy its abiding stimulant, fuel, and motive."[12]

The Bible pulls no punches about envy being "rottenness to the bones."[13] That rot is the subject of many biblical tales highlighting how far human beings will go when envy is afoot. It is important enough to make the list in the Ten Commandments with an admonition against coveting whatever it is your neighbor has. It is Cain's act of fratricide against his brother Abel that is perhaps one of the most famous of many acts in the Bible driven by unbridled envy.

Envy is the charging current animating the hate and enmity infecting many political and social disagreements. It allows the liquid fear (to borrow a perfect phrase from Polish sociologist and philosopher Zygmunt Bauman's seminal book on the issue[14]) we live in, to flow. As we've discussed, it is not organic but a contrived environment requiring constant development, nursing, and perpetuation.

True vs. Unwarranted Fear

Gavin de Becker, whom I got to know during our respective work during the O. J. Simpson murder trial (he as a security expert and me as an advocate on women's issues, including violence against women), is an authority on the prediction and prevention of violence and is much in demand internationally for his security expertise. His groundbreaking book, the aptly titled *The Gift of Fear: Survival Signs That Protect Us from Violence*, was first published in 1997 and remains one of the most important works on the subject.

De Becker explains that fear is a gift, as long as we are cognizant of what's happening and conscious of our response. He describes real fear as "a signal intended to be very brief, a mere servant of intuition. But though few would argue that extended, unanswered fear is destructive, millions choose to stay there."[15] Fear is indeed natural, but it is meant to be helpful and transitory, an emotion to motivate us and help us respond, in the moment, to danger.

Moreover, fear "is not a state, like anxiety," de Becker writes. "True fear is a survival signal that sounds only in the presence of danger, yet unwarranted fear has assumed a power over us that it holds over no other creature on earth."[16]

In de Becker's discussion about the differences between "true" and "unwarranted" fear, he warns us about unwarranted perpetual fear and its impact on our ability to respond to our intuition when urgently needed in the moment. This is where, he explains, we become inured to the feeling and are put more at risk by the impact of psychological exhaustion damaging our intuitive grasp of actual threats in our midst.

While de Becker's analysis is groundbreaking, I take issue with his assertion that millions *choose* to stay in fear. I contend that millions of us are unwittingly *conditioned* and *manipulated*, essentially trained, into fear on a mass scale by the establishment's Fear Industrial Complex. Just like my experience with the stalker in Times Square, fear is so prevalent and "normal" that it takes on a statelike condition as we become acclimated to it. This doesn't mean we adjust to fear; it means we become used to it, forgetting what it's like to live in psychological peace without unwarranted fear.

As our lives become increasingly hellish and depressing due to political incompetence, corruption, malevolence, and misadventure, today's neo-Democrats tell us to settle down and simply accept their ruinous "new normal." Just as domestic abusers insist their victims must accept chaos and deprivation, the left assumes we'll quit pushing back on anything if it's suddenly deemed "normal."

The implanting and maintaining of fear requires an ugly and sinister effort to convince a select group of people that they're doomed, that they have no future, and that there is nothing they can do about it. Because the monolithic and faceless "system" is racist, sexist, homophobic, or prejudiced in some other way or, even better, in multiple ways. There's only so much a society can take before mass anxiety also begins to manifest.

Mass Anxiety: The Spawn of Weaponized Fear

There are times when we owe our safety and even our survival to our sharp intuition and quick action in the face of imminent danger. A driver swerving to avert a collision, a mother grabbing her baby and fleeing their burning home, or a soldier desperately fighting for his life in battle. Fear and the instinct for self-preservation are powerful motivators that protect us.

Many of us have nightmares in which we face something we fear and are inexplicably frozen. Whether it's the desire to run, strike out, or yell, it's not an uncommon experience to be unable to move when facing horror and dread in the dream state. This is *anxiety*, which is a subset of fear.

We are all familiar with the "fight or flight" response to fear. It is a "primitive and powerful survival reaction," explains psychologist and researcher Dr. Rachael Sharman. "Once the brain has perceived a danger or threat, bucketloads of adrenaline course through our veins, increasing heart rate, pumping blood to muscles, and moving our attention toward a very singular focus: fighting off or getting away from the threat. We become so singularly goal-directed in that moment, we may not process (and therefore cannot remember) any extraneous details. . . . Many people report 'operating on instinct' with no clear memory of how they got away from or fought off a danger."[17]

Fear can be helpful when it serves as a momentary alert, prompting us to act. Anxiety, on the other hand, hurts us because it is an emotional state brought on in part by life experiences to "cope with adverse or unexpected situations."[18] Anxiety is a chronic state that can be brought about by an environment awash in fear-inducing events and messaging. It can be malleable and reduce our ability to cope properly with events in our lives. It is a state that makes us even more vulnerable to the constant hectoring by neo-Marxists and others on the left. This includes leading Democrats warning us that we are on the precipice of a planetary doom as they create severe and immediate economic, social, and cultural crises.

Let's look at a prime example of leftist propaganda intended to induce anxiety: climate change, which I address in greater detail in a later chapter. We know that the Earth's climate has changed, and temperatures have fluctuated dramatically throughout history, beginning long before humans even existed. Millions of years ago, for example, Antarctica was a swampy rain forest, not the ice-covered continent it is today.[19] More recently, glaciers covered much of North and South America, Asia, and Europe about 20,000 years ago, long before humans were burning fossil fuels.[20] So, yes, climate change is real. Places now in the deep freeze were once warm and filled with plants and animals, and places now home to billions of people, cities, suburbs, and farms were once buried under giant ice sheets. These climate changes were driven by natural forces.

Yet now the left tells us that unless climate change is stopped—in other words, unless we stop Mother Nature in her tracks—our planet and all living things will be quickly headed for irreversible disaster. The bells are ringing, the sirens are blaring, and we, like good, trained dogs, are supposed to panic.

The left is simply wrong to declare that climate change is an existential threat caused by human activity. In fact, the accusation that climate change is "man-made" is one of the most egregious examples of malignant narcissism. It is meant to convince us that our very existence is a horrible, dangerous thing, allowing this view to be weaponized as a handmaiden of fear and control.*

This particular issue is perfect for the Fear Industrial Complex that seeks to terrify us into doing its bidding. After all, what could be more frightening and motivating than the thought that the world will end soon unless we take urgent and drastic action? America's bumbling neo-Marxists seem to be channeling the French astrologer Nostradamus, who predicted almost five hundred years ago that the world would end in the year 3797.[21]

That end date is too far off to be useful for the fear merchants. Today's

---

* For the preeminent analysis of how leftist fearmongering and exploitation harms a true understanding of climate change, see Michael Shellenberger's crucial book, *Apocalypse Never: Why Environmental Alarmism Hurts Us All* (New York: Harper, 2020).

environmental alarmists claim the world will end much sooner unless we change our whole way of life and redistribute wealth and political power right away. If this causes energy shortages that cripple economies and literally leave communities in the dark, creates food shortages that lead to malnutrition and even starvation, and sends prices of many products soaring . . . well, buckle up and take it. Remember, fear and anxiety are the point. Leftist policies that deliver destruction are not a bug of this mendacity—they are a feature. Envy is a bitter and malicious handmaiden.

In January 2019, Representative Alexandria Ocasio-Cortez (D-NY), a self-proclaimed socialist, put Nostradamus's prediction on steroids by declaring definitively that the world will end in twelve years if climate change is not addressed. In a videotaped interview with Ta-Nehisi Coates at a public event, she said: "Millennials and people, you know, Gen Z and all these folks that will come after us are looking up, and we're like: 'The world is going to end in 12 years if we don't address climate change and your biggest issue is how are we gonna pay for it?'"[22] Her comments were delivered very seriously, and to applause.

Ocasio-Cortez repeated her doomsday warning months later, and then suddenly backtracked on Twitter after four months and summarily blamed the GOP: "This is a technique of the GOP, to take dry humor + sarcasm literally and 'fact check' it. Like the 'world ending in 12 years' thing. You'd have to have the social intelligence of a sea sponge to think it's literal."[23]

But the damage was done. Fox News reported: "A Rasmussen poll, conducted earlier this week, found 67 percent of Democrats believing that the U.S. has only 12 years to avert the 'disastrous and irreparable damage to the country and the world' stemming from climate change. Out of all total likely voters, 48 percent of respondents believed the apocalyptic claim."[24]

It's unfortunate, but not at all surprising, that Ocasio-Cortez—a former bartender who became the youngest woman ever to serve in Congress when she took office in 2019 at age twenty-nine—believes most Democrats have the brainpower of sea sponges. Perhaps that explains their willingness to do things that destroy so many lives. Her ridiculous claim that the world will end in 2031 builds on the kind of overwhelming fear and pathological anxiety that Democrats have long relied on to win voter support.

There has indeed been a disaster unfolding, ruining people's lives, but it's not a warming planet. It's the emotional and mental abuse perpetrated upon average people about climate change, creating an environment of liquid fear and mass anxiety.

This is just one tiny slice of the neo-Marxist and bureaucratic establishment's efforts on many fronts to frighten us into surrendering our autonomy and freedom to a massive government that pledges to protect us from contrived boogeymen. Climate is a perfect issue because predictions of future disasters can't be indisputably disproven until years or decades later.

The Method of the Marxist Madness

Earlier, I described to you how I was stalked in Times Square and how my instinctive reaction to my fear was to get away as quickly as I could. My mind was on autopilot, but it wasn't frozen. At a certain key point, my critical and logical mind came alive and allowed me to take control not only of that situation, but of my determination to confront my predicament and transform fear into resolve. Fortunately, I was able to escape my stalker without injury, unlike too many other women here and around the world.

When we are engaging with "real fear," as de Becker would call it, we act: "Real fear is not paralyzing—it is energizing."[25] These actions allow us to address the issue at hand, take control of our environment, and protect our personal safety. This is necessary fear, moving us to concern and the logic required to address that issue. As we cope with artificial fear constructed by politicians and other malign agents of the establishment, we are constrained in part by the fact that there is no immediate way to confront or resolve the fear. And that's part of the point.

Whether it's climate change, pandemics, crime, cancel culture, social chaos, or any other number of establishment and neo-Marxist schemes, there is no solution to address the anxious fear pounded into us by professional alarmists and their enablers.

"Progressive" policies focused on protecting criminals from justice rather than protecting the public from crime, along with the economic devastation of COVID-19 lockdown policies, have made walking anywhere in New York City past 9 p.m. a dangerous act. Defunding the police and enacting no-bail laws allows criminals, violent and otherwise, to remain on streets empty and quiet enough to be the setting for an episode of *The Walking Dead*.

We see this everywhere, especially when news reports in the summer of 2020 of the now infamously described "mostly peaceful" Black Lives Matter and Antifa riots were filled with images of small businesses on fire. The riots followed the death of George Floyd, a black man killed by a white Minneapolis police officer who was later convicted of murder. What we were seeing did not match what we were being told was happening. This creates a cognitive dissonance, adding to the sense of chaos and fear.

The left is good at one thing—organizing people to do its bidding, often under pretexts and through manipulation and lies. We don't need to imagine the impact of blending the malice and rage of envy with the anonymity of the mob mentality. We have seen this chaos—fomented by leftists in our own government and outside organizations like (but not limited to) Black Lives Matter and the fascist street gang Antifa—unleashed on civil society in the form of riots, arson, statue toppling, and personal violence. These groups want people to believe that their violence and riots are acceptable responses to social distress, but this is not true.

The left wants to instill immediate fear through specific violent events, but also to instill anxiety in all of us about *future* violence. The anxiety of unknown consequences is what pushes us off a cliff into an underlying chronic state of fear.

Most Americans were appalled and transfixed at the images of the rioting we saw from our windows, or on our TV or computer screens during the summer of 2020. We saw thugs burning down business districts, law-abiding citizens assaulted and murdered, police officers attacked, state and federal buildings vandalized and set on fire, and statues of historic figures damaged or destroyed. Our first understandable concern in the face of such obscene and repugnant violence is safety and survival.

In his book *How Fear Works*, Frank Furedi—a sociologist and analyst on issues including terrorism, fear, and cultural authority—points to Aristotle, who "wrote in his *Rhetoric* that 'fear may be defined as a pain or disturbance due to a mental picture of some destructive or painful event in the future.' The connection drawn by Aristotle between fear and visions of the future has important implications for understanding our current predicament."[26] Furedi adds:

> **In practice, anxiety about the unknown reinforces the public's concern about specific threats and habituates it to fear** [emphasis mine]. When society is habitually drawn towards worst possible outcomes it fosters a mood where fear can acquire a character of a habit, the acquisition of which endows fear with a banal and casual character.[27]

We are being habituated today into generalized fear by a number of disturbing developments designed to induce anxiety. These include Marxist rhetoric about America being irredeemably racist; demands to defund or even disband police departments; politicians accusing millions of Americans of being white supremacist terrorists; the Department of Justice announcing plans for terrorist investigations of parents who dare to confront local school boards; outrageous rhetoric and actions by the federal government and some state and local governments regarding COVID; and legacy media acting as the perfect handmaiden by perpetuating the negativity, accusations, and smears vomited up by the Fear Industrial Complex.

These are not unrelated situations. Nor are they wholly natural consequences of our modern world, as the progressive establishment would like us to believe. Instead, we are being subjected to accusations, emotional manipulation, crime- and violence-induced fear, health "emergencies," economic chaos, and cultural issues being deliberately exploited, contrived, and weaponized against us.

In *Liquid Fear*, Bauman's description of the emotion is an important addition to our discussion, about why it's such a malleable controlling tool that is so appealing to bullies, tyrants, grifters, and totalitarians:

> Fear is at its most fearsome when it is diffuse, scattered, unclear, unattached, unanchored, free floating, with no clear address or cause; when it haunts us with no visible rhyme or reason, when the menace we should be afraid of can be glimpsed everywhere but is nowhere to be seen. "Fear" is the name we give to our *uncertainty*: to our *ignorance* of the threat and of what is to be *done*—what can and what can't be—to stop it in its tracks—or to fight it back if stopping it is beyond our power [emphasis in original].[28]

Evading Murder-Suicide

Gavin de Becker's warning about becoming desensitized to our intuition when inundated with constant messages of danger is vitally important politically and socially, but also personally. His work has helped me understand a terrible event in my life that I want to share with you to illustrate how being caught in a perpetual state of fear and anxiety hampers our natural ability to manage our environment and puts us at even greater risk.

In my second book, *The Death of Right and Wrong*, I wrote about the suicide of my first partner in 1982, Brenda Benet. An actress in her midthirties, she was an alcoholic and had attempted suicide in the years prior to our relationship. I was sixteen when I first met her, and eighteen when I moved into her Los Angeles home nestled in the beautiful Mandeville Canyon section of Brentwood.

As the years go by and we get older, it's extraordinary how much more we understand about the various events in our lives, especially when we become the age of the person whose behavior so terribly altered our life. Only when I entered my thirties did I completely grasp the impact of this nightmarish experience on my teenaged self, and I am surprised I survived.

For decades, I felt guilt for not acting to stop Brenda's death by a self-inflicted gunshot wound and for not consciously recognizing the signs leading up to her act. And there were signs. With the help of psychotherapy, writing, my work, and my friends, I have come to terms with the trauma of being at her home when she killed herself while locked in a bathroom.

What I have never disclosed until now is the fact that Brenda's suicide was likely meant to be a murder-suicide—with me as the murder victim. I feel able to bring this to light now because it has been almost twenty years since I first wrote about the experience, and over forty years since the event itself. It has taken this long, but I now understand myself more and feel I finally comprehend the situation and my actions enough to share it with you.

I had not been paying attention to my intuition, or even to outright signals from Brenda about her intentions and capacity for violence. I had grown exhausted by her behavior and had adapted to a level of anxiety and fear that allowed me to cope with our roller-coaster relationship. Or at least I thought I was coping.

After arriving at her home for what Brenda told me would be lunch (I had ended our relationship and moved out two weeks earlier), I let myself in, and it was immediately apparent Brenda was in the downstairs bathroom near the front door. I could hear her pacing, and I could see the shadow of her movement in the light at the bottom of the door. I knew immediately, somehow, that she was going to kill herself.

For years, I explained it as "intuition," but more than that, it was the collection of signs I had collected in my subconscious for years. Suddenly, I connected the multitude of suppressed dots within seconds and knew what would happen.

I frantically begged Brenda to open the door and told her nothing was so serious that we couldn't work it out. She didn't respond, but continued pacing. At one point, I told her I was going to break down the flimsy door, which had a single-handle lock but no bolt. I was confident I could break it down with a swift kick or shove.

Upon telling Brenda what I was going to do, I heard her step back. The shadow on the floor indicated she was facing the door. As I prepared to throw myself into the door, I had an extraordinary and overwhelming sense of fear. At first, there was what felt like a physical restraint in front of me, almost like a massive hand placed on my torso, and I understood completely—it was as clear in my mind, as if in that moment someone else in that room was saying directly to me: "If you do this, you will die." It was like a batch of data being dropped into my mind.

Just as de Becker describes the issue of intuition and real fear, I was not frozen. I acted, but not by throwing myself against the door. I said nothing more, walked through a short hallway and around to the front door, and walked out of the house. As the front door closed, I heard Brenda fire the shot to her head that took her life.

At first, too afraid to go back into the house, I went to neighbors in an attempt to get help and to call the police (this was well before cell phones), but it was midday, and no one was home. Having no option, I summoned the courage and went back into Brenda's house and called the police. There was no movement in the bathroom, and the shadow under the door indicated she was on the floor. While waiting, I discovered a lone shoe box on a couch in the room attached to that bathroom. The box contained sheets of paper with handwritten notes. It was almost like a random diary in single pages outlining the suffering Brenda was experiencing, complaints, anger, guilt, and hopelessness. It was a crushing exposé of overwhelming psychic pain.

And then there was a note apologizing for killing me.

The note about the would-be murder didn't surprise me. That was what I sensed would happen just minutes before. I don't know why Brenda didn't come out of the bathroom to enact her plan or even shoot through the door. I can only surmise that she wanted both of us in the bathroom. Or perhaps, when it came right down to it, she had simply changed her mind.

It's difficult to assign logical decision-making to someone who has already transcended all instinct and decided to kill herself or others. To this day, I don't understand it. It will always remain an incomprehensible and unsolvable mystery.

This experience has compelled me in the decades that followed to want to know more and understand why people do what they do, and what can be done to mitigate the emotional and psychological pain afflicting too many of us, and women in particular.

My personal experience has helped shape my political and media work to focus on helping people understand what's happening in our lives and why. I suppose I am continuing to educate myself in the process. I am especially determined to make sure those who create and use the pain of others for their own benefit are exposed and defeated.

Looking back at that horrible day in April 1982, I understand now how my personal experience on the micro level with fear and anxiety allowed me to walk into an environment of existential danger. And it was the power of my "intuition" (finally allowing myself to connect the dots I had been ignoring) that broke through right when it was necessary, allowing me to not be a victim. All of us can have that breakthrough personally, politically, and culturally. Overcoming the impact of malignant forces is possible in every part of our lives.

Fear and anxiety afflict all of us at times in our lives. Our challenge is to understand their causes and overcome their consequences, all while learning more about ourselves and our environment. Read on, and you will gain insights into our collective and individual fears that will serve you well.

CHAPTER 4

Indoctrination Centers

Our leaders must remember that education doesn't begin with some isolated bureaucrat in Washington. It doesn't even begin with state or local officials. Education begins in the home, where it is a parental right and responsibility.

—PRESIDENT RONALD REAGAN[1]

The activists who have seized control of most American schools and colleges have rejected the admonition by President Ronald Reagan, above, and turned it on its head. They have transformed educational institutions into centers of indoctrination and propaganda dedicated to brainwashing young people from kindergarten through graduate and professional schools, erasing their individuality and dictating to them what to think.

The Thought Police running schools today are as intolerant of dissent as were their fictional counterparts in George Orwell's dystopian novel *1984*. Leftists are fervently committed to hunting down apostates. They brand the nonwoke as heretics and generate fear to pressure them to repent and submit to tyrannical Big Government control.

Today's inquisitional left seeks to create an environment of perpetual fear—not just in schools, but in every institution in our society—to destroy the individuality, independence, and autonomy of each of us, beginning in childhood. This has the potential to turn the American Dream into the American Nightmare, where we all live in perpetual fear of being canceled, ostracized, or punished in other ways if we dare deviate from rigid, woke dogma.

Make no mistake: the sinister goal of the leftist indoctrination centers masquerading as schools is to impose groupthink on students so they become social justice warriors in a bureaucratic army battling to transform America into an imagined Marxist utopia. They call it a utopia not because they believe it, but to cloak their ultimate goal—a totalitarian hell on Earth, which is always good for bureaucratic tyrants, and bad for everyone else. Schools have weaponized fear as a tool to take control of impressionable young minds and stop them from thinking for themselves. This also trains children to accept this sort of "schooling" after elementary grades.

Parents are the obvious obstacles to the success of this programming, so the true-believer educators do all they can to usurp parental rights by calling into question the intention and capability of mothers, fathers, and even the concept of family in general. The populace must be convinced that parenting is best left to professionals outside the home. Parents are still needed to procreate and feed and house their offspring. But the woke believe mothers and fathers should have little role in overseeing the education of their sons and daughters. Instead, the radicals believe that agents of the state (public school teachers and administrators) should be the primary influencers of children, for which the nuclear family must be maligned and smashed.

Napalm, Rubble, and Ash

As scrutiny of school curricula heated up during the COVID-19 lockdown and parents became more involved and vocal about what their children would be taught, the outright hostility by the left and the education establishment against parental rights and involvement became clear. An October 2021 opinion piece in the *Washington Post* titled "Parents Claim They Have the Right to Shape Their Kids' School Curriculum. They Don't,"[2] argued that parents insisting on being in charge of their children's education were using a "political tactic" to stop young people from thinking independently.

The authors of the article, an assistant professor of education at the University of Massachusetts Lowell and a freelance journalist, ask and answer their own question: "When do the interests of parents and children diverge? Generally, it occurs when a parent's desire to inculcate a particular worldview denies the child exposure to other ideas and values that an independent young person might wish to embrace or at least entertain. To turn over all decisions to parents, then, would risk inhibiting the ability of young people to think independently."[3]

In other words, the progressive agents of the state think their agenda is more important, smarter, safer, and better than what any pesky and intruding parent has in mind. Moreover, they insist that a parent providing guidance and a value system to a child is isolating and dangerous, yet somehow the stranger in a classroom deciding what is to be "inculcated" is noble and freeing. Ignore Mom and Dad, and bow down to Orwell's all-powerful Big Brother.

Watch out if the teachers' union doesn't get its way! Letting loose with the scourge of war analogies, they then warn that "conservatives are bringing napalm to the fight. . . . But as with any scorched-earth campaign, the costs of this conflict will be borne long after the fighting stops. Parents may end up with a new set of 'rights' only to discover that they have lost something even more fundamental in the process. Turned against their schools and their democracy, they may wake from their conspiratorial fantasies to find a pile of rubble and a heap of ashes."[4]

Yikes! Leftists want us to believe that parents ending up with scare-quoted "rights" are a threat to democracy and will only deliver a war-ravaged hellscape of rubble and ash. Okey-dokey. If anything, this screed confirms why strangers with a political agenda should be nowhere near the impressionable minds of children.

None of this is normal. Leftists rely on fear-based arguments about what will happen to children and society, if wokeism does not prevail.

One has to wonder, when did parents become the enemy who must be excised from their children's lives? At about the same time Marxist theory was securely implanted in much of the critical political and cultural infrastructure in this country.

Authoritarian movements have long believed that planting ideas in the minds of children can turn them into obedient adults to perpetuate even the most toxic beliefs far into the future. Once beliefs take root in young minds, they grow and strengthen over the years like an oak emerging from a seed, and the more they are woven into the child's identity, the more difficult it is to change them later in life.

Totalitarian regimes spend a great deal of time fostering this investment in future control. The Russian Bolsheviks created the Young Communist League, the Nazis created Hitler Youth, and Mao Zedong created the Red Guards. In 1976, the totalitarian Cambodian Khmer Rouge ordered all children over the age of seven to be "separated from their parents to live communally with Khmer Rouge instructors."[5] Unsurprisingly, Pol Pot, the Marxist genocidal leader of the regime, gravely warned: "Mothers should not get too entangled with their children."[6]

All these diabolical regimes tightly regulated what was taught in schools. Their goal was to indoctrinate young people and teach them to be more loyal to their political masters than to their own parents. This allows Big Government to rob us of our freedoms and turn us into obedient servants. It is a fundamentally anti-American effort because, in America, government has always been the servant of people—not the other way around. We must not let this change.

Behind the Zoom Glass

Many Americans were unaware of just how far off the deep end leftists had gone in their efforts to turn schools into assembly lines churning out woke robots until 2020. That's when COVID-19 lockdowns closed schools, forcing students to struggle to learn remotely, often using the Zoom platform from home on computers, tablets, or smartphones.

Parents—many of them working from home or newly unemployed

due to the pandemic—gained the ability to watch their children in these remote classes and were shocked to see the leftist garbage that teachers were feeding students in the name of "education." The teaching of race essentialism through the poisonous Critical Race Theory, books about sex acts, children "transitioning" gender in secret, the denigration of patriotism, and the view that America is inherently racist, sexist, imperialistic, environmentally destructive, and a force for evil abounded. Millions of parents were rightly outraged.[7, 8]

Obviously, we all understand that America is not and never has been perfect. No nation can claim the mantle of perfection, but our freedom of thought and speech makes it possible to try to become a better people and nation and allows us to determine when we make progress.

Children certainly need to be taught about slavery and racial discrimination, mistreatment of American Indian tribes, discrimination against women, and our other challenges. But they also need to be taught that these issues of the past have been largely corrected, and we remain vigilant about them in our continuing quest to fulfill the mission of the Constitution to "form a more perfect union."[9] They also need to be taught about other nations and peoples that have committed similar injustices—including the ones that still do today.

Above all, children need to be taught that the good in America far outweighs its shortcomings, and that America is the greatest nation that has ever existed. Much like what we tell our children and even ourselves as we get older—yes, we've had problems, made mistakes, and have regrets, but it's how we respond that matters, which is informed by our character. As individuals, the good in us also far outweighs the difficulties.

Many of us know the lifelong and dreadful impact of growing up in abusive homes where adults reinforced our negative self-view and berated us as "irredeemable." The Marxist agitprop and conditioning being unleashed in our education system is a haunting simile of what happens in an abusive home and has the same deleterious impact on the young minds subjected to it. Children growing up in fear become anxious, unfocused, and unsuccessful at personal relationships. Does that sound like any young adults you know? Moreover, a study from the National Scientific Council on the Developing Child at Harvard University reports that "early exposure to circumstances that produce persistent fear and chronic anxiety can have lifelong effects on brain architecture."[10]

The United States is a nation that replaced rule by kings, queens, and dictators with a representative democracy in which the people rule. A nation that provides us with more freedom and rights than any other. Moreover, it is exactly the negatives we have overcome and defeated that illustrate the power of freedom and the decency of the American people and the American Dream.

If America was the terrible place leftists make it out to be, people would be leaving here in droves. Instead, America is the home to more immigrants than any other nation—about 45 million people, making up 14 percent of the US population.[11] They come here specifically because of our past and what we strive to become: a strong and compassionate nation that is the leader of the free world militarily and economically. Those of us lucky enough to be born in the United States should honor, love, and appreciate it even more than the people desperate to come here.

Most American parents want their children to learn these facts in school so that young people understand how lucky they are to live in the United States and embrace patriotism to preserve our liberty for themselves and for future generations. Most parents also haven't been sitting at home, wringing their hands about Marxist theory, because they haven't had to until recently. It has been unthinkable for parents that sending their children to public school would endanger their moral authority over their own family and their right to guide their sons and daughters in the fashion that best suits their hopes for the future.

But here we are, in an upside-down world where politicians, union organizers, social workers, and activist teachers from kindergarten through graduate schools are shifting from teaching people *how* to think, to what to think.

Identity Politics and Triggering Genocide

The immediate demonstration on college campuses across the country celebrating the Iranian-backed terrorist group Hamas's genocidal slaughter of unarmed civilians, including children and infants, in Israel on October 7, 2023, reveals an important truth about the mind-killing agenda.

How can thousands of students paint signs saying, "From the River to the Sea," a slogan clearly advocating the return of all of the Jewish state to Palestinians? How do they defend ethnic cleansing? They don't even try, often because they're ignorant about what they're supporting. In fact, a survey found that a majority of those chanting that slogan couldn't name the river or the sea at issue. And a full 60 percent reduced their support for the slogan when they were informed that it was a call for the genocide of the Jews.[12] Ignorance is bliss, until it's not.

In November 2023, the House of Representatives censured Democrat Rashida Tlaib of Michigan for using the slogan, even as she denied its plain meaning. Tlaib has lived her whole life in Michigan, attending public school and a state college, presumably learning to accept propaganda without thinking much about it along the way.

Mind-killing is the destruction of the individual mind and sense of self with conditioning with identity politics, perpetual victimhood, hate and envy, nurtured with fear and racism. Every argument the extremist left makes is meant to facilitate brainwashing people into accepting the vile notion that other human beings are less than human or "irredeemably" evil because of the color of their skin or some other personal characteristic. This is how genocide is triggered, and it is the fuel that has fed the American university system for over half a century.

Watching thousands of people marching in support of a bloodthirsty terrorist group foaming at the mouth with a hatred of Jews was a frightening spectacle, but it wasn't organic or inexplicable. It was the result of teaching, stoking, and encouraging the cancer of racism and hate by Marxist theorists, professors, community "activists," teachers' unions, and the leftist public education establishment, including the Department of Education. How best to help metastasize the woke cancer? By mandating the scourge of "Diversity, Equity, and Inclusion" throughout the education system at every level.

When the curtain was pulled back on the shocking extent of Jew-hatred on American college campuses in the aftermath of the Hamas attack in Israel, one former college DEI director bluntly blamed the woke scheme for driving antisemitism on campuses.

"The blatant antisemitism on college campuses[13] has shocked millions of Americans over the past week and a half. But not me," wrote Tabia Lee, former DEI director at De Anza College in Silicon Valley. "I saw antisemitism on a weekly basis in my two years as a faculty 'diversity, equity and inclusion' director. In fact, I can safely say that toxic DEI ideology deliberately stokes hatred toward Israel and the Jewish people."[14]

Lee continued, "Some campus leaders and colleagues repeatedly told me I shouldn't raise issues about Jewish inclusion or antisemitism. I was told in no uncertain terms that Jews are 'white oppressors' and our job as faculty and staff members was to 'decenter whiteness.' I was astounded, but I shouldn't have been. At its worst, DEI is built on the unshakable belief that the world is divided into two groups of people: the oppressors and the oppressed."[15]

All of this is designed to frighten people and then use that fear to gain power, not just here but everywhere it's implemented. It's meant to make Israelis literally surrender, and Western civilization surrender its values and moral authority through silence, due to the shock and fear of witnessing unspeakable and inhuman atrocities. The intent of DEI is to divide people into two groups: the oppressed and the oppressor, and those who are trained to be afraid of speaking and those who are trained to be afraid of hearing. That this produced a hatred of Jews and fear in Jews is one of the foundational goals of the leftist powers that be.

Understanding the method to the madness doesn't make it any less alarming, but it does help us remain intellectually nimble enough to confront and defeat this cancerous tumor in education threatening the very survival of our country and Western civilization itself.

Anti-Parent Arrogance

Parents are a serious impediment to the goals of leftist activists, as their parallel agenda of crushing the American family by destroying the bond between parents and children is of utmost importance.

The revelation of the Marxist anti-parent arrogance of the left was dramatically illustrated in September 2021 by Terry McAuliffe, a former chairman of the Democratic National Committee and former governor of Virginia seeking reelection. In a debate with Republican gubernatorial candidate Glenn Youngkin, McAuliffe said, "I don't think parents should be telling schools what they should teach."[16]

With their candidate saying the quiet part out loud, the Democrats watched the Republicans turn the foot-in-mouth comment into an ad blasting McAuliffe, as Youngkin made preserving parental rights in education a centerpiece of his campaign.[17] Virginia voters elected Youngkin because moms and dads, unsurprisingly, had no intention of coparenting with the government.

McAuliffe's toxic view about the supremacy of teacher rights over parental rights is a foundational belief of the left. The powerful National Education Association, a three-million-member teacher union with a long record of funding Democratic political candidates,[18] echoed this view in a tweet in November 2022 that said: "Educators love their students and know better than anyone what they need to learn and thrive."[19]

Are we supposed to believe that teachers love their students more than parents love their own children? And believe parents are clueless when it comes to knowing what their children should be taught in school? The answer is yes. We are expected to believe it because the progressives, informed by their own leftist indoctrination and contempt for the average person, believe it.

What's really concerning is that once the attitude that government and its agents (school administrators and teachers) know better than parents what's best for children, the next logical step is to take children from parents to ensure they get a thorough indoctrination in government "reeducation centers." As already noted, it has happened and, horribly, is still happening.

Amnesty International—hardly a right-wing group—and many other human rights groups have reported that China has imprisoned more than one million Muslim Uighurs (a minority ethnic group) as part of a genocide designed to wipe out Uighurs as a distinct population. In addition to forced sterilizations to reduce the number of Uighur births, the BBC reported in 2021 that according to Amnesty International, "China has forcibly separated Uighur families by taking young children into state orphanages . . . without the consent of their families" for "re-education" to mold them into obedient followers of the Chinese communist regime.[20]

The Associated Press reported in October 2022 that invading Russian forces waging war against Ukraine "have deported Ukrainian children to Russia or Russian-held territories without consent, lied to them that their parents didn't want them, used them for propaganda, and given them Russian families and citizenship," in addition to offering them "patriotic education" to turn them into loyal Russian subjects. The Ukrainian government said nearly eight thousand children have been deported this way.[21]

Think this sort of forced removal of children from their homes to indoctrinate them with new beliefs could never happen in the United States? It already has. Hundreds of thousands of Native American children were forcibly (or sometimes voluntarily) taken from their families and sent to federal Indian Boarding Schools[22] between 1819 and 1969 for an assimilation and reeducation program to wipe out their cultures, religions, and languages. Parents and children were traumatized, and some children were physically and sexually abused.[23, 24] This was an example of Big Government ignoring parental rights and using its power and the weapon of fear to crush the individual and make an entire group of people submit to government orders.

Parental rights are a serious and existential issue because for as long as human beings have existed, mothers and fathers have been responsible for raising their children, serving as their moral arbiters and protectors. This is instinctual behavior. Most parents, however, don't have the time to homeschool their children, so they delegate the important tasks to teachers and schools (and prepay for that system through taxes), just as they delegate providing health care for their children to doctors.

But parents don't give *decision-making authority* about the care of their children's minds and bodies to teachers at the schoolhouse door, any more than they give medical decision-making power to doctors when children enter the exam room or hospital. This is why McAuliffe's claim that parents should butt out and leave it to teachers and school officials to chart the course of the education of their children struck such a nerve and helped cost him the election.

Parents Smeared as Domestic Terrorists

As elementary school Marxist curriculum became exposed courtesy of the pandemic lockdowns, parents around the country began exercising their First Amendment rights under the Constitution and showing up at school board meetings in 2021. They were protesting and challenging the substitution of indoctrination for education in schools, as well as long school shutdowns during the pandemic.

This engagement by local parents prompted the National School Boards Association (NSBA) to actually seek Big Government intervention to crush the protests. The association sent a letter to President Joe Biden warning that "threats and acts of violence" at school board meetings might amount to "domestic terrorism."[25] The letter actually suggested using the Patriot Act against parents who dared to become involved with the education of their own children.

In what must be one of the fastest turnarounds in federal government history, a short five days later, Attorney General Merrick Garland promptly issued a memo ordering the FBI, the Justice Department Criminal Division, and US attorneys around the nation to investigate the concerned parents due to "criminal conduct directed toward school personnel."[26]

Yet, true to one of my main warnings throughout this book, none of this was organic but instead the result of a request by the Biden administration, which apparently wanted an excuse to both terrify American parents into silence and harass and arrest those who would not comply.

According to emails obtained through a Freedom of Information Act request by a parents' group called Parents Defending Education,[27] "Education Secretary Miguel Cardona solicited the much-criticized letter from the National School Boards Association that compared protesting parents to domestic terrorists, according to an email exchange reviewed by Fox

News. The email exchange indicates Cardona was more involved with the letter's creation than previously known," reported the network.[28]

This was not the first revelation of collusion between the Biden administration and the NSBA. Previous emails indicated additional correspondence between the two for weeks before the letter to Biden was sent.[29, 30]

In the meantime, the ensuing exposure and outrage had an impact. The NSBA retracted its missive and apologized, admitting there was "no justification for some of the language included in the letter."[31] Despite this, in September 2023, two years after the original issuance of the memo, Attorney General Garland continued to refuse to rescind his directive targeting parents, saying "there's nothing to rescind."[32] Yet, according to whistleblowers, "the FBI opened investigations in every region of the country and relating to all types of educational settings."[33]

Schools Aren't What They Used to Be

Since schools today bear little resemblance to the ones many of us attended in the twentieth century, parental rights are particularly important. For most of American history, students were taught reading, writing, arithmetic, civics, American history, science, and other essential subjects and skills—along with, as famed anthropologist Margaret Mead put it, "Children must be taught how to think, not what to think."[34] With some exceptions in liberal enclaves, parents didn't have to worry about teachers on the loony left trying to radicalize their children.

The anti-individualist wokeism virus is in the process of consuming a great deal of our critical education infrastructure. The fact that this even has to be discussed is shocking. How did we get here? The left understands that indoctrinating children is key to fulfilling its agenda. That's because American parents have long raised children beholden to the values of a free people and country, and this is kryptonite to the barbaric and ruinous notions of Marxism. Gaining control of public education is a key Marxist objective, and that goal has been achieved with astounding success.

The schools of decades past did what they were supposed to do. They educated generations of students who made America the richest, most powerful, most prosperous, and greatest nation in the world. Unfortunately, schools have now been transformed by political correctness on steroids.

Now, rather than giving children the skills they need to succeed in their careers and as responsible citizens, woke schools waste enormous amounts of valuable class time on politically correct propaganda. Every fact-free hour of classroom and homework time devoted to stoking despair over gender identity, systemic racism, sexist oppression, police brutality, and capitalism is an hour taken away from learning about core school subjects.

One thing woke education does accomplish, however, is to create depressed, paranoid, angry, and fearful young people brainwashed into believing that America is a lost cause and her people are horrible and irredeemable bigots. This creates fear of the world, people in general, and parents in particular. The left works feverishly to instill envy and paranoia in young people to guarantee they'll grow up to be leftists themselves, perpetuating the Marxist virus.

Consider the case of Annabella Rockwell, at first thrilled to be accepted at Mount Holyoke College, a women's college in Massachusetts currently charging nearly $60,000 per year in tuition and fees. But like so many others, her dream turned into an indoctrination nightmare after she enrolled in 2011.

The *New York Post* described[35] Rockwell as having lived a charmed teenage life as the heiress of a pharmaceutical fortune. Before college, she had already lived abroad and competed as a figure skater. Describing herself as "open-minded," but having been raised in a "traditional" home, when it was time to go to college, she chose Mount Holyoke. "I was so excited about going to this renowned, respected school in Massachusetts," she told the *Post*. "I literally arrived there bright-eyed and bushy-tailed, I was just so happy."[36] Normally, the story would end there as another happy college tale. But not these days.

Rockwell described an environment resembling classic indoctrination impacting her own worldview so severely that she had to undergo deprogramming. She was lectured about "the patriarchy" working against her and was told that oppression, while not always apparent, was constant, ruining her life, and must be fought.[37]

"I left school [in 2015] very anxious, very nervous, very depressed and sad. I saw everything through the lens of oppression and bias and victimhood," Rockwell told the *Post*. "I came to the school as someone who saw everyone equally. I left looking for injustice wherever I could and automatically assuming that all white men were sexist. My thoughts were no longer my own."

Rockwell's relationship with her mother collapsed because she was convinced by professors to think of her parents as a problem and family as something to reject. "The professors encouraged alienation [from parents] and even offered their homes to stay in. They'd say, like, don't go see them, come stay with us for the holiday. Most of my classmates believed all this stuff, too. If you didn't you were ostracized," she explained to the newspaper.

The good news is that Rockwell's mother, appalled by what the college experience had done to her daughter, hired a deprogrammer to reverse the damage that had been done by the indoctrination. It worked, and now both women are telling their stories in an effort to warn other families that this isn't something that happens to other people—it can happen to anyone.

Annabella Rockwell's parents are lucky in that their business success allowed them to use extraordinary measures to come to the aid of their daughter, whose joy for life and happiness had been undone by miserable and malevolent leftists in control of a college. The first step for all parents is recognizing that what is happening is not normal, organic, or beneficial, and that it must be confronted. Most Americans, especially the families of those being indoctrinated, are themselves manipulated into surrendering to what is happening. This is why the anti-parent agenda exists: because leftists know that parental involvement ruins their entire scheme.

Smug Ignorance and Small Minds

It doesn't take a Lenin, Hitler, Mao, or Pol Pot to engineer and advocate for parents to be banished from their children's lives in favor of more glorious and masterful party apparatchiks. It is the especially small-minded who are attracted to the left's cultic program of authoritarian control.

Smugly ignorant politicians seem to believe they are morally superior to those not in public office and slouch toward tyranny whenever the opportunity presents itself. Their compulsion to indulge their conceit eventually reveals the banal contempt they feel for Americans in general and parents in particular.

Remind yourself: for some reason, so-called progressives (the favored euphemism for both economic Marxists and cultural Marxists) see parents as at least a problem for realizing their agenda, if not an outright enemy. Remember to ask: Why is that? What is it they are so obsessed with that it requires removing children from their parents' sphere of influence?

Case in point about small minds: Democratic US representative Eric Swalwell of California was one of the biggest boosters of the now disproven conspiracy theory that President Trump colluded with Russia to steal the 2016 election. Marc Thiessen at the *Washington Post* noted at the time, "During the Mueller probe, Swalwell repeatedly claimed without a shred of evidence that Trump not only colluded with Russia but also that he was an 'agent' of Russian intelligence. . . . Swalwell used his position as a member of the House Intelligence Committee to suggest that he had seen evidence the rest of us could not that Trump was a Russian operative—when we now know no such evidence existed."[38]

Not surprisingly, that same bad judgment and moral vertigo also drives Swalwell to be bothered by the idea that American parents expect to be in charge of their children's education.

When Republican senator Tim Scott of South Carolina tweeted that, "We are putting parents back in charge of their kids' education," Swalwell tweeted back: "Please tell me what I'm missing here. What are we doing next? Putting patients in charge of their own surgeries? Clients in charge of their own trials? When did we stop trusting experts? This is so stupid."[39]

Jonathan Turley—a professor at George Washington University Law School, an attorney, and a legal scholar—obliged Swalwell and explained exactly what he was missing. "These were curious analogies to draw since patients and clients are in charge of the key decisions in their surgeries and trials. What Rep. Swalwell is missing is called informed consent," Turley said. "What is most striking about Swalwell's reference to patients and clients is that, under his educational approach, parents have far more say in a wart removal or a parking ticket challenge than the education of their children. If anything, his analogies support the call for greater parental knowledge and consent."[40]

Parents play a crucial role in their child's education, and their opinions should be taken into account. The only reasons not to are always suspect. Remember, the ultimate goal is not to censor people directly. It is to scare everyone into increasingly censoring themselves, until they stop thinking freely their own thoughts.

The Woke Takeover

The woke takeover of American schools and colleges has reached an irrational level. Teachers, administrators, and school governing board members in elementary, secondary, and higher education now fear being denounced and losing their jobs for addressing a student by the wrong pronoun or saying anything that could possibly be labeled a so-called "microaggression." They also fear allowing students to have a free and candid exchange of ideas and to speak up in defense of (horrors!) traditional values and conservative ideas. Students are treated as if, and ergo taught that they are, confused infants who could melt at any time by being "triggered" by something they find disturbing.

The left wants "safe spaces" on school campuses, meaning they want campuses sealed off from any ideas that are not part of woke dogma. This, of course, reinforces the lie that any idea that challenges or deviates from the approved framework is itself dangerous. Rather than using schools to allow students to expand their minds—which was the original and imperative mission of the education system—the left wants to use indoctrination and fear to close student minds to the "wrong" ideas, meaning ideas that do not conform or pay allegiance to the leftist narrative, or that could provoke and inspire free thinking and even outright rejection of brainwashing itself.

Not content to subject only their students to woke brainwashing, some schools are even demanding reeducation for parents as well. For example, as the *New York Post* reported in October 2022, at least five New York City private schools that charge about $60,000 per year in tuition "are pushing woke training on parents in Soviet-like efforts to keep their kids on message." The schools call on parents to undergo "training in anti-racism" and "diversity, equity, and inclusion," and some require parents to write an essay and sign a pledge promising to support these woke values in their homes.[41]

With their demand for absolute viewpoint conformity, the schools might as well put a notice on their websites saying conservative parents need not bother applying for their children to attend. Or maybe the schools can next require parents to place listening devices in their homes so the Thought Police can monitor their conversations with their children to make sure there are no deviations from the woke script.

The problem is so serious that it led former Trump administration secretary of state Mike Pompeo to say in an interview in November 2022 that "the most dangerous person in the world is [American Federation of Teachers president] Randi Weingarten. It's not a close call." Pompeo added: "If you ask, 'Who's the most likely to take this republic down?' It would be the teacher's union, and the filth they're teaching our kids, and the fact that they don't know math and reading or writing."[42]

In her response to Pompeo's spot-on remarks, Weingarten perfectly illustrated exactly why the leftist education mob is inculcating our children with the scourge of identity politics. Instead of addressing Pompeo's critique and the concerns across the country about her malfeasance and the destruction of the American education system, Weingarten accused Pompeo of bigotry.

The British newspaper the *Guardian* reported: "Weingarten, who has been president of the AFT since 2008, [said] she thought Pompeo was attacking her because she is 'Jewish, gay, teacher and union.' 'It's all of the above,' Weingarten said. 'It's an anti–public school strategy. The antisemitic tropes are there. The anti-gay tropes are there. It's anti-union. It's anti-teacher. It's all of the above. But the effect is it really hurts what teachers are trying to do to help kids every single day.'"[43]

So Pompeo is supposedly a bigot and wants to hurt children. The End. Discussion Over. Commence with the Cancellation.

This is the only strategy the left has ever known. It is global, it is as old as the hills, and it is becoming the sole focus of the public education system in our nation. Weingarten's response is the epitome of the gaslighting that leftists have always relied on because they cannot survive being confronted on the details of the issues. Their goal relies on the shutting down of debate and critique, and the pursuit of censorship in the name of "safety." Ironically, safety is supposedly only possible when the public has been conditioned to live in fear of, well, everything.

In the twenty-first century, identity politics as a vehicle for control and annihilation through fear has become refined and especially dangerous due to the left's control of the bureaucratic state, the legacy media, Big Tech, and the education system. The only way the left survives is to make sure students churned out by woke schools are brainwashed into believing this madness. Students may not be functionally literate,[44] but they sure know how to destroy someone by accusing them of being racist, sexist, or whichever of the many phobic iterations that have been concocted.

Enough Is Enough

The indoctrination doesn't start in the Ivy League. The left wants their mind-killed soldiers *ready* by the time they get to college. At the very latest, elementary school is where the conditioning begins.

One father in New York City decided enough was enough and removed his daughter from an elementary school that was subjecting his nine-year-old to CRT. "Little children don't need to feel bad about the color of their skin. That's what they're teaching them, to feel bad about who they are. Schools are supposed to be teaching you confidence," said Harvey Goldman in an interview with Fox News.[45] He added that most parents and teachers are "scared to say something." When he confronted school administrators, he said they told him there was nothing he could do about the curriculum. If he didn't like it, he could withdraw his daughter from the school. And that's just what he did.

The Goldman family's experience is not an outlier. In New York City, an underground network of parents is working to expose and fight the increasingly woke culture in city grade schools. The *New York Post* reported on the growing movement and spoke with Bion Bartning, a father "who is Mexican and Yaqui [an Indian tribe] on one side and Jewish on the other, [and] said he was especially dismayed by how [schools] across the country force kids to label themselves based on their skin color. Sometimes kids are even given a palette and made to choose the color that best fits their skin, he said. 'I don't fit into any of those race buckets,' Bartning told the *Post*. 'I think it is wrong to be teaching kids these socially constructed race categories. It's a destructive ideology, teaching children to be pessimistic and full of grievance rather than being optimistic and full of gratitude. It goes against all the values I was raised with, and there are many out there who feel as I do. This is a movement with a lot of people.'"[46]

Another New York parent described what one private school was teaching children in the name of CRT. "The fourth graders learned about astronauts and inventors—but only black ones. They no longer learn about Thomas Edison. The math curriculum is a joke; they've dumbed it down. No more birthday celebrations are allowed and no holidays are allowed. They did away with Columbus Day but now they celebrate the end of Ramadan and the Chinese Lunar Year."[47]

Parents of children in several New England private schools formed a protest group in 2021 called Parents United after they were shocked to learn their children were "being taught what to think, rather than how," said cofounder Ashley Jacobs. She said some students were told never to use gender-specific language and were told to reconsider their own gender identity. Jacobs said schools didn't allow students to express unwoke views, so students were afraid to say anything in class because they might get in trouble or offend someone. Parents said schools were spending too much time on ideological issues and not enough time on academics.[48]

In another example, Florida Republican governor Ron DeSantis signed the Parental Rights and Education bill into law in March 2022 to bar discussion of gender identity and sexual orientation in kindergarten through third-grade classrooms. The law also requires that any presentation of the topics to students in older grades be "age-appropriate or developmentally appropriate." What a concept! This is so commonsensical it's hard to believe it became controversial. Yet woke radicals became apoplectic over the Florida legislation, falsely labeling it the "Don't Say Gay" bill. Taking their cue, the media went into hysterics.[49]

The good news is that the coordinated Outrage Theatre hasn't stopped other states from following Florida's commonsense lead on the most basic parental rights. Alabama enacted its version of the Florida law in April 2022, and similar bills were introduced in at least twenty other state legislatures.[50]

CHAPTER 5

Destroying Individualism

I was not born to be forced. I will breathe after my own fashion. Let us see who is the strongest.

—HENRY DAVID THOREAU[1]

One of the most disturbing aspects of wokeism is its condemnation of the concept of the individual in favor of the concept of group identity. The American ideal has always been for each of us to be treated as an individual and to advance based on our abilities and hard work. This was the foundation of the American Dream.

But socialism and communism subsume the individual to Big Government in the name of supposedly advancing the greater societal good when in fact the complete opposite is the result. While capitalism encourages individual initiative, innovations, entrepreneurship, and the accumulation of wealth, Marxism looks on rewarding these qualities as selfishness. The Marxist view is at the core of wokeism, and it is being force-fed to millions of children in school today.

In woke schools, children are no longer being taught to look at themselves and others as individuals, but as members of particular racial, ethnic, religious, gender, and other groups. What is the practical effect? Imagine this: Sally is ten years old and white, so she is taught under Critical Race Theory that she is part of the oppressor class, benefits from white privilege, holds white bias, and must atone for the sins of past generations, leaving her upset and confused. Her friend Mary is also ten years old and is black, so she is taught under Critical Race Theory that she is oppressed and victimized by systemic racism that pervades every aspect of life, leaving her upset that people of Sally's race are working against her ability to succeed. The ten-year-old girls had always looked at each other as individuals, each unique in her own way but with many things in common that were more important than their difference in skin color. Yet through CRT, they are to view each other through a racial lens.

CRT's obsession with racial differences encourages group stereotyping and prejudice, made worse by calls for "equity"—meaning that group advancement and equal outcomes, rather than individual achievement and equal opportunity, have become the new standard of fairness.

This focus on group identity flies in the face of the hopes of civil rights icon Dr. Martin Luther King Jr., who told an estimated 250,000 people[2] at his famous speech at the March on Washington for Jobs and Freedom in 1963: "I have a dream that my four little children will one day live in a nation where they will not be judged by the color of their skin but by the content of their character."[3] That's what our fictional Sally and Mary want—and it's the dream of equality we should all share.

Equality and equity are not the same. The former should be revered. The latter, reviled. Equality is anathema to the left because, by relying on individualism, it fosters tolerance and respect. Equity, on the other hand, demands an erasure of the individual and elevates only the faceless group. Seeing other people as complete and unique individual human beings facilitates empathy by reminding us of the humanity in each person. It's the power of seeing a person as a member of the human race as opposed to a generic representative of a particular group identity.

That's exactly the problem for the left. If you train people to see only groups and foster hate between those groups, eventually one of those groups will demand the elimination of the others. Critical Race Theory, and all Marxist critical theories, essentially train people to see people unlike themselves as subhuman, normalizing the resentment and eventual hatred of outgroups as oppressors.

Equity: A Marxist Word Game

The left uses the fear of being labeled a bigot, particularly a racist, to prevent people from questioning or challenging their agenda. They achieve this by training people to self-censor on social issues, especially those related to race, using fear. The ultimate goal is to present every anti-human leftist mission as a benevolent and necessary intervention against racism, making it psychologically difficult for those conditioned by fear to criticize or challenge destructive ideas. The price to pay otherwise could include social ostracization and the loss of employment. The left has constructed a system to punish those accused of wrongthink, and the accusation of "structural racism" is a way to maliciously label the majority of Americans as racist.

A case in point is the Marxist equity agenda, which replaces the American commitment of equal opportunity for all with the malignant "equal outcomes" of CRT. When you know the specifics, it is obvious that equality and equity are very different, even though the terms sound similar and are conveniently tossed around interchangeably by leftists. Leftists know Americans are committed to equality; it's in our DNA. Their conflation of the two terms is deliberate—not only to confuse, but to cloak the fraudulent concept of equity from scrutiny and complaints.

Equality is a goal we should all strive to achieve. It requires that each of us be treated fairly and justly as an individual, regardless of the demographic categories into which we fall. The civil rights movement in the 1950s and 1960s fought for equality and won long-overdue victories, outlawing segregation and other ugly vestiges of racism.

The women's movement won victories, giving women the right to vote in 1920, and later opened up careers and colleges to them. This was the beginning of an effort to expand how women viewed themselves in and out of the home. Women, like men, should be able to build lives that best suit them. Some prefer the traditional role of stay-at-home mom and homemaker, others focus on their careers, and most blend the two roles. Ultimately, the American Dream is different for everyone, but all Americans should have the same access and opportunities to pursue their uniquely personal aspirations. Outcomes, though, are up to the individual, not the collective.

The gay rights equality movement led to the legalization of consenting homosexual relations, protected gay people from discrimination on the job and elsewhere, and ultimately brought about legalized same-sex marriage. The drive for equality also succeeded in getting colleges, along with the federal and state governments, to provide more financial aid for students so that bright young people could get a higher education even if their families couldn't afford to foot the bill. Teaching students today about the benefits of these actions to promote equality is a good thing and should be encouraged.

Equity, on the other hand, isn't a dream; it's a cancerous nightmare. It requires remedying past discrimination by discriminating against someone else now. Yet students are being indoctrinated in schools around the country at every age level to embrace "equity" and even our federal government is pouring money into its promotion and use.[4]

Don't be fooled by the new language—it's part of all the old and failed leftist theories that have destroyed lives and countries for centuries. We have seen this scourge of centralized planning and complete social control (requiring the annihilation of the individual) implemented by every failed communist, fascist, and other totalitarian nation. And now American leftists are arguing for it to be implemented here as they actively seed the academies, our government, and culture with this repugnant notion.

The War on Merit

No one willingly acquiesces to psychological imprisonment and severe personal limitations applied by a government. Even leftists have to couch their schemes in rhetoric appealing to fairness and freedom. The notion of the left's equity scheme is not only unnatural at its core, but there's only one way to truly achieve it—by artificially culling the field of high achievers who illustrate how different human beings can be.

Most of us are average people and are more than happy with our lives and accomplishments. In America, being middle class provides the best quality of life in human history. Among the many things history has shown is that not all people are the same, and our republican government and the values that inform our lifestyle of freedom expect that and are especially geared for a nation that expects and embraces the power of the individual. Some people are high achievers in their chosen fields, gaining fame for their work and lives, while others enjoy their achievements with less acclaim.

One high school in Virginia illustrates just how vile and destructive people can become when pursuing the nefarious goal of equity. In December 2022, former *Wall Street Journal* reporter and parent advocate Asra Nomani reported that for years, two administrators at the Thomas Jefferson High School for Science and Technology in Alexandria, Virginia (where her son was a former student), deliberately withheld notifications of National Merit Awards won by students. Why? All in the name of equity, of course.

She writes in *City Journal*: "For years, two administrators . . . have been withholding notifications of National Merit awards from the school's families, most of them Asian, thus denying students the right to use those awards to boost their college-admission prospects and earn scholarships. This episode has emerged amid the school district's new strategy of 'equal outcomes for every student, without exception,'" Nomani reported.[5]

Moreover, "School administrators, for instance, have implemented an 'equitable grading policy'[6] that eliminates zeros, gives students a grade of 50 percent just for showing up, and assigns a cryptic code of 'NTI' for assignments not turned in. It's a race to the bottom. An intrepid Thomas Jefferson parent, Shawna Yashar, a lawyer, uncovered the withholding of National Merit awards," the article alleges, after she learned her son had been one of the 1,200 students whose award had been hidden from him and his family.[7]

Yashar's son was tapped by the National Merit organization as a commended student, recognizing his position in the top 3 percent of students nationwide. Overall, these awards and the attendant recognition open the door to millions of dollars in college and corporate scholarships. But the honored students and their parents never knew about the award because, Nomani alleges in her exposé, school administrators decided their mission to promote the rancid goal of equity was more important.

One of the administrators involved in the shocking deception admitted it was, in fact, intentional, according to *City Journal*. The reasoning he claims is a perfect example of the gaslighting the left relies on in an effort to disguise the social and educational carnage they're implementing.

"In a call with [high school parent] Yashar, [the TJ director of student services] admitted that the decision to withhold the information from parents and inform the students in a low-key way was intentional. 'We want to recognize students for who they are as individuals, not focus on their achievements,' he told her, claiming that he and the principal didn't want to 'hurt' the feelings of students who didn't get the award," Nomani reported in *City Journal*.[8]

As the community became aware of the story, outraged parents of TJ students wrote a letter to state and county education leaders demanding that the two school officials allegedly responsible be fired.[9] The local ABC affiliate 7News also reported that Virginia lieutenant governor Winsome Earle-Sears responded via social media, stating, "This is reprehensible. I have reached out to the Governor and Attorney General and asked for an investigation. Our children's education is not a zero-sum game. We cannot punish success in order to have 'equal outcomes at all costs.'"[10]

As the firestorm intensified, Fairfax Public Schools released a statement that reads in part, "As part of our ongoing review into this matter, Fairfax County Public Schools' (FCPS) current understanding is that the delay in notifying National Merit Scholarship commended students was a one-time human error in the fall of 2022 only. Once the issue regarding the fall 2022 notifications came to light, counselors sent emails and made follow-up calls to each college where these students had applied and informed them of the National Merit Scholarship Commendations. To suggest a deliberate intent to withhold this information would be inaccurate and contrary to the values of FCPS."[11]

At first, this revelation was about one high school, but as the state's attorney general announced an investigation into the matter, it was revealed that more than a dozen high schools withheld merit awards in the noxious name of "equity." We have two options here—either a leprechaun magically compelled more than a dozen high schools to take the same obscene action against gifted and hardworking students, or it's a deliberate agenda item for progressives that they discussed, planned, and implemented.

Make no mistake, the Marxist war on merit is nationwide. We have been alerted to the destructive leftist agenda in our schools mostly by accident during the last two years. Fox News reported on Virginia governor Glenn Youngkin's response to the revelation of how widespread the merit award scandal really is: "Despite school systems blaming the delay in notifying students as an administrative oversight, Republican Virginia Gov. Glenn Youngkin said the 'golden ticket' was withheld from students 'for the purpose of not wanting to make people feel bad who didn't achieve it. All of a sudden, we see it spreading around to the rest of Fairfax County,' Youngkin told WJLA. 'They have a maniacal focus on equal outcomes for all students at all costs.'"[12]

Nomani was even more blunt: "Withholding the National Merit awards from children is immoral, unethical and downright cruel, if not illegal. It's emblematic of a war on merit that has become a war on kids."[13]

People are different, and the results of all of our endeavors will be different. No school can pledge the woke maxim "equal outcomes for every student, without exception" without committing first to the artificial manipulation of outcomes and the leveling-down it requires.

Some note that this is a "bizarre turn" for the woke mob. But not really. It is what the left has always done. Leftists exploit and weaponize the natural human desire for fairness and opportunity to create a system that crushes the potential of the gifted throughout society. It could be because they don't know any better, but it has happened so many times in history that this excuse is hard to swallow. The left requires citizens with a perpetual sense of victimhood tightly controlled by a small cadre of Masters of the Universe. This can only be achieved when the people believe the best is behind them, and their survival relies on the kindness of government strangers.

The left's agenda has always had three steps: envy, chaos, and control. I used to be on the left, and I understand the attraction to its arguments.

That attraction only lasts as long as one is naive and inexperienced. When the truth of the matter becomes apparent, the left is exposed as exploiters of well-meaning people, maintaining power by quashing the individual, implementing censorship, and criminalizing dissent.

With all we know, if anyone asks you to accept and embrace "equity," the short answer should be no. The long answer should be: hell no.

The Woke Race to the Bottom

In the meantime, the results of the National Assessment of Educational Progress, published in October 2022, showed a big drop in reading and math scores among nearly 450,000 fourth and eighth graders tested around the US.

Among fourth graders, only 36 percent were proficient in math, and only 33 percent were proficient in reading. As if that weren't alarming enough, scores were even worse among eighth graders, with a mere 26 percent proficient in math and just 31 percent proficient in reading.[14] The drop in scores can't be blamed entirely on school closures during the pandemic because test scores of reading ability also dropped from 2017 to 2019 (before the pandemic began), while math scores were relatively flat during that same period.[15]

An international test last administered in 2018 measuring student achievement in 78 countries also showed disappointing results for American students. The Program for International Student Assessment—administered to 600,000 fifteen-year-olds to assess their performance in math, science, and reading—ranked the US in 25th place when scores in all three areas were combined together. China had the highest ranking. A breakdown of student scores in the three areas tested showed American students ranked 13th in reading, 18th in science, and a dismal 37th in math.[16,17] Clearly, US students could be doing better. If they were subjected to less leftist indoctrination and were afforded more time on genuine education in school, it seems obvious their performance would improve.

It's not as if we aren't spending enough. America spends more per student than any other major developed nation, and its teachers are well ahead of international averages as well. However, in the last two decades, the number of administrators in America's public schools has nearly doubled.[18]

Schools are preparing students for failure and, ultimately, seeding envy that can come from seeing others succeed. As an example, in 2021 Oregon suspended their "essential skills" requirement for high school graduation. Through 2029, students "don't need to prove mastery of reading, writing, or math to graduate, citing harm to students of color."[19] And exactly how is it helping young people by allowing them to enter society if they are functionally illiterate? This is the ultimate abandonment of children by our system, and yet guarantees more victims for leftist organizers.

As discussed earlier, fostering envy among the people the left uses is at the core of its mission of fear and compliance. Riots, looting, arson, vandalism, and even assault, rape, and murder are acceptable tools to accomplish this mission. When hope is taken away and replaced with envy (and ultimately hate), human beings lose as Marxism and totalitarian governments thrive.

What are graduate, medical, and law schools to do as grade schools,[20] high schools, and colleges turn out poorly educated students due to, in part, the focus on social justice and woke indoctrination?

They ignore that applicants have no idea how to adequately read, write, or comprehend the basic complexities of daily life. But hey, at least they know their pronouns, when they'll need a "safe space," and the finer points of how to cancel people who dare to not conform.

For medical students, the victim pool of this Marxist scheme encompasses not just their future patients subjected to "social justice" health care, but the students themselves, who presumably started their academic careers wanting to be healers. Instead, many will emerge from medical schools indoctrinated as social justice warriors dressed in white coats.

The lowering of academic standards to promote racial and ethnic diversity, combined with the growing amounts of class and homework time devoted to woke indoctrination in schools and colleges, is producing a generation of students less qualified to perform jobs in the real world once they leave the shelter of their far-left schools.

In 2005, fifteen years before the COVID-19 lockdown and school closures, alarm bells were already ringing about the decline of literacy among the college educated. "The National Assessment of Adult Literacy," developed by the Education Department's National Center for Education Statistics, found "that the average literacy of college educated Americans declined significantly from 1992 to 2003. But it also reveals that just 25 percent of college graduates—and only 31 percent of those with at least some graduate studies—scored high enough on the tests to be deemed 'proficient' from a literacy standpoint, which the government defines as 'using printed and written information to function in society, to achieve one's goals, and to develop one's knowledge and potential,'" reported *Inside Higher Education*.[21]

Just a few months later, in 2006, another national survey, this time by the American Institutes for Research (AIR), and funded by the Pew Charitable Trusts, found equally alarming results[22]: "Twenty percent of U.S. college students completing four-year degrees—and 30 percent of students earning two-year degrees—have only basic quantitative literacy skills, meaning they are unable to estimate if their car has enough gasoline to get to the next gas station or calculate the total cost of ordering office supplies." Moreover, they found "more than 75 percent of students at two-year colleges and more than 50 percent of students at four-year colleges do not score at the proficient level of literacy. This means that they lack the skills to perform complex literacy tasks, such as comparing credit card offers with different interest rates or summarizing the arguments of newspaper editorials."[23]

Skip ahead and it becomes clear that colleges did not heed the disturbing news years earlier about college students being functionally illiterate at graduation. The *Wall Street Journal* reported in 2017 about the results of the Collegiate Learning Assessment test taken at two hundred colleges: "At more than half of schools, at least a third of seniors were unable to make a cohesive argument, assess the quality of evidence in a document or interpret data in a table, *The Wall Street Journal* found after reviewing the latest results from dozens of public colleges and universities that gave the exam between 2013 and 2016."

Also in 2013, half of college graduates *agreed* with the assessment that they're unprepared for the workplace, with a *Time* magazine assessment noting the reaction among employers about new crops of the college educated: "The problem with the unemployability of these young adults goes way beyond a lack of STEM skills. As it turns out, they can't even show up on time in a button-down shirt and organize a team project."[24]

Not surprisingly, a 2023 survey found employers particularly blunt about what they find problematic with new college graduates. "88% say college graduates from the last three years are less prepared for the workforce than in years prior. Seventy percent say recent college grads lack preparedness due to their work ethic, 70% think they lack communication skills, 71% say they are 'entitled,' and 43% think they lack technological skills."[25]

Corrupting Our Medical Establishment

This development is concerning in all fields, but particularly so in health care. After all, having skilled doctors, nurses, and other health professionals can make a critical difference in patient care and in saving lives when dealing with health crises.

Responding to wokeism and calls for more diversity in the medical profession, more than two dozen US medical schools no longer require students to take the difficult Medical College Admission Test (MCAT), in use since 1947, to be admitted.[26] The test, which takes 7.5 hours to administer, was created to measure the knowledge students need in order to master the curriculum in medical school and become skilled doctors.

However, as *U.S. News & World Report* reported in June 2022: "Some say the MCAT impedes low-income pre-meds of all ethnic backgrounds, especially those whose parents did not attend college or who were raised in rural areas, and that the test particularly deters pre-meds from underrepresented racial groups, including black and Hispanic students.

The average MCAT score within these demographic categories is lower than the norm—a phenomenon MCAT skeptics attribute to systemic inequalities that hinder the educational opportunities of certain populations."[27] In other words, it's all the fault of systemic racism.

Keep in mind, if someone is taking the MCAT, it means they've also just gone through four years of pre-med in college with a focus on preparing for that test. If someone is completely unprepared, wouldn't that be obvious to the student's professors, family, friends, and even themselves? And then, wouldn't the goal be to recognize the problem and adjust to get back on track? That would be and is what those interested in medical school would normally do . . . unless they've been conditioned to believe that their woke indoctrination is more important, and that test scores don't matter.

Journalist Heather Mac Donald explores this issue with her "Corruption of Medicine" essay in *City Journal,* where she relays this story about, among other things, the impact on student priorities of Yale's pass-fail grading system combined with anti-racist advocacy, now a core element of medical training:

> A fourth-year Yale medical student describes how the specter of Step One [of the United States Medical Licensing Examination focused on basic medical knowledge and leading to residencies] affected his priorities. In his first two years of medical school, the student had "immersed" himself, as he describes it, in a student-led committee focused on diversity, inclusion, and social justice. The student ran a podcast about health disparities. All that political work was made possible by Yale's pass-fail grading system, which meant that he didn't feel compelled to put studying ahead of diversity concerns. Then, as he tells it, Step One "reared its ugly head." Getting an actual grade on an exam might prove to "whoever might have thought it before that I didn't deserve a seat at Yale as a Black medical student," the student worried.[28]

This corruption of priorities is not the fault of the students, but a result of the environment that the left has deliberately created to further its degrading cultural agenda. Students are being trained to care more about dogma than science. More about politics than medicine and patients. The students are being defrauded, and our society is being strangled and denied high-quality medical care.

Sick with Woke

The Association of American Medical Colleges (AAMC), which advises and represents medical schools and also advises the national accreditation agency for medical schools, issued a report in 2022 telling the schools that medical students should be taught "diversity, equity and inclusion competencies." That means, the AAMC states, that future doctors must learn a slew of woke concepts, such as "intersectionality," which it defines as "overlapping systems of oppression and discrimination that communities face based on race, gender, ethnicity, ability, etc."[29]

Medical students must also be able to discuss "the impact of various systems of oppression on health and health care (e.g., colonization, white supremacy, acculturation, assimilation)." The AAMC said these and other politically correct lessons should be something practicing physicians learn as well because doing this is as important as learning about "the latest scientific breakthrough."[30]

What on Earth does any of this have to do with health care? It's important to understand diseases that disproportionately affect people of African or Asian descent, as an example, or customs of some religions that may affect treatments, but that is learning about specific potential patient populations and transcends politics. We want and deserve, above all else, to know that our doctor was focused on learning about medical care in medical school, so he or she has the excellent education, training, skills, experience, and bedside manner needed to do a good job taking care of us. This is basic common sense.

But the corruption of our important institutions marches on as though every day is May Day. The American Medical Association,[31] founded in 1847, recently established the AMA Center for Health Equity, from which in 2021 it conjured up an "equity plan," declaring in a press release their woke bona fides with "AMA releases plan dedicated to embedding racial justice and advancing health equity."[32]

With pronouncements worthy of the most rigorous Marxist struggle sessions, the association declares: "The American Medical Association (AMA) today released an ambitious strategic plan to dismantle structural racism starting from within the organization, acknowledging that equity work requires recognition of past harms and critical examination of institutional roles upholding these structures. The framework of the plan—which is central to the work of the AMA Center for Health Equity and the responsibility of AMA leadership, membership, and external stakeholders—is driven by the immense need for equity-centered solutions to confront harms produced by systemic racism and other forms of oppression."[33]

And exactly how will this be implemented? Fox News reports: "Much of the 86-page document includes buzzwords typically found in other organization's [*sic*] 'equity' plans but is unique in explicitly acknowledging its use of CRT. . . . The AMA commits to '[e]xpand medical school and physician education to include equity, anti-racism, structural competency, public health and social sciences, critical race theory and historical basis of disease.' The document follows other programs, including a 'land acknowledgment' for indigenous people. It criticizes the concept of treating everyone equally and, like previously reported materials, it disparages the idea of meritocracy."[34]

This document, still unbelievably from the American Medical Association of all places, reads as though it was written by Marxist apparatchiks determined to make sure the evil bourgeoisie understand they are the problem and will be treated as such. This demonizing and blaming is part and parcel of the politics of fear. It is old, typical, and destroys everything it infects.

Do No Harm

Writing in an op-ed published by the *New York Post* in September 2022, Dr. Stanley Goldfarb, who is chairman of the nonprofit group Do No

Harm, and registered nurse Laura L. Morgan, a program manager at the organization,[35] warned: "Elite medical schools are deliberately recruiting woke activists, jeopardizing their mission of training physicians."[36] Goldfarb is a kidney specialist, retired professor, and associate dean at the University of Pennsylvania Medical School. Do No Harm is operated by health professionals and policymakers with the mission to "Protect healthcare from a radical, divisive and discriminatory ideology."[37]

In their op-ed, the pair wrote that Do No Harm reviewed the application process for the top fifty medical schools in the US and found that nearly three-quarters "ask applicants about their views on diversity, equity, inclusion, anti-racism, and other politicized concepts. The clear goal is to find the students who will best advance divisive ideology, not provide the best care to patients. . . . Recruiting woke activists instead of the most qualified candidates will both undermine trust in health care and lead to worse health outcomes for patients. That's the last thing medical schools should do."[38]

When Goldfarb tweeted in 2022 that the underrepresentation of blacks and Hispanics in medicine might be due to individual qualifications of students rather than racism, the chair of the University of Pennsylvania's Department of Medicine, Dr. Michael Parmacek, emailed faculty and students to denounce Goldfarb's "racist statements," and offered mental health counseling to anyone traumatized by reading the tweet.[39]

Calls followed to fire Goldfarb from his position as an editor at UpToDate, a medical reference publication used by millions of doctors.[40] Bowing to the woke mob, the publication fired Goldfarb. "I'm disappointed in UpToDate," he told Fox News. "Rather than stay focused on great medicine, they bowed down to cancel culture bullies. The focus on identity politics in medicine promoted by political activists is harming care, and will drive away talented medical professionals."[41]

Alarmingly, wokeism is not just diverting the attention of medical students and doctors from medical education to social justice propaganda. It is diverting funding away from potentially lifesaving medical research. As Heather Mac Donald wrote in *City Journal* in the summer of 2022: "The NIH [National Institutes of Health] and the National

Science Foundation are diverting billions in taxpayer dollars from trying to cure Alzheimer's disease and lymphoma to fighting white privilege and cisheteronormativity. Private research support is following the same trajectory."[42]

For example, Mac Donald said that the Howard Hughes Medical Institute—one of the largest charitable funders of basic science in the world—has made promoting diversity in the ranks of medical researchers its top priority. The institute announced in May 2022 that it was awarding $1.5 billion to scientists to promote a "happy and diverse lab where minoritized scientists will thrive and persist."[43] Hmm . . . I have a sneaking suspicion that patients dying of incurable diseases—including black and Hispanic patients—just might appreciate it more if the funds were used to find ways to keep them alive.

CRT and other woke indoctrination being applied in medical schools and advocated for by leftists is performing exactly as Marxists had hoped. Race-based criteria are also being used to determine who gets medical care. For example, guidance issued by the Biden administration in late 2021 limited the use of then-scarce oral antiviral drugs and monoclonal antibodies for the treatment of COVID-19 to patients at "high risk" of severe illness or death from the disease. This sensibly included people who are elderly, obese, diabetic, pregnant, or have chronic kidney disease or cardiovascular disease. But the guidance also said "race or ethnicity"—meaning being black or Hispanic—should also be considered a risk factor, even if the black or Hispanic person was young and healthy.[44]

Several states—including New York, Utah, and Minnesota—quickly announced they would favor minorities in deciding who should get the drugs. "Non-white race or Hispanic/Latino ethnicity should be considered a risk factor, as long-standing systemic health and social inequities have contributed to an increased risk of severe illness and death from COVID-19," a memo from the New York State Health Department said.[45]

In a similar vein, Dr. Michelle Morse (the chief medical officer in the New York City Health and Mental Hygiene department) and Dr. Bram Wispelwey (an instructor at the Harvard Medical School) authored an opinion piece published by the *Boston Review* in March 2021 advocating preferential treatment of black and Hispanic patients in health care.[46] "After more than five decades of colorblind law . . . the stubborn persistence of racial inequities—both in health care and across society at large—gives the lie to the effectiveness of colorblind policies," the two wrote. They called for incorporating anti-racism and Critical Race Theory into health care.

Christopher Rufo, a researcher with the nonprofit Discovery Institute and a critic of Critical Race Theory, blasted the entire premise: "The 'equity' ideology has permeated all of our elite institutions," Rufo said. "Now medical professionals are setting the conceptual framework to deny medical treatment to Whites in order to achieve 'non-disparate' outcomes. This is a moral crime, a violation of the 14th Amendment, and a direct contravention of their oath to 'do no harm.'"[47]

Information Is Power

The left uses issues surrounding civil rights and personal freedom specifically to promulgate division and fear. They are obsessed with controlling speech and information because they know information is, in fact, power. Controlling education is the necessary step if they have any chance at successfully "fundamentally transforming" America, which at this point appears to be transformation into a dumpster fire. It's undeniably time for a course correction, and we need to move quickly or it will be too late.

CHAPTER 6

The Bureaucratic Tyranny of Fear

Neither a man nor a crowd nor a nation can be trusted to act humanely or to think sanely under the influence of a great fear.

—BERTRAND RUSSELL[1]

Two prescient dystopian novels—Aldous Huxley's *Brave New World* (published in 1932) and George Orwell's 1945 masterpiece *Animal Farm*—warn us of the grave dangers humanity faces from the utopian totalitarianism that robs individuals of their freedom and destroys everything it claims to save. Both books indict tyranny brought on by ruling elites, and show how identity politics have been used to crush the human spirit.

This is exactly what callous authoritarians—socialists, communists, fascists, and the deceptively named "progressives"—have used against modern civilization for over one hundred years. Leftists have seized control of governments through lies and perpetuate their cancer through the bureaucratic system. It is what the left has always done, and what we must fight now to prevent the cancer from metastasizing.

Widely considered prophetic, Huxley's *Brave New World* portrays a nightmarish society under authoritarian rule that conditions individuals into conformity and a passive enslavement through the use of technology and drugs. Sound familiar? In large part, *Brave New World* is a blistering critique of technology and the degree to which tyrants will crush humanity when they have the chance. Huxley anticipated the spread of modern technology with uncanny accuracy, and watched with increasing alarm as it developed throughout the first half of the twentieth century.

Set in the year 2540, Huxley describes the tyranny of the governing "World State," where human reproduction is controlled in laboratories and people are genetically engineered to meet the prearranged goals of the government. Individuality is conditioned out of people, and meaningful relationships do not exist because "every one belongs to every one else." Sounds a bit like "it takes a village," yes? People are kept under control through a drug called "soma" that creates artificial feelings of happiness and suppresses any desire to resist or rebel.

When reading *Brave New World* as a teenager, I never dreamed the world Huxley conjured up in his imagination could be remotely possible. But now as I write this, I am stunned at our current situation culturally and politically, realizing we are in the horrible grip of what Huxley warned us was possible.

While Huxley's concerns focused on the dangers of technology, Orwell also understood people were at the center of any imagined dystopia of the future. In *Animal Farm*, published in 1945, Orwell was intent on revealing the true nature of fascism and its necessary partner of totalitarianism and its impact on the choices and behavior of the people (or in his book, the animals) implementing their supposed egalitarian utopia.

In a simple allegory symbolizing the 1917 Russian Revolution, Orwell tells the story of abused and overworked farm animals who rebel against the human farmer who is their oppressive master and proceed to establish their version of a utopia with egalitarian rules. Eventually the pigs, who have become the leaders, ignore the rules, manipulate the other animals, and establish a ruling society much like the one they rebelled against. Still pretending to embrace equality, the pigs adopt an absurdly contradictory slogan: "All animals are equal, but some animals are more equal than others." In real life, Russian revolutionaries who preached universal equality followed the same course, replacing the tyrannical rule of the czars with an even more tyrannical communist dictatorship.

In *Animal Farm*, the pigs use propaganda, fear, and force to maintain authority, as opposition is suppressed. For Orwell, his book wasn't just a warning about Soviet Russia, but about the nature of the left itself—exploiting important and serious issues to rise to power, and then using newfound influence to consolidate control.

Orwell understood that the real goal of leftist revolutionaries is not to solve the problems that lifted them to power. The Marxist goal is to achieve power, using lies about a better future free of victimhood and suffering to reach their goal. It is the ultimate vicious circle, benefiting the few who become rich and powerful in the process. The left's natural totalitarian instinct co-opts important issues, weaponizes them, rides them to death in pursuit of power and money. In the end, civilizations are destroyed as they fall victim to the abusers and mass murderers masquerading as leaders and politicians.

Once a pervasive atmosphere of fear is created, both authors recognized, it becomes a perfect cudgel to beat any opposition into submission. The true danger illustrated in both books is a small technocratic elite who insist that the world outside is terrifying, and only they have the knowledge and experience to keep that danger at bay.

From Deplorables to "Semi-Fascist"

The left promotes Big Government by criticizing and condemning the intent and abilities of citizens. After all, why would you need an all-encompassing government if people were competent enough to run their own lives? As the agents of the state reduce individuals to a commodity to be used or abandoned, it's inevitable that bureaucrats slouch into the notion that the only thing the little people are really worth is the tax dollars they generate to keep the living entity of government functioning and alive.

We are at a point with our bureaucratic state that the citizen must be kept distracted and in fear. Keeping the average citizen out of the hair of the Masters of the Universe is job one. How better to accomplish this than by pitting groups of Americans against each other? And how better to do that than by condemning one group of people as dangerous domestic terrorists simply because they're conservatives? Or because they support Donald Trump? Or because they oppose the establishment's favored policy and positions?

You can live in fear of the apocalypses they predict, or you can live in fear of being found out you don't believe them.

The Marxist worldview relies on a condemnation of average people and their value to excuse the necessity of an all-powerful state. But you don't need to be a Marxist to be willing to destroy people to appease the Gods of Money and Power. Just ask Hillary Clinton and Joe Biden. Clinton unlocked the door to characterizing average citizens as enemies of society with her insulting description of Trump supporters as a "basket of deplorables." Biden put those attacks on steroids when he lashed out at Trump supporters as "semi-fascist" and threats to democracy.

There's a tradition in politics to go after your political opponent. We expect debates, insults, and accusations. It's part and parcel of the political process as we get to know who and what the candidates are made of. We take much of it with a grain of salt. But today's Democratic Party decided it was time to smear and condemn American *voters* who happen to disagree with them on policy or support their political opposition.

The strategy to attack and define American citizens as an internal enemy had begun in September 2016, just two months before the presidential election. Hillary Clinton started the ignominious decline when she attacked Donald Trump *supporters* during an event in New York City. *Time* magazine reported: "Democratic presidential nominee Hillary Clinton lashed out at many supporters of Donald Trump Friday. . . . 'You could put half of Trump's supporters into what I call the basket of deplorables. Right,' Clinton said, drawing laughter and applause as she addressed about 1,000 donors at an LGBT for Hillary fundraising gala in New York City. 'The racist, sexist, homophobic, xenophobic, Islamophobic—you name it.' Adding that Trump had 'given voice' to many of those elements through his campaign rhetoric and retweets, she continued that, 'some of those folks—they are irredeemable, but thankfully they are not America.'"[2]

Here was an American presidential nominee, former senator, secretary of state, and first lady exhibiting contempt for and smearing tens of millions of Americans as irredeemable bigots. This was not an unscripted riff. It was a narrative Clinton repeated multiple times, including during in an interview with an Israeli television station.[3]

This was inevitable, because the core of the new Democrats is underlying contempt. It is what both Huxley and Orwell warn us about—the resentment, envy, and inhumanity that feed the political left. Pitting citizens against each other and creating suspicion, resentment, and paranoia about one's neighbor foments fear and a sense of vulnerability. It sends a message that only a massive government can help you because your neighbors and communities are too far gone.

Two days after her hate speech, Clinton expressed "regret" for the remarks. Amazingly, her regret was not for attacking American citizens, but for using the word *half*. She noted in a statement: "Last night I was 'grossly generalistic,' and that's never a good idea. I regret saying 'half'—that was wrong."[4] She never clarified how much less than half of tens of millions of voters she assigns as "irredeemable." But that was the point. The damage was done and the tone set.

There was no mistake made in Clinton's 2016 rhetoric and no lesson to learn, because the left meant to begin characterizing citizens as an internal enemy. Fast-forward to Joe Biden's 2020 presidential campaign, which picked up that baton and kept swinging. In August 2022, just prior to the midterm elections, Biden made a clear comment to specifically malign Trump supporters, whom he called "MAGA Republicans." Biden used the four-letter word as an insult, but the term comes from Trump himself. MAGA is short for the "Make America Great Again" campaign slogan from Trump's 2016 and 2020 presidential campaigns, a motto embraced by Trump supporters. Biden continued using the term in his attacks on Republicans in his 2024 reelection campaign.

Criminalizing the Opposition

Politico reported in 2022: "At a Democratic fundraising event in Maryland, the president denounced his predecessor and followers he labeled as 'extreme' Republicans. . . . 'What we're seeing now is either the beginning or the death knell of extreme MAGA philosophy,' Biden told Democratic donors in the Washington suburb of Rockville. Calling out those he labeled as 'extreme' Republicans, Biden said: 'It's not just Trump, it's the entire philosophy that underpins the—I'm going to say something . . . it's like semi-fascism.'"[5]

Biden is famous for saying things off script. He mentions when "they" will be mad at him if he takes a question, or "they" have told him who to call on at one of his rare press conferences. Calling tens of millions of private American citizens "fascist" (half, whole, or venti) is not something one does casually. It's discussed and decided upon. Biden was primed to make sure he said it and in a manner that would be heard and remembered. So he actually announced he was going to "say something." That's how invested leftists are in demonizing and isolating the American people. It's an act of desperation and the place where the left has always gone in the countries it parasitically consumes.

Douglas Murray—an author, political critic, and journalist—noted this about Biden's remark and the White House *joining in* on the well-worn leftist strategy of using the power of government to criminalize opposition:

> When she was asked about the comments, White House Press Secretary Karine Jean-Pierre went further. From the White House briefing podium she said that MAGA Republicans are an "extreme threat to democracy, to our freedom, to our rights." It is "one of the most extreme agendas we have seen," she declared. . . . Yet it is insulting their way out of an argument that Biden and his accomplices are doing. They are not trying to correct their opponents. They are trying to anathematize them. They are using the strongest words in the political dictionary to try to declare them non-persons. . . . It is the same with the way in which some people on the left have used the word "racist" in recent decades. They used it so much because they found it so useful. It covered people in a coat of slime which it was exceptionally hard to get off. For

while calling someone a racist is easy, disproving it or getting a correction is very hard.[6]

None of this is a gaffe by thoughtless people; it's an intentional strategy implemented by bullies to gain and maintain political power. When pressed about the divisive nature of Biden's comments, Jean-Pierre went so far as to state directly that opinions not deemed "mainstream" are extremist. "And, again, we see a majority of Americans who disagree. And so when you are not with where the majority of Americans are, then, you know, that is extreme. . . . That is an extreme way of thinking."[7] (For his entire presidency, a majority of Americans disapproved of Biden's performance as president. Wouldn't that make all the citizens who approve of him extremists?)

It's incredible that Jean-Pierre says the federal government considers people who hold opinions that differ from the Democrats' preferred narrative to be extremists—a word chosen for specific reasons. *Extremists* is the word the US and other national governments use to describe terrorists.

That very night, Biden delivered a live, prime-time address to the nation. The campaign-style rally was held at Independence Hall in Philadelphia, where in 1787 the Constitution was debated and finalized before it was sent to the states for ratification. Directly behind Biden the building was awash in a bloodred light, with Biden framed by two marines in the background. He then drowned in irony, using classic fascist imagery to declare Trump supporters a danger to the country, with outrageous rhetoric that could easily be switched out in a speech about ISIS or al-Qaeda:

"Too much of what's happening in our country today is not normal. Donald Trump and the MAGA Republicans represent an extremism that threatens the very foundations of our republic," Biden said. "The Republican Party today is dominated, driven, and intimidated by Donald Trump and the MAGA Republicans. And that is a threat to this country."[8]

The majority of Americans considered the speech divisive and "fearmongering."[9] The imagery was so startling, even liberals were critical.[10]

Biden ran as a "uniter" to get us back to "normal" after four years of Trump. The theme of his inaugural was "America United." To highlight just how significantly Biden voters were misled, the key to his inaugural address was this statement: "We can join forces, stop the shouting and lower the temperature. For without unity there is no peace, only bitterness and fury. No progress, only exhausting outrage. No nation, only a state of chaos. This is our historic moment of crisis and challenge, and unity is the path forward."[11]

What an astounding fraud. But if there was any doubt about what the establishment agenda really is, the Biden team wanted to make sure everyone knew the federal government was looking with a jaundiced eye at tens of millions of Americans who supported, or might be thinking about supporting, former president Trump.

Frightening Americans into silence and retreat remains the goal by signaling that the federal government—from the highest office in the land down the chain of command—will come after you in a way that will ruin your life if you support an opponent of the regime.

A Swamp of Corruption, Crisis, and Fear

Keeping Americans afraid to speak their minds, to participate in politics, and to criticize the establishment is at the core of progressive agenda. The left can win power based on lies, but it can never sustain support once the people realize the leftist utopia is really Dante's *Inferno*.

We now have a history of victimized people and ruined nations as evidence of the left's grift and malevolent intentions. The people of the collapsed Soviet Union, Cuba, Venezuela, China, North Korea, and many other nations finally understood—for many, too late—the fact that any iteration of Marxism and the left is not a salve, it's a cancer.

It's one thing to be dealing with a totalitarian dictatorship where there is no constitution or bill of rights that ostensibly protect you from government overreach, corruption, and crime. But the federal bureaucratic state has convinced itself it is the only thing that matters; that it is the living entity on which the country relies. It is now so big and administered by faceless bureaucrats (much like Biden's executive office) that worry about accountability does not exist, emboldening the system even more.

To illustrate the swamp of corruption, crisis, and fear plaguing the US government, below are some examples that made headlines during the Trump presidency and afterward.

FBI Corruption

Durham Report/Framing of Trump

Most Americans were shocked to learn the extent to which the FBI actively worked to undermine Donald Trump's 2016 candidacy for president. The operation to frame him as a Russian spy (absurd on its face) continued after he became the president-elect, and proceeded even after he became president. It took years, but only after Special Counsel John Durham's 306-page report was released in May 2023 was the extent of the scheme made clear.

The *Washington Times* reported: "Mr. Durham said FBI agents were so eager to pursue Donald Trump, both as a candidate and then as president, that they heralded 'seriously flawed information' and abandoned their 'own principles regarding objectivity and integrity.' Mr. Durham wrote that the FBI's behavior was 'seriously deficient' and caused the agency 'severe reputational harm.' The report details how the Clinton campaign, through operatives paid to dig up dirt on her opponent, gave the FBI some of the flawed information, possibly as part of a plan to 'vilify Donald Trump by stirring up a scandal claiming interference by Russian security services.'"[12]

Also revealed by the Durham Report: "Clinton allegedly approved a proposal from one of her foreign policy advisors to tie Trump to Russia as a means of distracting the public from her use of a private email server," the *Washington Times* reported.[13]

Moreover, then–CIA chief John Brennan briefed President Barack Obama and other top officials on "alleged approval by Hillary Clinton on July 26, 2016, of a proposal . . . to vilify Donald Trump by stirring up a scandal claiming interference by Russian security services," according to reporting by the *Post* in 2020.[14, 15]

This vile effort to engage in what some have considered a coup against a president of the United States was successful in a significant way—half the nation was consumed by the fear that larger, darker forces were at work. That only the government could save them from this modern Manchurian candidate. As a deliberate misinformation campaign it was not only designed to personally smear Trump but to make everyone in his orbit, and American voters, afraid of him.

Social Media: The FBI Subsidiary

After being outraged by the censorship and banning of accounts on Twitter, Elon Musk (along with other investors like Sequoia Capital and Andreessen Horowitz)[16] bought the social media platform for $44 billion in October 2022. In his commitment to transparency, Musk selected six independent journalists to investigate internal files and documents, and report on what they found regarding censorship at the platform and any government involvement.

Now known as the "Twitter Files," part of what was exposed included the "constant and pervasive" contact between Twitter employees and the FBI. Other reports addressed the suppression of evidence from the laptop computer belonging to President Biden's son Hunter, blacklisting of conservatives, and the Twitter suspension of Trump's account.

Former *Rolling Stone* reporter Matt Taibbi, one of those tapped by Musk to review the Twitter Files, released his report titled "Twitter Files, Part Six: TWITTER, THE FBI SUBSIDIARY."

The *Washington Examiner* reported on Taibbi's investigation:

> The FBI was not the only one to flag content. The Department of Homeland Security and several state governments notified Twitter of content they thought was problematic. Some of this was done through the Partner Support Portal, an outlet constructed by the Center for Internet Security, a partner organization with the DHS. "What most people think of as the 'deep state' is really a tangled collaboration of state agencies, private contractors, and (sometimes state-funded) NGOs. The lines become so blurred as to be meaningless," Taibbi concluded.[17]

Jonathan Turley, a legal scholar and a professor at George Washington University School of Law, explains further: "The 'Twitter files' revealed an FBI operation to monitor and censor social media content—an effort so overwhelming and intrusive that Twitter staff at one point complained internally that 'they are probing & pushing everywhere.' The reports have indicated that dozens of FBI employees worked on the identification and removal of material on a wide range of subjects and that Twitter largely carried out their requests."[18]

These reports just touch the surface of the main federal law enforcement agency using Twitter as a proxy to carry out an unconstitutional assault on everyone's First Amendment right to free speech. While that is alarming enough, the pre-Musk Twitter regime's cooperation with a government censorship operation without any significant legal resistance shows us the danger of the private sector's willingness to collude with government if their political aims coincide. Finding this out years later, after the damage had been done, is not reassuring and does not solve the problem.

One of the major benefits for the FBI and progressives in general was the banning and suspension operation implemented by Twitter, apparently on behalf of or at the request of the FBI. This made the average person afraid of losing their Twitter or social media accounts. Today, social media acts as a significant communication tool for millions of Americans. People rant, organize, entertain, inform, and help others. The threat of banning or suspension, especially of someone like Donald Trump, sends a message to everyone else: if social media companies can do it to him, they can do it to you. Self-censorship becomes the solution out of fear, and can even cause some to doubt their own intentions and value.

For the left and progressives (a misnomer if there ever was one), that's exactly the point and the goal.

As is often the case in history, the only reason this outrageous operation stopped and was exposed is because one man—Elon Musk—was as outraged as many of us were. As one of the richest people in the world, he was able to buy the platform. As more confirmation of the Biden administration's willingness to run afoul of the Constitution in their effort to control and squash dissenting speech, a unanimous 5th Circuit Court of Appeals upheld a federal district court judge's finding that the Biden White House and the FBI unconstitutionally "coerced" or "encouraged" online censorship.[19] The Biden administration appealed this decision to the United States Supreme Court, illustrating how desperate the establishment is to maintain control of what people learn about. It is also a threat to the status quo when the hoi polloi embrace and enjoy the ability to be heard on the issues of the day. Whatever the SCOTUS outcome on this issue, the progressive interest in censoring what the public can say and information they can see will remain and likely increase.

We got lucky this time, but we can't rely on luck and the perfect storm of circumstances to survive the malign intentions of a government gone wild.

The Open Southern Border

The erasure of, and consequential chaos at, our southern border created by Biden administration policies speaks directly to the agenda of the corrupt bureaucratic state—creating and maintaining crisis and corresponding fear. When our own government is directing a type of orderly dismantling of the very existence of our southern border, that alone is fear-inducing for the citizens relying on the national, economic, and personal security of what is supposed to be a controlled point of entry. When this unlocked door is interpreted as an open invitation for unbridled entry, the inevitable and uncontrollable rush by millions of people to enter this country without the usual identity and background safeguards impacts everyone watching the human catastrophe unfold.

The building of the border wall was well underway by late in Trump's term, and other border security efforts had been implemented, resulting in unheralded success at securing the southern border.[20] Despite this success, or perhaps because of it, on the day he became president, Biden issued executive orders reversing Trump's border policies.[21] Representative Steve Scalise (R-LA) noted: "Most of the problems we're seeing at the border were created by Joe Biden himself, starting on his very first day in office as president when he sent a message throughout the world that America's border is open by doing things like halting construction of the wall, reinstating catch and release, terminating the Remain in Mexico policy, the Northern Triangle agreements."

The consequences? In February 2023, border patrol chiefs testified to the House Committee on Oversight and Accountability that the border crisis is "overwhelming."[22] But that wasn't even the worst of it. Yet. On December 18, 2023, the United States hit a shocking milestone. "The besieged U.S. southern border saw a record number of migrant encounters in a single day on Monday, as thousands flooded into Eagle Pass, Texas, amid a broader surge in recent weeks that has left authorities overwhelmed. There were over 12,600 migrant encounters on Monday, Customs and Border Protection sources told Fox."[23]

If that wasn't alarming enough, at the end of October 2023, the *Washington Examiner* and Center Street reported,[24] "More than 10 million people have been reported illegally entering the United States since President Joe Biden took office in January 2021, the greatest number in history and of any administration. They total more than the individual populations of 41 states."

Moreover, in a Pew Research Center in February 2024 we learn,[25] "The U.S. Border Patrol had nearly 250,000 encounters with migrants crossing into the United States from Mexico in December 2023, according to government statistics. That was the highest monthly total on record, easily eclipsing the previous peak of about 224,000 encounters in May 2022." Other reports reveal concern about Chinese illegal immigration breaking records at the southern border.[26] But it's not just the southern border, as Hot Air reports, "Chief Patrol Agent Robert Garcia's territory is the Swanton Sector. This includes portions of Vermont, New Hampshire, and New York. Garcia is based in Swanton, Vermont. He is sounding the alarm that illegal crossings are up. Since October 1, 2023, when FY 2024 began, Border Patrol agents have apprehended more than 2022, 2021, 2020, and 2019 combined."[27]

In the midst of this extraordinary situation, Center Street reports during the 2023 fiscal year, "CPB agents apprehended the greatest number of known or suspected terrorists (KSTs)—736—in a single year in

US history." How many terrorists did it take to implement the catastrophic September 11 attacks? Nineteen.

We all know what dangers lurk within the unprecedented number of unauthorized immigrants entering this country illegally.[28] Sex trafficking and drug trafficking are making the cartels richer and more powerful than ever, while destroying American lives.[29] In 2021, over 108,000 Americans died of a drug overdose. This is an "an all-time high and was the first time overdose deaths topped 100,000 in a calendar year."[30, 31]

This isn't happening because leprechauns got bored and waved a wand. It is the result of governmental policies that they do not change despite the obvious chaos and carnage. It is a situation that is overwhelming, distracting, and frightening. And that's the point.

This is a perfect example of reminding ourselves of our earlier conversation, about the difference between allowing fear to push us into a paralyzed retreat, and using it as a signal to engage and work to overcome the problem. Like a bad health diagnosis—we *must* know so we can be proactive in confronting it. Remember, as Gavin de Becker tells us, fear is a gift, when managed consciously and with purpose.

Americans everywhere are impacted by this disaster, which contributes to most of our cultural and social ills—drug abuse, crime, homelessness, sex trafficking, human trafficking, economic uncertainty, and the specter of terrorism. An open, uncontrolled border makes a mockery of law and order and signals that the government is not in charge. If there ever was a problem that envelops all the issues that make people unsure and afraid, it's this one.

COVID

All of the above is just the tip of the fear iceberg. Fearmongering takes many forms, and when you're attempting to implement it against a free society like ours, the effort takes on a number of different layers. The manipulation of the American people during the COVID-19 crisis was normal for certain bureaucrats. Dr. Deborah Birx, who was part of the COVID Response Team in Trump's White House and was the chief proponent of lockdowns, wrote *Silent Invasion*,[32] a book in which she bragged about misleading then-President Trump and the country about the issue.[33, 34]

As reported by Libby Emmons at the *Post Millennial*,[35] often Birx was deliberately deceitful about what she did. At one point in the book she admits to deliberate and active subversion of administration messaging:

> After the heavily edited documents were returned to me [by the White House], I'd reinsert what they had objected to, but place it in those different locations. I'd also reorder and restructure the bullet points so the most salient—the points the administration objected to—no longer fell at the start of the bullet points. I shared these strategies with three members of the data team also writing these reports. Our Saturday and Sunday report-writing routine soon became: write, submit, revise, hide, resubmit. Fortunately, this strategic slight-of-hand worked. They never seemed to catch this subterfuge.[36]

Moreover, Birx wanted lockdowns, so she went about manipulating the president of the United States to achieve her goal. Last time I checked, misleading someone doesn't count as "science." Emmons reports, "Despite not having adequate data . . . [Birx] writes that in March 2020, she met with the President, and her plan was to obfuscate her intentions for economic shutdowns, knowing that Trump was wary of anything that would tank the economy he had worked so hard to build. 'I couldn't do anything that would reveal my true intention,' she writes, 'to use the travel ban as one brick in the construction of a larger wall of protective measures we needed to enact very soon.'"[37] Birx, who had reportedly been lobbying then President-Elect Biden for a job in December 2020, suddenly announced her retirement instead. She cited the public criticism of her hosting a family gathering for Thanksgiving after warning Americans to restrict gatherings to "immediate households" during the holiday citing the dangers of COVID. But the rules perpetuating fear itself do not apply to those who manage the Fear Industrial Complex. The BBC reported, "It emerged on Sunday she had travelled from Washington to one of her other properties, on Fenwick Island in Delaware, where she was joined by three generations of her family from two households. While in Delaware, she did an interview with CBS in which she noted that some Americans had 'made mistakes' over Thanksgiving by travelling and they 'should assume they were infected.'"[38]

When caught flouting the rules she promoted for everyone else, she attempted to deflect, explaining she went to prepare the house for sale, and just happened to "have a meal" with family.[39] Eventually, she admitted the distress of the lockdowns were taking a toll, telling Newsy and as reported by the *New York Post*: "Birx said she took her Thanksgiving jaunt to Delaware because her parents were so down in the dumps, they 'stopped eating and drinking'—a justification ripped by people who said it was her coronavirus restrictions that prevented them from seeing their own dying loved ones. . . . 'My daughter hasn't left that house in 10 months, my parents have been isolated for 10 months. They've become deeply depressed,'"[40] continued Birx. "My parents have not been able to see their surviving son for over a year. These are all very difficult things."[41] We know, Deborah. We know. What apparently wasn't difficult was misleading the president, treating the American people like shmucks, and then ignoring your own regulations and rules that destroyed the lives and families of others. Thanks for the memories, Deb, and for illustrating the nature of the Fear Industrial Complex.

Meanwhile, her mentor, Dr. Anthony Fauci, the head of the National Institute of Allergy and Infectious Diseases and leader of the national COVID response, remained head of the NIAID and also accepted Biden's offer to become his chief medical adviser in January 2021, only to retire in December 2022. But with each passing day there are more startling revelations about what exactly happened with the federal response to COVID, and how the search for answers and the truth was often maligned as "conspiracy theories." Those who presented alternative views were sometimes demonized, shut out of the conversations, and even canceled.

Even the *New York Times* couldn't ignore the absurdity, publishing an excellent opinion piece looking at Fauci's involvement in the war against the lab leak theory. How the media dutifully pushed the narrative was noted: "The MSNBC host Nicolle Wallace called it 'one of Trump-world's most favorite conspiracy theories.' Twitter added warning labels to posts that argued for lab leak; Facebook banned such posts altogether for several months in 2021 before reversing the decision. NPR called it a 'baseless conspiracy theory' in a tweet, and the foreign affairs expert Fareed Zakaria wrote (and repeated on CNN): 'The far right has now found its own virus conspiracy theory.'"[42]

Looks like everyone got the memo.

And now? A February 2023 *Wall Street Journal* headline, "Lab Leak Most Likely Origin of Covid-19 Pandemic, Energy Department Now Says."[43] Then on to a January 2024 Fox News report about comments from Dr. Francis Collins, the former head of the NIH: "Fauci's ex-boss now says COVID-19 lab leak theory was credible, despite previous claims it was a distraction."[44]

However, nothing tops Dr. Anthony "I-Am-the-Science" Fauci's admission during a closed-door interview with the House Select Committee on Coronavirus Pandemic in January 2024. When asked about what was behind the idiotic six-feet social distancing rules forced on Americans, he told lawmakers they "sort of just appeared."[45, 46] While alarming, it's not surprising. Many wondered how it was that a virus would be kept at bay as long as you stay in prearranged circles situated six feet apart at a park. With an answer like this from a man in his position, the urgent question becomes, what else "sort of just appeared" and then was presented as a legitimate, scientific action to combat a virus?

Well, how about mask wearing? In a *New York Times Magazine* story (I'm sure worthy of framing!) a few months after his retirement, Fauci was asked about the efficacy of masks and presented with data from Pakistan showing their marginal benefit. Dr. I-Am-the-Science then made an admission: "From a broad public-health standpoint, at the population level, masks work at the margins—maybe 10 percent. But for an individual who religiously wears a mask, a well-fitted KN95 or N95, it's not at the margin. It really does work."[47] Oh, like a doctor? Such a slippery answer from the man who told us "cloth coverings worked as well as surgical masks."[48] While couched as an expert's medical advice, with what we know now it's more like an idea that sort of just appeared.

None of that stops COVID, but it sure creates fear, uncertainty, isolation, and mass anxiety.

Now we know the rules and regulations that destroyed people's lives might as well have been delivered by a leprechaun and "just appeared." But these mandates, pronouncements, and warnings sure facilitated fear itself. And we know when made afraid, we'll be more inclined to do as we're told. In 2021, Fauci was excited when recounting this expectation in an interview: "It's been proven that when you make it difficult for people in their lives they lose their ideological bullshit, and they get vaccinated."[49]

Fauci and his gang seemed quite informed about how to fearmonger and force people to do things. Last time I checked, that wasn't "science," it was bullying, gaslighting, and harassment. We are supposed to revere Fauci and trust him completely because of his almost forty years of work as a doctor and public health expert at the NIH. But if he was relying on the "Just Sort of Appeared" method, and the "Marginal at Best" theory, one could argue that he was indeed an expert—for the Fear Industrial Complex.

The *New York Times Magazine* story title was "Dr. Fauci Looks Back: Something Clearly Went Wrong." It featured a picture of Fauci adjusting his tie, as though he's looking in a mirror. If he keeps looking, it just may dawn on him who that "something" just might appear to be.

This is the attitude that controls the bureaucratic state. The bureaucrats eventually believe only they know best, and all the peons should be grateful that they're in charge.

Abandonment of Law and Order

At the height of the COVID pandemic we were all dealing with mask mandates, senseless lockdown rules, fearmongering about hospitals being overloaded, and a host of other daily warnings and alerts. Politicians like former New York Democratic governor Andrew Cuomo—who later resigned in disgrace to avoid being impeached after he was accused of sexually harassing nearly a dozen women—were treated as rock star lifesavers for imposing restrictions on the freedom of people in their states. At the same time, progressives were setting the stage for a surge in crime. New York State's "bail reform law" eliminated the bail requirement for people charged with many crimes. New York City joined New Jersey, Chicago, Philadelphia, and other jurisdictions across the country implementing what would become the precursors to a crime surge.

CBS News reported on the predictable results for the first year of freeing defendants without requiring them to post bail in New York: "Starting in the summer [of 2020], there was an overall spike in crime, mirroring trends seen in cities across the nation. The year ended with a 97% increase in shootings, a 44% increase in murders, 42% increase in burglaries and 67% increase in car thefts in the city. The NYPD made arrests in 32% of shooting incidents."[50]

In 2022 crime continued to rise. The *New York Post* reported crime "skyrocketed" that year by 37 percent. "Grand larceny has shot up 49% so far this year over last year as of Sunday—from 18,058 to 26,908. Auto theft has spiked by 46.2%, from 4,855 to 7,100. Robbery is up 39.2%, from 6,530 to 9,091, and burglaries increased by 32.9%, from 6,251 to 8,305, the numbers show. Felonious assault rose by 18.6% and rapes saw an 11% increase so far this year over 2021."[51]

There are no signs of the crime wave stopping. In 2023 felony crime reports were up 6.4 percent from the previous year. As for those blaming the pandemic for the crimeapalooza happening in blue cities with no-bail policies, that 2023 statistic represents a 35.6 percent jump from the prepandemic period.[52]

Americans experience the impact of rising crime on their lives every day. The good news is more of us are realizing the deleterious impact of defunding the police and other liberal policies and attitudes. Paul Bedard at the *Washington Examiner* reports, "With violent crime hitting home across the nation, more people are coming to the defense of police to decry the liberal 'defund' movement. In a new survey . . . the National Sheriffs' Association found that 60% oppose defunding police operations, 44% 'strongly.' And the reason is simple: Crime is up. In fact, the new NSA/TIPP Survey showed that 42% blame the defund movement for reduced community safety."[53]

Keeping people unstable financially with higher prices, controlling their movements through fear of random crime and violence, afraid of being silenced if they utter an unapproved political opinion, or even visited by the FBI or arrested if they dare to participate in local politics, is a despicable package that Huxley and Orwell would not be surprised to see. After all, they also saw it all in the first half of the twentieth century.

A Warning from Justice Gorsuch

It will likely take years for any complete investigation into the federal government's COVID debacle. One thing is for sure, it is serving as a prime example of government using and creating fear to force people to comply with orders that otherwise make no sense. But as we know, once we're conditioned with fear, logic-based decision-making goes out the window as emotion takes over.

In the meantime, the government received a scathing review from Supreme Court justice Neil Gorsuch about the handling of COVID in general, noting "fear and the desire for safety are powerful forces." The court was addressing a lawsuit related to the ending of the Title 42 public health order in March 2020 allowing the US to quickly expel immigrants at the border during the pandemic. Gorsuch took the opportunity to comment about what the government had done and the impact on our civil liberties. Fox News reported on his statement: "One lesson might be this: Fear and the desire for safety are powerful forces. They can lead to a clamor for action—almost any action—as long as someone does something to address a perceived threat," the justice wrote. "A leader or an expert who claims he can fix everything, if only we do exactly as he says, can prove an irresistible force. We do not need to confront a bayonet, we need only a nudge, before we willingly abandon the nicety of requiring laws to be adopted by our legislative representatives and accept rule by decree."

Gorsuch then gave examples of how the US may "have experienced the greatest intrusions on civil liberties in the peacetime history of this country," noting:

> Executive officials across the country issued emergency decrees on a breathtaking scale. Governors and local leaders imposed lockdown orders forcing people to remain in their homes. They shuttered businesses and schools, public and private. They closed churches even as they allowed casinos and other favored businesses to carry on. They threatened violators not just with civil penalties but with criminal sanctions too. They surveilled church parking lots, recorded license plates, and issued notices warning that attendance at even outdoor services satisfying all state social-distancing and hygiene requirements could amount to criminal conduct. They divided cities and neighborhoods into color-coded zones, forced individuals to fight for their freedoms in court on emergency timetables, and then changed their color-coded schemes when defeat in court seemed imminent. . . . The concentration of power in the hands of so few may be efficient and sometimes popular. But it does not tend toward sound government.[54]

Gorsuch understood completely what politicians and government were doing with COVID, and the opportunistic use of fear to gain power and crush the human spirit. He also knew there must be a statement denouncing it. That this passionate defense of personal freedom and condemnation of outrageous government action would come only from a justice decried by liberals as a conservative menace tells you all you need to know about the condition of today's supposed progressive agenda. Once again, we are blessed to have one person in a particular position on whom we can rely to do the right thing, while reminding the country what's at stake.

A Global Cult Menace

For the left, groupthink is key. No matter what country they inhabit, no matter the background, leftists surround themselves with like-minded people, believe they have sole possession of the truth, demonize those who think differently, forbid and condemn debate, and punish those who dare to challenge ideology and public narratives. We see this cultlike behavior from the left and progressives everywhere in our society and around the world. It explains the rise of cancel culture, censorship, and the increasing inclination to destroy that which does not conform.

What we're dealing with in the United States is not exclusive to us—it is part of a global menace. I often mention to my radio and television audiences that if you want to know what the left has planned, just look at Los Angeles, San Francisco, New York, London, and Canada. The reliance on fear is also not new to our generation; it has been recognized as a tried and true element of power for millennia. Aristotle describes the universality of the emotion that was as relevant when his *Rhetoric* was written in 350 BC as it is to us today:

> To turn next to Fear, what follows will show things and persons of which, and the states of mind in which, we feel afraid. Fear may be defined as a pain or disturbance due to a mental picture of some destructive or painful evil in the future. Of destructive or painful evils only; for there are some evils, e.g. wickedness or stupidity, the prospect of which does not frighten us: I mean only such as amount to great pains or losses. And even these only if they appear not remote but so near as to be imminent: we do not fear things that are a very long way off: for instance, we all know we shall die, but we are not troubled thereby, because death is not close at hand. **From this definition it will follow that fear is caused by whatever we feel has great power of destroying or of harming us in ways that tend to cause us great pain. Hence the very indications of such things are terrible, making us feel that the terrible thing itself is close at**

> **hand;** the approach of what is terrible is just what we mean by "danger." **Such indications are the enmity and anger of people who have power to do something to us; for it is plain that they have the will to do it, and so they are on the point of doing it** [emphasis mine].[55]

Little did various Masters of the Universe in the United Kingdom know how they were proving Aristotle right. Keep in mind, what the leftist establishment does in London (or Los Angeles and New York) is a window into what the worldwide left is planning or is already implementing. In this case, courtesy of a powerful investigative series from the UK's *Telegraph* newspaper called "The Lockdown Files," the British people were finally informed about the incompetence and malevolence fueling pandemic decision-making among officials and ministers.

Leading the way off the cliff is a man called Matt Hancock, the now former health secretary who was directing the COVID response. It was leaked WhatsApp messages that exposed their reliance not on science, but on fear, to manipulate and control the people of England. The *Telegraph* reported:

> Throughout the course of the pandemic, officials and ministers wrestled with how to ensure the public complied with ever-changing lockdown restrictions. One weapon in their arsenal was fear. "We frighten the pants off everyone," Matt Hancock suggested during one WhatsApp message with his media adviser. The then health secretary was not alone in his desire to scare the public into compliance. The WhatsApp messages seen by The Telegraph show how several members of Mr Hancock's team engaged in a kind of "Project Fear," in which they spoke of how to utilise "fear and guilt" to make people obey lockdown.[56]

The WhatsApp messages in the *Telegraph* reveal deliberate, cynical, and shocking choices to manipulate the British people by frightening them as they pushed for a new lockdown. The conspiring to manipulate the country with how and when to "deploy the new variant" rhetoric to the media as the mechanism to "frighten the pants off everyone" as the excuse to continue the lockdown is astonishing. The *Telegraph* reported:

> The conversation started with a discussion about a fear that Sadiq Khan, the London Mayor, could attack the Government for plunging the capital into its own lockdown—just as Andy Burnham, the Mayor of Greater Manchester, had waged a battle in his city a few months earlier. . . . That led them into a discussion about when to "deploy" the new variant, although Mr Hancock was seemingly wary that it could have led to closing schools.[57]

Project Fear worked. A month later, January 2021, the country went into its third national lockdown.

Hancock resigned his post in June 2021 not because of his Monster-on-the-Hill decision-making as health secretary but because he had been exposed, on camera, cheating on his wife.[58, 59] Doing the right thing in any job, and in life, is a moral choice. As is being faithful to your spouse.

UK Scientists Admit Using Fear Was Totalitarian

Using fear wasn't exclusively the idea of Hancock or of the other fools in the UK and around the world who wouldn't let a good crisis go to waste. People like Hancock had backup from the system, which isn't hard to imagine. The bureaucratic state all throughout Western civilization is steeped in groupthink and relies on itself for protection and encouragement.

Scientists in the UK, however, are now admitting that their own actions and decision to use fear to control people during the pandemic was "totalitarian." Once again, the *Telegraph* reported the news to the British people:

> Scientists on a committee that encouraged the use of fear to control people's behaviour during the Covid pandemic have admitted its work was "unethical" and "totalitarian." Members of the Scientific Pandemic Influenza Group on Behaviour (SPI-B) expressed regret about the tactics in a new book about the role of psychology in the Government's Covid-19 response. SPI-B warned in March last year that ministers needed to increase "the perceived level of personal threat" from Covid-19 because "a substantial number of people still do not feel sufficiently personally threatened."[60] *

Members of that team spoke with Laura Dodsworth for her book *A State of Fear*, which examines the governmental reaction to the pandemic. One member was blunt with this confession to Dodsworth:

> In March [2020] the Government was very worried about compliance and they thought people wouldn't want to be locked down. There were discussions about fear being needed to encourage compliance, and decisions were made about how to ramp up the fear. The way we have used fear is dystopian. The use of fear has definitely been ethically questionable. It's been like a weird experiment. Ultimately, it backfired because people became too scared.[61]

But don't worry, Dodsworth was reassured by another team member that although mind control can be bad, they used it in the good way: "You could call psychology 'mind control.' That's what we do . . . clearly we try and go about it in a positive way, but it has been used nefariously in the past."[62] Got it.

---

* Original spelling maintained.

In May 2021, the UK established the UK COVID-19 Inquiry,[63] with public hearings scheduled to go through 2026, and a report not expected to be issued until the 2030s. How convenient for all those responsible as government scrambles to protect itself. "Inquiries," as Americans know all too well (think Benghazi and Durham), may turn up important information, but rarely is anyone held responsible. It has been the ultimate Kabuki theater.

Canada's Fake Wolves Fear Experiment

Conveniently, as COVID was disrupting daily life around the planet, the Canadian military decided October 2020 would be a good time to unleash a fear experiment on rural Nova Scotians.

A letter ostensibly from the Nova Scotia government was sent to residents warning them about wolves being released in the area. The problem was the letter was fake, and was eventually found to be the beginning of a Canadian military experiment on how the population would react to a fearful situation.[64]

Vice reported: "The Canadian military is taking heat after news broke that a mock letter, penned by 'information warfare specialists' in a reserve unit, made its way into the hands of civilians warning the public about a fictitious pack of grey wolves on the loose in the province of Nova Scotia. The incident also involved playing sounds of wolves howling in the woods through a loudspeaker."[65]

Moreover, in the reporting by the *National Post*, which broke the story, it's revealed the project was also training for the military to "hone its expertise for launching propaganda missions at home and abroad."

Canada's Department of National Defence sent out its own version of Baghdad Bob to address the controversy. He insisted "the fake letter wasn't meant to be released to the public and an investigation is underway to determine how that happened. The letter was an aid for the propaganda training. [The spokesman] said he didn't know why the loudspeaker was set up to transmit wolf sounds and that will be investigated as well,"[66] according to the *National Post*.

If the letter wasn't meant for the public, then for whom was it meant? With this absurd response, instead of setting up fear experiments targeting private citizens to hone their propaganda technique, perhaps the Canadian military and government should mandate training on how to ignore their inner fearmongering totalitarian.

What Should Be the Role of Government?

All the above examples illustrate the fundamental difference in the way leftists and conservatives view the role of government.

Because of its contempt for the average person leading to an inflated overestimation of themselves, leftists view government as the solution to all our problems, able to eliminate (or at least greatly reduce) poverty, inequality, racism and other ills, ushering in a golden age of "social justice." At least that's what they tell us.

The contempt and groupthink they are mired in also require the silencing of those who disagree, and the complete conformity and allegiance to the Marxist agenda. If only government were bigger, taxes were higher so the rich and corporations paid their "fair share" (a vague term with no commonly accepted definition), and government regulations were more far-reaching, most people would be better off in this view.

All of this is the excuse with which to manipulate societies into accepting the view that the individual is incompetent to run their own lives, and only political bureaucrats know what's best and can save society from itself. This has been the animating force driving the massive growth of government since President Franklin Delano Roosevelt began creating an alphabet soup of new federal agencies and giving them broad new powers to do things America's founders never imagined should be federal responsibilities.

Marx popularized the phrase "From each according to ability; to each according his needs," summing up his view of a world in which talent and merit are irrelevant and bring no reward.[67] In reality, no society on Earth has ever achieved this false end stage of communism because it is really meant to punish human nature, destroy the talented, and condemn the desire to succeed. Marxism is the cancer of envy, normalized and rewarded.

The leftist obsession with "equity" (meaning equal outcomes, as opposed to the far better path of equal opportunities) was espoused by Karl Marx. He said this would lead to a supposed communist paradise where private property and money would ultimately be abolished. However, such a "paradise" would also abolish incentives to work hard, innovate, and advance the cause of human progress. Why would pioneers of science and industry like Andrew Carnegie, Thomas Edison, Henry Ford, Walter Chrysler, John D. Rockefeller, J. P. Morgan, Steve Jobs, Elon Musk, and many others accomplish all they did and risk everything on untested ideas if they had no prospect of financial success, and if extreme government regulations punished them for their creativity and productivity?

Conservatives understand it's no accident that the free enterprise system limits government power, incentivizes individual initiative, and is the key to economic success and innovation. They also know this system enables the flourishing of human rights and the preservation of liberty specifically because the people gain and maintain their own power, keeping government in line.

Conservatives also understand that Big Government is usually not a benevolent parental figure taking care of the citizenry, but rather an iron-fisted oppressor forcing the population to bow down to the almighty bureaucratic state.

If Aristotle, Huxley, and Orwell could magically come back to life and view the suffering brought about by Big Government tyranny around the world since their deaths, we can imagine them saying in unison: "We told you so. Now do something about it." Doing something means deliberately cutting government down to a manageable size (many of the agencies that exist now serve only to maintain the behemoth of government while subjecting the citizens to federal diktats and edicts), and strengthening the freedom of individuals, and the businesses and organizations they create, to build a better future for us all.

It's a simple cure, but like all change threatening the establishment status quo, it requires courage to implement.

CHAPTER 7

Propaganda and Witch Trials

The mob I now faced carried no ropes or guns. Its weapons were smooth-tongued lies spoken into microphones and printed on the front pages of America's newspapers. It no longer sought to break the bodies of its victims. Instead it devastated their reputations and drained away their hope.

—SUPREME COURT JUSTICE CLARENCE THOMAS[1]

Mass media are the indispensable weapon the worldwide left relies on to spread its lies, misery, and fear. This is why the malevolent left has always coveted controlling the tools of communication in society to frighten, harm, and control the populace. The modern age has provided the world mass electronic media. It can be a wonderful, life-enhancing medium, but for the left it has been a terrible weapon with which to frighten, harm, and control. It was inevitable it would become an irresistible method with which the corrupt would spread their misery and fear without limit.

Understanding the power of the media, the American left has been remarkably successful at dominating communication platforms in the US and around the world. This explains why the Marxist agenda of fear is so easily dispersed through most of mainstream news media and becomes the prevalent "frame" or "spin" as chaos drives the left's ideological war against the free-market system and individual rights and freedom.

Radical leftists, having embedded themselves within the American academic, political, and media establishments, know that their victimhood agenda would naturally be rejected by the vast majority of people everywhere. So leftist radicals have embraced a propaganda campaign to romanticize, incentivize, and normalize their Marxist claims of victimhood to justify overturning the old order. For this existential lie to work, the left has infiltrated and seized control over much of the media to weaponize mass communications to successfully brainwash and manipulate as many people as quickly as possible. And, as we've learned, they will use government to coerce media to censor and crush unapproved voices and ideas.

Make no mistake—the radicals of 1960s didn't just disappear into Haight-Ashbury's drug-ridden side streets, stake out tents in Berkeley's parks, or set up candle and incense shops following the Woodstock countercultural music festival. The red-diaper babies* that came after them went to college, where they were churned out as journalists, politicians, lawyers, community organizers, and activists working for nonprofits pushing the far-left agenda. A short three generations later we're seeing the tragic result of the left's focused effort to control our cultural and social infrastructure, including media, government, education, and law.

In the twentieth century, radical journalists have become evangelists for wokeism—the new religion of the left that preaches an apocalyptic

---

* For the best historical biography about the communist left in 1960s America, see David Horowitz's important classic *Radical Son,* where he explains "red-diaper babies" was the designation "we used to identify ourselves as children of the Communist left." The term eventually expanded to describe the children of those who were just sympathetic to the aims of the Communist Party and ultimately was applied to leftist agitators who had no radical upbringing but were considered driven by what Horowitz calls "obscure personal rage." What we're dealing with today is a confluence of these catalysts.

fear of gathering oppression, rejection of free speech, equality of outcomes, and the necessity of discrimination against some groups for justice. They want us to fear being labeled as bigots if we embrace traditional American values, American exceptionalism, and a positive view of American history and our nation's place in the world. They praise millionaire sports stars who disrespectfully kneel when our national anthem is played as heroic "social justice warriors."

These journalists deride police seeking to quell rioting and looting in cities across the nation as racist oppressors. They denounce parents and government officials as backward and prejudiced for wanting to shield children in early elementary school grades from lessons about sex. They elevate "progressive" Democrats and socialists as the true patriots who will usher in better futures for the downtrodden, soak the rich and corporations with sky-high taxation, impose an enormous regulatory burden on businesses, and transform life as we know it in a fanatical crusade against climate change. Their goal is not just to use fear to attract the biggest audiences, but to use fear as a powerful weapon to push a leftist Big Government agenda.

Control of media is the linchpin for the success of the entirety of the Marxist agenda. America's liberal news media—made up of the vast majority of US news organizations and most of the journalists they employ—are now unabashedly in the Marxist business of fomenting fear and anxiety as a means of controlling what we think and what we do. It is *fear itself* they covet; fear itself without resolution but the chronic, unsolvable perpetual kind of fear meant to drive people into a compliant state of mass anxiety.

It's not one act, one story, or one event. The impact on us results from a combination of efforts. The media want us to think what's happening in this country is a natural and organic meltdown. The Democrats love phrases like "new normal" and "painful transitions," which is Joe Biden's favorite trope. Barack Obama loved telling us about his plans to "fundamentally transform" the country.

How has that been working out for all of us?

Leftist journalists don't sit under looming portraits of Karl Marx, plotting the next Bolshevik revolution. Their efforts are much more insidious. For activist liberal journalists, propagandizing for Democrats is the natural and appropriate thing to do. After all, these journalists believe they are so much more enlightened and public-spirited than the millions of hardworking and patriotic Americans they smear as semi-fascists clinging to politically incorrect religious and traditional values. After all, what makes us "deplorable" is our unwillingness to confront the apocalypses coming from pandemics, climate change, Trump's foreign string pullers, systemic racism, and whatever number of other frights-of-the-day may be useful.

These smears are designed to reinforce and spread contempt for the average American. When I was on the left, I recall everyone being inspired and encouraged by rhetoric casting conservatives as evil and hopeless enemies. When I worked with journalists to create stories and get coverage of the liberal policies I was supporting, it was genuine teamwork. There was no pretense about it. I reflect on those times and the fact that every aspect of my work, including with media, reinforced my leftist ideology and sense of rightness. Everyone felt the same way; everyone understood. In order for that to work, we were to not watch or listen to "the enemy." It was crazy to even consider having friends who were not activists or "in the fold."

Now I know why. Because the moment a different idea appears, or an action is challenged, or someone you may grow to respect questions the false reality that has been built around you, the walls begin to crack. Listening to "evil" conservative media was especially forbidden. Speaking with conservatives was existentially dangerous because then you would find out just how much your feminist "mentors" had lied to you. And I speak from experience.

This is at the heart of the leftist obsession with censorship and controlling what people read, hear, see, and are "allowed" to say. Leftists understand that their arguments and narratives, when challenged and exposed, fall apart. They operate through lies and manipulation that cannot be maintained when even glanced at in the light. They also understand the power of even one voice when it presents the truth.

From Cancel Culture to "Depersoning"

What is now called "cancel culture"—destroying the lives of dissenters, nonconformists, and others deemed troublemakers for the establishment—is an old weapon of the left. The dead Soviet Union and current Russian regime, Cuba, Venezuela, North Korea, and the cancerous Chinese Communist Party have long histories of using murder, imprisonment, and "disappearances" to cancel journalists, political opponents, activists, and noncompliant influencers. For us, another term might be "depersoning," because the goal is to shut people out of every part of life. Both cancel culture and depersoning seek not just accountability for a perceived wrongdoer, but destruction of their public life and ability to participate in society. The mob wants them to be unemployable, undatable, unfriendable, unwanted in restaurants or on planes, shouted down in every venue, and excluded from everything, including family.

The individuals featured in the following case studies have been written about extensively for years by those who recognize the injustice done to them at the hands of a burgeoning totalitarian government and its media handmaidens. The following commentary about Justice Clarence Thomas, Justice Brett Kavanaugh, and President Donald Trump provide important and specific examples of the vile collusion of the Democrat-Media Axis and how consistent, focused, and vicious their war against the foundation and values of this nation has been.

These three cases also share a particularly important element: sensationalized stories threatening the reputations, careers, and even lives of the targets involved in leaking the core accusation by a member of the government to the media.

In our first case study, what Thomas called his "high-tech lynching" began when President George H. W. Bush sent his Supreme Court nomination to the Senate in July 1991. The attempt to derail-by-smear Thomas's confirmation began when a former coworker, Anita Hill, provided a confidential statement to the Senate Judiciary Committee alleging sexual harassment by Thomas. And voila, NPR's Nina Totenberg and Tim Phelps of *Newsday* each suddenly obtained a copy and reported on Hill's unsubstantiated allegations.[2]

In our second case, the Kavanaugh virtual assassination circus went public when Christine Blasey Ford gave an interview to the *Washington Post* in July 2018, alleging that a drunken Kavanaugh had sexually assaulted her in high school in 1982. After approaching media, Blasey Ford then made the same unsubstantiated allegation to Representative Anna Eshoo (D-CA). Eshoo then gave a letter from Blasey Ford to Senator Dianne Feinstein of California, who was the ranking Democrat on the Senate Judiciary Committee.[3]

Our third case, in what some argue amounted to a coup attempt against Trump,[4] became public when FBI director James Comey gave confidential notes of a meeting with Trump to a college professor friend with the request that the individual provide it to the media, which the friend dutifully did.[5] This unethical subterfuge was designed to allow Comey to say he didn't leak the notes to the media, even though he used his friend as the middleman to do exactly that.

None of these premeditated character assassinations were organic or natural. They were all plots that required cooperation and amplification by the media.

This is one of the goals of normalizing the abnormal—making us accept something completely destructive and wrong as the "new normal." Many of you are familiar with the following events, but now think of them within our context of the spreading of fear beyond the target and the necessary involvement of the media in the "fake news" attack. We previously saw how the goal of spreading huge, amorphous fears is having the mind-killed turn over power to a technocratic elite. They want you to believe the only path to safety is obeying the authoritative and high-status. And who does the left is believe is more authoritative and high-status than journalists?

Justice Clarence Thomas

In 1991, Clarence Thomas withstood one of the most obscene and egregious assaults by liberal media in memory. Thomas's comment that opened this chapter comes from his wide-ranging 2007 memoir, *My Grandfather's Son*, in which he recounted his October 1991 Senate confirmation hearing for the Supreme Court. It became what was for most Americans, as he described it, a "high-tech lynching" concocted by Democrats and their allies in the media. Thomas is a black man who grew up in poverty and achieved professional success in government with humility and keen skepticism. Liberal groups protested his appointment to an appellate court on ideological grounds, but they really came out in force when a seat opened on the high court.

Democrats were still riding high from shooting down Robert Bork, whom Reagan had nominated for the court. This time, they knew they would need more.

Thomas testified for hours on his own behalf, and after that concluded, he found himself suddenly accused of sexual harassment in the press after someone leaked FBI documents. A public feeding frenzy began as Democrats began calling for his withdrawal.

Sound familiar?

The Senate allowed Anita Hill, a woman who had previously worked for Thomas at two other government agencies, to accuse him of sexual harassment during the nationally televised hearings.

Much like Justice Kavanaugh, it was Thomas's passionate response to the horrific and unsubstantiated allegations against him that shocked Americans out of their media-induced stunned trance. His remarks brought viewers of his confirmation hearing back to the stark reality of what was unfolding in front of them. After unequivocally denying every lurid and absurd accusation, Thomas said in part:

> I am here for my name, my family, my life, and my integrity. I think something is dreadfully wrong with this country, when any person, any person in this free country would be subjected to this. This is not a closed room. There was an FBI investigation. This is not an opportunity to talk about difficult matters privately or in a closed environment. This is a circus. It is a national disgrace. And from my standpoint, as a black American, as far as I am concerned, it is a high-tech lynching for uppity blacks who in any way deign to think for themselves, to do for themselves, to have different ideas, and it is a

> message that, unless you kowtow to an old order, this is what will happen to you, you will be lynched, destroyed, caricatured by a committee of the US Senate rather than hung from a tree.[6]

Yes, it was about race, but that was secondary to what I contend was the main point to be signaled and understood by just about everyone, which Thomas also notes in his statement. This was about how the system would treat any threat posed by those who challenge the liberal and bureaucratic status quo. It was a message by the establishment to blacks, women, gays, and everyone else that they had better behave and comply with the left's fast-talking snake oil salesmen. No identity would keep you from being sent into the coliseum to be mauled to death by wild animals.

Thomas has lived with the smears now for over thirty years. In an excellent 2022 essay in the *Federalist*, cultural and media critic Tom Elliott describes the experiences in Thomas's life that have helped to craft this American hero. In discussing the continuing media assault on a black man who dares to be independent, in "Why the Racist Left Smears Clarence Thomas as an 'Angry Black Man,'" Elliott writes:

> Supreme Court Justice Clarence Thomas is "a person of grievance" harboring "resentment, [and] anger," reported no less an authority than Hillary Clinton during an appearance last week on CBS [in 2022]. In ignoring Thomas's ideas to smear his temperament, Clinton pulled from the same playbook leftists have been using against Thomas since even before his 1991 confirmation hearings.[7]

For Marxists, we are all an attraction to highlight the suffering brought about by noncompliance, which they use to threaten and control society at large. But one voice can break the spell and reveal the fraud of the left. The bureaucratic elite knows this, and Thomas knows this. And while in his case it was about race, it was also about conforming and complying.

Justice Brett Kavanaugh

The Democrats' template of destruction was fanatically utilized against now-Justice Brett Kavanaugh in 2018. The anti-Thomas and -Kavanaugh displays were designed for the progressive media to inflict the kind of pain and destruction that can only come from repeated and widespread calumny. It also serves as a warning to everyone watching—if we can do this to them, we can do it to anyone. The kind of sexual allegations made against these two men are designed to be impossible to refute (how do you prove a negative?) as the smears move at the speed of light courtesy of the Democrat-Media Axis.

Defending yourself against the woke zealots who design your cancellation requires being able to *prove your innocence*, turning due process on its head. Proving your innocence now is just as impossible as it was in 1692 and 1693 for the roughly two hundred women and men accused of witchcraft in Salem, Massachusetts—or for the tens of thousands of people (mostly women) executed as witches in Europe from the 1300s through the 1600s.[8]

The vile and shocking Democrat-Media Axis smear campaign against Kavanaugh during his 2018 Senate confirmation hearings for the Supreme Court was a pure contrivance; propaganda at its most desperate and howling. It began, as so many do, as a last-minute accusation leaked to the media. An additional Senate hearing was staged to investigate the lurid and unproven allegations against Kavanaugh, and accusers were produced, making outrageously absurd accusations, all without evidence, against him. Just before a confirmation vote was to be taken.

The left had deployed one accuser against Thomas, but he was confirmed anyway. So progressives escalated and found three people to scream "Witch!" at Kavanaugh in hopes they would succeed in sinking his nomination. It was a show of shows.

In fact, Kavanaugh didn't have to just prove his innocence. According to the media, he bore the guilt of every human being who has ever been sexually assaulted. According to legacy media, we lived in a time of pervasive sexual trauma that only the government could heal. As *Time* magazine put it, "Most of all, the hopes and fears of women and men who have lived with the trauma of sexual violence were riding on the credibility of Ford's testimony. Her treatment in the halls of power and her reception by an expectant public would send a signal to countless survivors wrestling with whether they should speak up."[9]

Courtesy of that legacy media, the inferno that followed the accusations leveled against Kavanaugh was worthy of Dante. Americans and the world were exposed to a choreographed and irrational display of the Democrat Party's alliance with liberal media as they worked in concert to destroy an innocent man simply because his politics did not match theirs.

Through unabating news coverage, those watching the disgraceful spectacle were to be, consciously and subconsciously, instilled with enough fear for everyone. For those supportive of Kavanaugh and suspicious of the power of government in general, it was a fear that can only come when an out-of-control leftist government shows you its goal is to destroy whoever does not comply.

For liberals, feminists, and the cadre of woke Democrats and leftists, they were being gaslit by the bizarre and conspiratorial nonsense that a drug-dealer gang-rapist was going to be on the Supreme Court. It was the Democrats' veritable fearapalooza, and they couldn't stop themselves despite what it would do to the country, to the Court, and to the American people.

The virtual assassination was planned and produced with, as historian and author Daniel Boorstin would likely tell us, the "purpose of being reported or reproduced." It was obscene propaganda and emotional-torture porn, meant to completely destroy Kavanaugh, his family, those who supported him, and even strangers who were incredulous about the outlandish allegations. It was a fear-fest packaged for a greedy and obedient media to spread libel about a decent man who committed the crime of being a conservative and a man of faith.

Media reports of the outlandish claims against Kavanaugh included sanctimonious assertions by journalists and liberal senators that we must "believe the women," regardless of the absurdity of their claims, as if being female makes it absolutely impossible for someone to tell a lie.

The "politically correct" message was clear: anyone (including millions of women) who even doubted Blasey Ford's preposterous claims must be an incorrigible sexist who hates women. This is so nonsensical it would be funny if the harm done to Kavanaugh and our nation was not so serious.

Incredibly, we were lectured about how Kavanaugh was not even worthy of the presumption of innocence, because of his "ideological agenda," with one Democrat senator saying, "I put his denial [of being a rapist] in the context of everything that I know about him in terms of how he approaches his cases."[10] Moreover, at least one senator actually declared publicly that the burden was on Kavanaugh to *prove his innocence.*[11]

This is how people accused of wrongdoing are treated in dictatorships. It is the opposite of justice, socially and culturally destructive, and completely un-American. The Democrats know this and embraced it with gusto.

Women: The Left's Favorite Targets

Not to be missed is how horrifically the Democrats—the supposed "champions of women"—have been using us like dirty dishrags for generations. We have been the left's most successful grifting target. They only see our issues as opportunities with which to manipulate and profit. The Kavanaugh hearing put that fact in stark perspective.

The generational effort to help victims of sexual violence access justice was shockingly damaged by the slow-motion train wreck the world witnessed during the Kavanaugh hearings. As a feminist advocate for women most of my adult life, I can tell you ours was not a demand to destroy due process for the accused or an insistence that accusers be automatically believed simply because they were women. Quite the opposite, in fact. If you need to ask people to ignore the principles of real justice, then you are telling people the accuser can't be trusted. Ours was advocacy asking society and the justice system to simply take women seriously and treat them fairly when they came forward with an accusation.

The Democrats' position condemning due process, saying the accused must prove his innocence, and the accuser's veracity was not to be questioned, are exactly the positions you take when you know your allegation is false and can't survive scrutiny. It reinforced the scurrilous belief that women used victimhood as a weapon against men. It had taken generations of advocacy to persuade Americans about the truth—that domestic violence, sexual violence, and sexual harassment were serious issues, and that women did not use these experiences as a pretext for attention, personal benefit, or their own malign intentions. The Democrats and media politically weaponized sexual harassment and sexual violence claims in an attempt to keep a brilliant jurist off our nation's highest court, simply because liberals didn't like his views, illustrating just how shallow and repugnant they really are.

Turning Supreme Court hearings into a political spectacle was infuriating and loathsome. This circus did monumental damage to efforts to curtail the serious problem of sexual misconduct and was an insult to women who have genuinely suffered from such abuse. It also damaged those decades of work convincing people of the truth that women wanted only justice, not contrived revenge.

In the end, the Kavanaugh hearing was nothing more than a televised witch trial produced by our own government.

It was supposed to be the cancellation of Kavanaugh not only because he was deemed the enemy of the American left, but because every man and woman who is like him is deemed the enemy. The attempted public destruction of this man—and, by proxy, his entire family—was also a warning to every American who admires and aspires to be like him, and admires his professional and personal accomplishments. "Be afraid!" it screamed at everyone who might dare to not genuflect to leftist orthodoxy.

A cloud of envy envelops everyone engaged in this carnage. Kavanaugh's accomplishments alone made him suspect to the left, before ideology even comes into it.

This travesty was only possible because of a triad of collusion: a major American political party, its representatives in the Senate, and the legacy media. In the end, Christine Blasey Ford had her allegations against Kavanaugh disputed by the one woman she said was her witness and present at the alleged assault. As of this writing, Blasey Ford is a professor of psychology, and had a memoir released in 2024 focusing on—you guessed it—her testimony against Justice Kavanaugh.

Another accuser recanted allegations that Kavanaugh had raped her in a car, admitting that she fabricated the story to "get attention."[12] The lawyer for another accuser alleging Kavanaugh sexually assaulted her at Yale, stated publicly his client wasn't even sure it was Kavanaugh.[13] A third accuser, brought forth by the now-infamous attorney (and currently incarcerated on fraud convictions on other matters)[14] Michael Avenatti, alleged Kavanaugh orchestrated a gang rape during a high school party. In 2018, both Avenatti and his client were referred to the Department of Justice by the Senate Judiciary Committee for criminal investigation.[15] The Committee alleged the "individuals made materially false, fictitious, and fraudulent statements to Committee investigators." In 2019 and 2023,[16] Senator Chuck Grassley sent letters to the DOJ and FBI asking for updates on the status of the referrals. As of this writing, the senator has yet to receive a response.

But the damage was done to Kavanaugh and the country, courtesy of a liberal media deciding to be the American *Pravda* for the Democratic Party, and a justice system that is increasingly weaponized against what it perceives as political opponents of the ever-growing liberal, bureaucratic state.

The Compulsion to Confess[17]

Confirming the political agenda at the heart of the accusations was Blasey Ford's attorney, whose remarks Mollie Hemingway* reported on for the *Federalist:*

> The attorney for a woman who made unsupported allegations of sexual assault against Supreme Court Justice Brett Kavanaugh admitted that she and her client Christine Blasey Ford were

* For the most comprehensive and acclaimed investigation of the coordinated attack on Justice Kavanaugh, read Mollie Hemingway's and Carrie Severino's 2019 bestseller *Justice on Trial: The Kavanaugh Confirmation and the Future of the Supreme Court.*

> motivated by their support for abortion. . . . **Tarnishing the reputation of a justice who would have the power to overturn abortion law *Roe v. Wade* "is part of what motivated Christine," her attorney Debra Katz said. "Elections have consequences, but he will always have an asterisk next to his name,"** she said of Kavanaugh [emphasis mine].[18]

It was much more than an asterisk next to his name. It was a target. In June 2022, one month after a leaked draft opinion indicating the court was preparing to overturn *Roe v. Wade* was published by *Politico*, an armed man was arrested near Kavanaugh's home. Fox News reported:

> Nicholas John Roske, 26, of Simi Valley, California, was carrying a gun, ammunition, a knife, pepper spray, a screwdriver, zip ties, and other gear when he was arrested by Montgomery County Police Department officers in the early morning hours Wednesday, according to a criminal complaint. Roske, who is charged with attempted murder of a federal judge, told police that he was upset about Kavanaugh's positions on Roe v. Wade and the Second Amendment, the complaint said.[19]

A catastrophe was averted when Roske called 911 and told the operator he was "having thoughts," and wanted to kill Kavanaugh and himself. He also had texted his sister confessing to the plan. Authorities credit her with getting him to abandon the plot.[20] After his arrest in June 2022, he was indicted by a grand jury for attempted murder and has pled not guilty.[21]

The impact of smears like the ones conducted on Thomas and Kavanaugh go far beyond the original time frame of the pseudo-event itself. Part of the role of the liberal media is to continue, ad infinitum, the condemnation of the enemy with an asterisk. Cornell Law School professor William A. Jacobson reminds us the attempt on Kavanaugh's life "did not take place in a political vacuum. Democrats have a years-long effort to delegitimize and demonize the Supreme Court, through vile obstruction of nominations, as happened with Justice Kavanaugh, and threats to pack the court. . . . That an unhinged activist would act violently against this backdrop was not surprising."[22]

President Donald Trump

It was confirmed, through both the Robert Mueller and John Durham special investigations, that there was no truth to the crazy 2016 campaign season claim that business titan and then–presidential candidate Donald Trump was a spy for Russia. It was all a lie. It wasn't a mistake or a misunderstanding. It was a deliberate hoax, imagined first in Hillary's chardonnay-soaked brain and then implemented by her political machine in league with various stooges in the federal government and the entire Democrat media machine backing it up.[23]

A major project was launched and became an attempt to ruin and remove a duly elected president. You don't decide to falsely accuse the most powerful man in the world of being a traitor and expect that person to remain in office. The goal isn't to ruin their dinner. It's to eliminate them from every single arena in life.

The crux of the claim was that Trump was committing treason and colluding with a hostile government to win the 2016 presidential election. This fiction was also meant to frighten the American people enough to allow the government itself the leeway to act officially to destroy Trump, his family, and associates and then ultimately remove him from his elected office.

This establishment temper-tantrum wish-fantasy was produced and proliferated by people in our own government and other powerful political elites. It relied on shock value and fear in an effort to turn the American people against their president; it required government agencies leaking every action, the media spooling out small scoops on who was being "investigated" and for what, and talking heads speculating that this must be the tip of the iceberg.

The media were the mechanism used to spread that hoax, and somehow, none of them determined that a story accusing Trump of the completely absurd was . . . absurd. The *New York Times* and the *Washington*

Post were awarded Pulitzer Prizes for their coverage, while even the most modest of unbiased investigations would have revealed the supposed Trump-Russia collusion story was fake.

What their work did reveal is that those previously respected newspapers and much of the legacy media stopped being reporters and behaved instead as partisan activists and stenographers for the Democratic Party.

With the revelation that all he was accused of was part of an elaborate political hoax, Trump sent a letter to the Pulitzer board requesting that it rescind the prizes to the *Times* and *Post*. Not surprisingly, the board refused. Rescinding the prizes would have amounted to a confession that the foremost liberal newspapers in the United States performed as propagandists spreading fear and chaos in the name of defending the bureaucratic status quo.

As we look back, the Russia hoax was a shocking abuse of power and a flagrant display of the disregard the American political establishment has for the will of the people and the rule of law. Many exceptional books, columns, and television and radio commentary have exposed the details of this attempted coup of a duly elected president. Like the Thomas and Kavanaugh catastrophes, the attack on Trump was exclusively reliant on the liberal media to make the lie come alive, and amplify it without questioning or care.*

After Attorney General William Barr announced that "the Special Counsel's investigation did not find that the Trump campaign or anyone associated with it conspired or coordinated with Russia in its efforts to influence the 2016 US presidential election,"[24] Gregg Jarrett pulled no punches in describing the media's putrid role in this fraud against both Trump and the American people:

---

* Gregg Jarrett, an attorney and Fox News legal analyst and commentator, has written what many consider the definitive analysis and critique of what the Democrat-Media Axis has attempted to do to Trump. Jarrett's bestselling books—*The Russia Hoax: The Illicit Scheme to Clear Hillary Clinton and Frame Donald Trump*, and *Witch Hunt: The Story of the Greatest Mass Delusion in American Political History*—are must-reads for anyone wishing to be fully informed about the debacle.

> Many journalists were . . . reckless and malevolent. Most of them never bothered to examine the facts, evidence and the law. They refused to do their jobs. Instead, they abandoned objectivity and suspended their sense of fairness. They allowed enmity to obscure their judgment. In the process, the media squandered credibility, its only currency.
>
> It is no wonder that many Americans have little trust in journalists to be honest in their reporting. Will network brass take action to punish those who so egregiously exaggerated or, in some cases, even lied to Americans? Not a chance. Network chiefs were complicit cheerleaders. The media, together with Democrats, are already parsing and pivoting.[25]

If the past ten years have taught us anything, it's that none of us can predict the future. Trump's ability to disrupt was less about his nature and more about the establishment's shock at the unplanned and completely unexpected nature of the American people embracing Trump as evidenced by his 2016 win for the presidency. They were caught by surprise because they had forgotten about the American people in general, believing power and money would all flow naturally to them as the "system" was firmly in place. And yet, ironically, it was exactly those same forgotten men and women who delivered Trump into the White House.

Ultimately, the establishment was blinded by their own smug overconfidence as the media placated, assured, and massaged the system's apparatchiks day and night, and they began to believe their fiction was reality.

Off with Their Heads!

Young progressive journalists are increasingly trying to impose their woke sensibilities on their own news organizations. Like political commissars in the old Soviet Union and China who enforced communist orthodoxy, or the Thought Police in Orwell's novel *1984*, progressive journalists have gone to extremes to impose their standards of what is politically correct and to make everyone fear violating those standards.

This would be comical if the consequences weren't so serious. Reporters, editors, and other newsroom employees must now live in fear that they will lose their jobs if they write, edit, or broadcast anything that angers the left—not just among their audiences but among their colleagues. Their fear is not unfounded, and as a result, it's safe to assume that many journalists must be censoring themselves to avoid deviating from liberal orthodoxy.

One of the journalists falling victim to the woke mob was James Bennet, the powerful editorial page editor at the *New York Times*, who was considered a contender to eventually become executive editor. But in June 2020, Bennet made a career-ending move by committing the unpardonable sin of publishing an op-ed by Senator Tom Cotton, a conservative Republican representing Arkansas.

There is absolutely nothing unusual about the content of the op-ed, titled "Send in the Troops." It expresses the very reasonable and commonsense view that "as rioters have plunged many American cities into anarchy," US troops should be sent to the cities under the Insurrection Act to restore order. The rioting was sparked by the killing of George Floyd, an unarmed black man, by a Minneapolis officer who knelt on his neck for over nine minutes. The officer was later convicted of murder for the brutal crime.

Pointing out how rioters had looted and burned stores, shot and assaulted police officers, and even murdered a retired black police captain, Cotton wrote that "the rioting has nothing to do with George Floyd, whose bereaved relatives have condemned violence. On the contrary, nihilist criminals are simply out for loot and the thrill of destruction, with cadres of left-wing radicals like Antifa infiltrating protest marches to exploit Floyd's death for their own anarchic purposes. These rioters, if not subdued, not only will destroy the livelihoods of law-abiding citizens but will also take more innocent lives."[26]

Cotton then noted accurately that "during the 1950s and 1960s, Presidents Dwight Eisenhower, John Kennedy and Lyndon Johnson called out the military to disperse mobs that prevented school desegregation or threatened innocent lives and property."[27] Back then, liberals praised these actions.

Four days of furor ensued, as *Times* staffers and others said Cotton's op-ed endangered black people. This charge was preposterous because Cotton never called for rioters or peaceful protesters to be shot or otherwise assaulted by the military, the police, or anyone else. Cotton said nothing remotely racist in his piece, and the words *black* and *African American* never even appear in the op-ed.

Bennet defended himself in a tweet (since deleted), saying the role of the op-ed page was to publish competing opinions and that the Cotton essay advanced debate. *New York Times* publisher A. G. Sulzberger at first defended Bennet but then gave in to the woke mob and forced Bennet to resign. The newspaper has left the op-ed on its website but has put a groveling editor's note running an extraordinary 317 words on top that reads like the forced confession of a political prisoner in North Korea, concluding that "the essay fell short of our standards and should not have been published."[28]

Bennet stayed silent on his forced resignation for over two years, but in October 2022, he spoke out in an interview to blast Sulzberger. Bennet said the publisher "blew the opportunity to make clear that the *New York Times* doesn't exist just to tell progressives how progressives should view reality. That was a huge mistake and a missed opportunity for him to show real strength." The former editorial page editor said Sulzberger "set me on fire and threw me in the garbage" to win "the applause and the welcome of the left," including subscribers who expect "the *Times* will be *Mother Jones* [a far-left magazine] on steroids."[29]

The end result of this disgraceful episode is clear. First, *Times* editors who want to keep their jobs must now be reluctant to publish any more op-eds from Republicans, at least without heavy editing to water down conservative opinions. Second, the *Times* opinion pages are now even more hostile to conservative opinion and less ideologically diverse than they were before the Cotton furor. In fact, the *Times* announced it would publish fewer op-eds going forward, said they would undergo closer review, and renamed outside opinion pieces "guest essays" to make clear they are not written by the newspaper's employees.

Then–*New York Times* opinion staff editor and writer Bari Weiss tweeted in response to the Cotton episode: "The civil war inside The New York Times between the (mostly young) wokes [and] the (mostly 40+) liberals is the same one raging inside other publications and companies across the country." In a long Twitter thread, she added that the "New Guard" (woke young staffers at the newspaper) believes that "the right of people to feel emotionally and psychologically safe trumps what were previously considered core liberal values, like free speech." And in another criticism of the New Guard, she added: "The New York Times motto is 'all the news that's fit to print.' One group emphasizes the word 'all.' The other [the New Guard], the word 'fit.'"[30]

Proving the accuracy of Weiss's complaint, *Times* staffers called for her to be fired for daring to criticize her colleagues on Twitter. After being targeted for continuing harassment, she resigned and posted her resignation letter on her personal website, writing:

> My own forays into Wrongthink have made me the subject of constant bullying by colleagues who disagree with my views. They have called me a Nazi [despite Weiss being Jewish] and a racist . . . some coworkers insist I need to be rooted out if this company is to be a truly 'inclusive' one, while others post ax emojis next to my name [on company Slack channels]. Still other New York Times employees publicly smear me as a liar and a bigot on Twitter with no fear that harassing me will be met with appropriate action. They never are.[31]

Weiss added that "intellectual curiosity—let alone risk-taking—is now a liability at The Times. Why edit something challenging to our readers, or write something bold only to go through the numbing process of making it ideologically kosher, when we can assure ourselves of job security (and clicks) by publishing our 4000th op-ed arguing that Donald Trump is a unique danger to the country and the world? And so self-censorship has become the norm. . . . If a person's ideology is in keeping with the new orthodoxy, they and their work remain unscrutinized. Everyone else lives in fear. . . . Op-eds that would have easily been published just two years ago would now get an editor or a writer in serious trouble, if not fired."[32] Weiss has since gone on to create a very successful independent news operation.[33]

With all we've seen, you would not be incorrect in thinking those woke *New York Times* staffers sure have a lot of passion about keeping people safe from the idea of keeping people . . . safe. Until it's not the convenient political position. Mara Gay, an editorial board member of the paper and considered one of its leading "progressive" voices, was very public with her own outrage against Cotton's op-ed in 2020, tweeting at the time, "Running this puts black people in danger. And other Americans standing for our humanity and democracy, too. @nytimes."[34] Her tweet, in part, led to the firestorm that followed.

Fast-forward four years to 2024, an election year when defunding the police and de-criminalizing crime has put New York City and so many other blue cities, in the grip of crime waves. Inexplicably, polls are also showing Americans across the board are deeply unhappy with the downward plunge in the direction of the country.[35] Enter New York governor Kathy Hochul announcing that she would be deploying—wait for it—*the troops* supposedly to help quell the crime and violence plaguing the system. One thousand members of the National Guard and State Police were dispatched to *perform bag checks* (specifically only to "deter" crime) throughout the New York City subway system.[36]

Right on cue, über-woke Mara Gay, still on the *New York Times*' editorial board, chimes in but, hold your horses! She has an entirely new perspective. As though it was an opinion delivered to her by a leprechaun, Gay now thinks law and order and deploying the troops as a way to fight crime is *fine and dandy*.[37] Heaping approval on Hochul's plan to use the military to supposedly deal with subway crime, she wrote, "New York City cannot function without a thriving subway . . . ensuring that the system not only is safe but feels safe is paramount," noting that Hochul's decision was "the right one." In her genuflection on using the National Guard in this fashion she noted that if this "can provide even some psychological comfort, nudging additional riders back to the subways, it could help the system become safer."

That's quite the leap. From insisting just the *idea* in an op-ed of using troops to quell murderous urban riots "puts black people in danger" (even though many of the victims of the riots were also black), but totally no problem to actually implementing it to make subway riders "feel safe." She is also tacitly acknowledging in her comments that actual law enforcement is not at play, but simply getting more people into the system is the goal. As long as there is no actual law and order, we're good. Perhaps that adds to her comfort zone.

Understandably, the astonishing turnaround is accurately being described as rank hypocrisy.[38] But it's also more than that—it is an open illustration (and confession) of the left's commitment to chaos and victimhood through unrelenting crime. And even when it gets so bad that it can't be ignored, their solution is to deploy troops, not to arrest people, but to perform security theater. This subjects the law-abiding to an even more onerous experience, while still not bothering to deploy the transit police onto subway trains to write tickets, and act on crime as it unfolds. It is security theater at its most pornographic.

Meanwhile, a few weeks after the troops were stationed as security models, a man on a subway train was shot by his own gun during a chaotic and violent scene recorded by another straphanger's cellphone. When asked by reporters about that crime despite the presence of the National Guard, Hochul quipped her plan was "working as expected."[39] Indeed.

Another example of wokeness gone wild costing a journalist his job is the case of David Mastio, who was deputy editorial page editor at *USA Today* and had worked as an opinion journalist for thirty years. He was demoted at the flagship Gannett newspaper in August 2021 (and later left the paper) because he tweeted that "People who are pregnant are also women."

Writing later in an op-ed in the *New York Post*, he said: "That idea was forbidden because a 'news reporter' covering diversity, equity and inclusion wrote a story detailing how transgender men can get pregnant . . . the LGBTQ Employee Resource Group and the newsroom 'diversity' committee thought I should be fired. . . . Gannett's top editors and publishers are filling the company with a cadre of young college graduates who share a narrow 'woke' ideology that is alien to the values of most of its readers."[40]

It is a sad realization that the liberal media have been consumed and destroyed by Marxist woke enforcers. This hurts the industry itself, but even more importantly, it harms America. Principled media presenting a spectrum of perspectives on the issues are important for the health of our republic. Right now, virtually the full burden of presenting TV news outside the framework of the Democrat-Media Axis is on the shoulders of Fox News, the relatively small number of similar news organizations, and independent media and journalists.

Fox Derangement Syndrome

This obsession with controlling the conversation explains the unhinged reaction by the establishment's cultural, political, and media infrastructures to the emergence and success of Fox News.

Suddenly, in 1996, the liberal, Democratic, and establishment nightmare had an awakening—no longer were they the only source of TV news. There was now an alternative source for news and commentary that was not part of the Democrat-Media Axis. Unlike all the news organizations under the control of the liberal establishment, Fox News took conservative opinions seriously, rather than dismissing them as the bigoted and backward views of "right-wing nuts" to be marginalized or condemned.

Even Fox News's original slogans—"We Report, You Decide" and "Fair and Balanced"—caused outrage in the leftist circles I was in during my time as a left-wing community organizer in the mid-1990s. It was heresy to believe average Americans could come to their own conclusions about issues in the news without the "guidance" of enlightened liberals telling them what to think. Even the suggestion that regular people could decide on the issues for themselves was an empowering reminder of reality and was damaging to the decades-long inculcation of helplessness and fear doled out by the leftist media.

In 1996, I was in the midst of my tenure as president of the Los Angeles chapter of the National Organization for Women. I distinctly remember when Fox News launched, as there were ads with their slogan plastered all over the city at bus stop shelters. As a friend of mine and I were driving by one such shelter, she said with a mash-up of disdain and mockery: "Oh, look, I've heard about that. It's *conservative*," replete with an eye roll and sigh. The more the merrier, I opined. After shooting me a disapproving side-eye, her response surprised me and stayed with me all these years. "What do they mean, 'We report, you decide'? Decide what? What is there to *decide*?" she asked in all seriousness and with the added mockery of scary air quotes.

Generally, then and now, many liberals in deep-blue cities like Los Angeles, New York, and Washington, D.C., live in leftist news and information bubbles, watching and reading only news stories that support their oh-so-progressive worldview. The only way they can encounter different opinions that will provoke them to think, reexamine, and even refine their long-held beliefs is to take a detour in the media ecosystem to destinations like talk radio, the *Wall Street Journal*, the *New York Post*, or—beginning in 1996—Fox News. Before 1996, with the exception of talk radio, there were no media platforms offering programming that approached the conservative point of view fairly or seriously. Back then, the internet was in its infancy, and most conservative websites did not yet exist.

Having lived most of my adult life in Los Angeles—a city where everything people hear and see reflects the liberal or leftist point of view—I, like millions of others, never considered my opinions or their being echoed back to me as "biased." It was simply the only reality we knew, like people growing up on a remote tropical island believing everyone on Earth lived in the idyllic midst of beaches, palm trees, with an average temperature of 73 degrees in the winter. My friends consisted of liberal activists, journalists, and actors, and we all held the same beliefs. When those opinions (truly considered the Truth) are never challenged, and you never encounter an alternative point of view, those beliefs become even more reinforced as unassailable.

My exchange passing the bus shelter with my friend was a few years after I had started my radio show in Los Angeles, and I had already realized that there was more to be said and more perspectives than our own. "Yes, what is there to decide?" I quizzically answered back and laughed.

She didn't get it. She then warned me that, considering my work for years as a feminist community organizer, this new "weird" network, as she called it, would probably call me for interviews. She stated as a given that I would not grant any Fox News interview requests. "You don't want to give them any legitimacy!" she warned. On the contrary, I told her it would be fun to talk with people who needed a talking-to.

She was, and still is, an actress. We're both older, and she is quite a bit more famous now than she was then. It has been decades, and we are still good friends. Our politics actually haven't changed, but our commitment to personal freedom and civil liberties has grown, and is now considered "conservative." To this day, we laugh at our Fox News bus-shelter exchange.

While being open about my political predilections, if she were to "come out of the political closet," so to speak, her career would be over. She, like many of my friends in a similar situation, leaves it to me to be vocal about the issues and the conservatism that will not just save our nation but return us to the values we all embrace—freedom of speech, freedom of religion, freedom from government intrusion into our lives, and the freedom to be ourselves without being threatened or canceled.

Just six years after noticing those Fox News ads, it became clear I wasn't the only one who thought hearing more perspectives on the news was a good idea. As *Forbes* reported in February 2022:

> The latest cable news ratings show that, **every year since January 2002** [emphasis mine], Fox has been #1 in total day and primetime viewership as well as #1 in the key 25–54 demo. A 20-year record that, while not only unprecedented across the cable news landscape, is also likely to continue this year. . . . Last month alone, Fox had 95 of the top 100 cable news telecasts for the month, including the top 91 cable news telecasts.[41]

The cable network ended 2023 by announcing it was finishing the year as the "most watched network for the 8th straight year."[42] The powerhouse then began 2024 with an even more remarkable achievement—at the end of January the Fox News Channel was officially number one for twenty-two *consecutive* years in all four key categories of news ratings measurement,[43] confirming again that Americans are not afraid of differences of opinion, and very much prefer to decide for themselves what to make of the news of the day.

Fox News presented a disturbing new reality not just for leftist progressives but also for center-left liberals who never really had to accidentally encounter or entertain ideas other than their own. Talk radio was the only real outlet for genuine debate and conversation, and that was furiously being marginalized by the left's Thought Police. Fox News represented a challenge to the status quo in that conservative ideas and arguments would suddenly be available on television for millions of Americans. This presented an immediate threat to the near-universal media control the Democrats had enjoyed since the 1960s, fueling the Democrat-Media Axis.

The liberal media and their narrative of fear is so fragile that the creation of one alternative network providing genuinely diverse opinions on the issues continues to be seen by the comfortable progressive establishment as an existential threat. The left's fight against intellectual freedom and a marketplace of ideas has intensified over the years as it seeks to demonize conservative ideas and traditional American values in order to generate fear.

Contrary to the belief of many that Fox News only attracts Republicans, it actually draws a significant number of Democrats and independents to its cable network, a fact noticed in 2021 when data first showed more Democrats watched Fox News than CNN during prime time.[44] That's because people other than conservatives also want reliable information, understand the difference between news and opinion, and can handle disagreements and opinions that contradict their own. Go figure.

The left knows they can't survive politically with free speech and people are able to hear and engage in a vibrant debate of issues and ideas, which is why they're desperate to squelch it. Americans, however, are voting with their clickers. In December 2023 it became clear that voters had made their choice about who they could trust: "The latest New York Times/Siena poll found that Fox News was the single news source voters said they 'turn to most often,' beating out CNN, MSNBC, and a host of other news sources in the December survey."[45]

While we know these days it's impossible to avoid news that can be frightening, Americans have been through a lot and are a tough bunch. We saved the world in two world wars, and were born of dreams, revolution, and taking chances. We want information and news so we can properly assess what's happening in the country, and more confidently determine how it impacts our lives and the future. With whatever the news brings, we choose information over ignorance, and determination over fear.

Today, we are at a crossroads and must decide which path our nation will choose—freedom from fear itself and its tiny tyrant boosters, or surrender to the controlled predictability of totalitarianism. In other words, we will continue to observe, learn, and . . . decide.

CHAPTER 8

Manipulating Reality

We are not afraid to entrust the American people with unpleasant facts, foreign ideas, alien philosophies, and competitive values. For a nation that is afraid to let its people judge the truth and falsehood in an open market is a nation that is afraid of its people.

—PRESIDENT JOHN F. KENNEDY[1]

It's funny how much can change in just a few decades. Like shape-shifters, in sixty years, the Democrats have gone from embracing President Kennedy's support for freedom of speech and trusting the American people to transforming into bullies, censors, and authoritarians working to crush the life out of both. In the last half century, Democrats have joined forces with liberal media to form what amounts to a Democrat-Media Axis that is the antithesis of the Democratic Party in the Kennedy era.

Kennedy's quote comes from his remarks delivered in February 1962 on the twentieth anniversary of the Voice of America (VOA). The Kennedy Library explains the intent of his speech was to reinforce "the necessity of freedom of information and complete truthfulness of the media."[2] We still embrace that objective, but for today's Democrats and progressive media, his comments would be condemned as a defense of hurtful, racist, and violent expressions.

Kennedy uttered these words with a purpose. He had witnessed the spread of the virus of communism from the Soviet Union to Eastern Europe, China, Cuba, and elsewhere. He understood that communist dictatorships—like the dictatorships he and millions of others in the American military bravely battled in World War II—all seized control of the media to spread their poisonous propaganda. In 1962, we were only seventeen years out of World War II, twenty years from the founding of the VOA, and in the midst of the Cold War with the Soviet Union.

The new president was of a generation that watched the Office for War Information and its offshoot (the VOA) become infested with influential leadership and staff harboring pro-Soviet and communist views and knew this was affecting VOA operations and programming.[3] Kennedy also believed strongly that the "open market" of ideas was critical and that media honesty with the American people centered on facts was vital to maintain the nation's strength and founding principles.

Ted Lipien, a former officer with the Voice of America and Radio Free Europe/Radio Liberty during the Trump administration, writes: "Previously classified US government documents show that following the start of Voice of America radio broadcasts in February 1942 in response to the dangers and the turmoil of the Second World War, the first group of VOA managers and journalists uncritically embraced and eagerly promoted various Soviet propaganda lies."[4]

Moreover, he notes, "Almost all of VOA's early pro-Soviet propagandists in the 1940s were radically left-wing US federal government officials, employees, and contractors who were hired without extensive security and background checks."[5]

Through the first half of the twentieth century, it became abundantly clear to Kennedy's generation that radio was a harbinger of the power and importance of mass media. Like any object, depending on whose hands it was in, it could be a force for good or a weapon inducing misery and fear.

Communist propaganda aimed at the American people was not in the United States, or humanity's, best interest. The left, however, operates within the presumption that the American people are drooling infants who need to be manipulated and controlled. For our own good, of course.

Kennedy's argument, as is mine, is the complete opposite of the miscreants on the left. We are part of the majority of Americans who understand and expect that the people can handle a myriad of ideas and make their own decisions accordingly. We also summarily reject the left's reliance on gaslighting, lies, and fear, all nursed by contempt for those enjoying life. In the age of modern media, actively confronting and condemning the propagation of fear and lies by Marxists and their fellow travelers is even more vital.

Leftists in particular, and people devoted to Big Government in general, don't have the same regard for the average person as Kennedy did. They are afraid of the people because they have contempt for us. We have now come full circle from what the most beloved Democratic president in the modern age wanted to accomplish—reforming the VOA into an entity that respected American values and relied on the truth. Instead, over the next sixty years, the left doubled down on its successful efforts to control government media while spreading its infection into the private broadcast networks and media writ large. Kennedy is gone, but the left is still here and remains obsessively committed to destroying anyone who refuses to conform and bend a knee.

This matters because what I term the Democrat-Media Axis—the Democratic Party, liberal journalists, and Big Tech media enablers—are as obsessed with controlling what we think, say, and do as in Kennedy's time. The world's leftists are still incompetent, miserable, and unhinged in their pursuit of power and money, tormenting everyone around them, yet they remain singularly focused on destroying everything the United States stands for—especially individual freedom and Western values.

Marxist totalitarian leaders believe they must exercise total control of public messaging and communication. They use public humiliation, shame, and executions of inspirational individuals to ruthlessly stay in power. While regimes can't directly control each individual in a nation, they expect populations to submit if they see enough examples of harm inflicted on those who dare not to conform.

"Good Night and Good Luck"

As we fight to stop Marxist totalitarian madness from destroying our country, it's important to remember that most news organizations haven't always been lapdogs of the left. Many are still committed to bringing all information for a variety of points of view to the public discussion. Knowing this history is important because it reminds us that journalism can attract good people and that human nature is not predominantly bad or disturbed.

When it comes to inspiration about journalism and news, many of us think about Edward R. Murrow, the CBS radio and later TV journalist who rose to fame reporting on World War II from Europe. His signature sign-off, "Good night and good luck," created a bonding of trust with his listeners as he broadcast from London during the Nazi bombing "Blitz" on the city.

Murrow gave us wise guidance when he said in a 1954 TV broadcast: "We will not walk in fear, one of another. We will not be driven by fear into an age of unreason, if we dig deep in our history and our doctrine, and remember that we are not descended from fearful men—not from men who feared to write, to speak, to associate and to defend causes that were, for the moment, unpopular."[6]

Journalists like Murrow (and they still exist) have long enjoyed trust and respect in the United States and are meant to be protected from governmental control by the First Amendment to the Constitution. They provide us with vital information about our communities, states, nation, and the world—everything from storm warnings to alerts about criminals on the loose, to actions by government at every level, to wars.

Objectivity was embraced as a goal when radio news began on August 31, 1920, with what is believed to be the first broadcast newscast on a station in Detroit.[7] Radio news gradually spread across the nation as other stations sprouted up.

Little did we know how powerful (and influential) the first coast-to-coast news report broadcast by NBC would be. The highly emotional recorded description by announcer Herb Morrison of the May 6, 1937, explosion of the hydrogen-filled German dirigible *Hindenburg*[8] shocked and arguably changed the way Americans viewed the world around them and defined the power of news reports. Airing the day after the catastrophe, listeners could imagine themselves there as the passenger zeppelin attempted to land during an afternoon of periodic thunderstorms in Lakehurst, New Jersey, killing thirty-six passengers and crew members.[9]

"The effect of the Hindenburg recordings on audiences was startling," Cary O'Dell wrote in a 2002 essay for the Library of Congress. "Never before had such a large audience heard such a blow-by-blow description of such a horrific occurrence. For listeners, the news of the day suddenly became active, proximate, and real. News gathering and reporting was altered too."[10] The immediacy of radio news and the ability of listeners to hear events unfolding enhanced the credibility of reports.

War of the Worlds

These days, we see fake news spread like a virus in an effort to get clicks on the internet. Conspiracy theories and deliberately false stories meant to smear those who irritate the powers-that-be are, in part, what is destroying public trust in the media. In 1938, the goal wasn't for clicks, of course. Instead, it was for ears. The drama and power of the 1937 *Hindenburg* report and its impact on the public just one year later inspired a creative team and their production of what could be considered the first broadcast of deliberately fake news.

On October 30, 1938, Orson Welles and his *Mercury Theatre on the Air* broadcast an adaptation of the 1898 H. G. Wells novel *The War of the Worlds* on the CBS radio network. In the novel, a narrator conveys the story, but for the radio adaptation, Welles decided to present it as breaking news, delivered by a reporter.

The adaptation deliberately copied the style of the Herb Morrison report on the *Hindenburg* crash to deliver what sounded like a series of urgent breaking news bulletins about a successful Martian invasion of New Jersey taking place as the broadcast aired.

"Sunday evening in 1938 was prime-time in the golden age of radio, and millions of Americans had their radios turned on. But most of these Americans were listening to ventriloquist Edgar Bergen and his dummy 'Charlie McCarthy' on NBC and only turned to CBS at 8:12 p.m. after the comedy sketch ended and a little-known singer went on," the History Channel tells us. "By then, the story of the Martian invasion was well underway."[11]

On the eightieth anniversary of the broadcast in 2018, in a special for its magazine, Peter Tonguette at the National Endowment for the Humanities wrote:

> For much of its duration, the program was presented as a faux newscast. Consequently, Welles, who was then all of twenty-three, had somehow persuaded a portion of the public that Martians were annihilating Earthlings. The *New York Times* headline painted the picture: "Radio Listeners in Panic, Taking War Drama as Fact."
>
> So, seated among a semicircle of eagerly scribbling reporters, Welles wore an oh-so-serious expression and spoke in sincere, thoughtful tones. "I know that almost everybody in radio would do almost anything to avert the kind of thing that has happened, myself included," Welles said. "Radio is new, and we are learning about the effect it has on people. We learned a terrible lesson."[12]

Despite some people claiming the audience reaction was overblown and that the radio play would never have been mistaken for a real broadcast, during a 1955 television show, Welles admitted that the hoax and impact wasn't an accident. "We made a special effort to make our show as realistic as possible," Welles said in an episode of the BBC television series *Orson Welles' Sketch Book*. "That is, we reproduced all the radio effects, not only sound effects. Well, we did on the show exactly what would have happened if the world had been invaded. We had a little music playing and then an announcer coming on and saying, 'Excuse me, we interrupt this program to bring you an announcement from Jersey City.' "[13]

Looking back on something like this has allowed the world to consider this an example of classic entertainment, including the fear that surrounded it. But the reaction of panic and terror at the time was genuine and certainly not entertaining. *The War of the Worlds* broadcast is an early example of how taking advantage of listeners' trust in a new communications medium could easily be exploited for publicity and attention. It was, as Welles noted the next day, a "terrible lesson." But perhaps for others, not so terrible an example, as we all know too well today.

"Mostly Peaceful" Riots

A disappointing majority of liberal journalists don't even try to be objective, despite their claims to the contrary. Like the proverbial wolf in sheep's clothing, they attempt to disguise who they are: partisan Democratic activists embedded in their media platforms. We see the results of their flagrant left-wing bias every day. Welles presented deliberately fake news to his audience. Today we have the same problem, but we also have to guard for lies by omission from the media, and the deliberate gaslighting of the audience.

One of the best examples of gaslighting and propaganda is represented by the remarkably absurd news coverage of the Black Lives Matter and Antifa riots of 2020 that swept across the US (an issue I cover more extensively in our last chapter). In this case, we see every classic element of propaganda, including manipulation, omitting or distorting facts, and lying or misrepresenting something that is on its face completely different from what is being described. One of the goals of gaslighting and cultic brainwashing is to have the targets begin to question what their own senses are telling them. Marxists can only win when they convince us to literally not believe what we see with our own eyes.

Liberal news organizations were fearful of portraying riots following the murder of George Floyd for what they were—lawless rampages involving property damage, injuries, and the loss of life—because they didn't want to make the left look bad and be accused of racism. In addition, the leftist media sought to normalize violence in the name of "equity." Telling average Americans that violence is a natural response to leftist grievances and should be expected tells them that their new normal is a Hobbesian state-of-nature, where massive government involvement and a dramatic change of the American system and society is the only answer.

Facilitating that narrative were statements from the organizer of Black Lives Matter in Chicago. After a night of mass looting in the city, the activist insisted to a throng of protesters and media that "'I don't care if somebody decides to loot a Gucci or a Macy's or a Nike because that makes sure that that person eats. That makes sure that that person has clothes,' [Ariel] Atkins said, according to NBC Chicago. 'That's reparations. That is reparations. Anything they want to take, take it because these businesses have insurance. They're going to get their money back. My people aren't getting anything.'"[14] The effort began to "reimagine," normalize, and even romanticize crime, violence, and riots, as raging against the machine. And it's quite safe to say that no one looted a Gucci bag or a pair of Nike kicks to eat them. A major publisher even coughed up a book with a title clear enough to help along the new messaging, "In Defense of Looting."

It's all gaslighting, but also a message that otherwise vile, ugly, and dangerous mob action should be thought of . . . differently. And so it was with the BLM "protests."

Liberal journalists engaged in verbal gymnastics to often describe the riots as "racial justice protests" and asked their audiences not to believe in reality or to grow more fearful about what the future has in store for them.

For example, during rioting in Minneapolis at the end of May 2020, as reporter Ali Velshi of MSNBC stood in front of a burning building, he absurdly said he was witnessing "mostly a protest" that "is not generally speaking, unruly." Velshi then sought to make excuses for the arson and looting taking place around him by saying that "it does have to be understood that this city has got, for the last several years, an issue with police, and it's got a real sense of the deep sense of grievance of inequality."[15]

During August 2020 rioting in Kenosha, Wisconsin, in a now infamous scene, a CNN reporter stood in front of a car that had been set on fire while an on-screen banner read: "Fiery but mostly peaceful protests after police shooting."[16] Should we describe September 11, 2001, as a day of "mostly peaceful" flights? Should we describe Hurricane Katrina as a "mostly peaceful" time on the world's oceans? The liberal media simply couldn't bring themselves to say anything derogatory about urban looters and rioters. This was because, for liberal journalists, job number one was legitimizing the unhinged and organized urban riots by Marxist and anarchist groups as normal and expected behavior because . . . Trump.

Newsrooms controlled by a supermajority of liberals and Democrats wasn't an organic development, but a deliberate mission pursued with a fanatical focus. Liberal activists flock to journalism today because they understand that their agenda of fear and chaos flows from the control of mass media. They don't want to simply report the news; they want to change American society and the world.

A Simmering Fear All Their Own

How successful has the left been at taking control of the media and weaponizing it as an instrument of "social justice"? Consider this *New York Times* story from 1992 about a study revealing how far reporters' political sympathies had shifted to the left. In an article headlined "Increasingly, Reporters Say They're Democrats," the newspaper reported on a survey of 1,400 journalists nationwide showing a dramatic increase in the percentage of reporters who are Democrats:

> The report released in Washington showed that more than 44 percent of reporters now say they identify themselves as Democrats, up from about 36 percent in 1971. As the number of newsroom Democrats has increased, the number of reporters who say they are Republican has fallen from more than 26 percent in 1971 to about 16 percent. The survey, conducted

> by telephone, is the third in a series of studies of journalists' attitudes since 1971.[17]

Fast-forward to 2014, and another long-term study of reporters' sympathies and attitudes revealed just how successful the left had been. A mere 7 percent of reporters identified as Republicans:

> A long-term study of reporters' leanings and attitudes, "The American Journalist in the Digital Age," shows that the drift toward liberalism has been going on for years within journalism. In 1971, Republicans made up 25.7% of all journalists. Democrats were 35.5%, and independents were 32.5%. Some 6.3% of responses were "other."
>
> By 2014, the share of journalists identifying as Republican had shrunk to 7.1%, an 18.6 percentage point drop. From having near-parity with the journalist Republicans in the 1970s, Democrats today outnumber Republicans today by four to one.[18]

As of 2023, the number of journalists identifying as Republicans collapsed to just 3.4 percent.[19]

Flooding the marketplace with propaganda is only possible when liberal activists are in control of the national conversation. For leftist activists and the establishment, it takes an enormous amount of energy to keep control of narratives and facades. All the energy at the national level is spent on projecting a particular image, outrage, protests, displays, press conferences, and publicizing demands. Perpetual victimhood is the expectation, and it remains the singular organizing principle.

No one naturally wants to be a victim, so how do you move people along into that hopeless pit? With fear-based propaganda about what is in store for the public—particularly women, gays, and people of color—if conservatives have power or are even allowed to be heard. Riots, of course, will conveniently further that narrative, but the leftist plate is full of strategies to bully and gaslight us into retreat and then surrender.

When you have contempt for those you are supposed to be serving, there will be unintended consequences. Every day, we see the deleterious effects of the fear itself the liberal news media promulgates via the strategies they use against us. The American people have noticed. The result is less trust and more suspicion of the media in general, creating a simmering fear all its own.

After all, what happens when the news industry you believed would keep the powerful in check was doing the bidding of the system itself? Bias is damaging and irritating, but it is also a dangerous signal that one of the important pillars of democracy has abandoned its duty, understandably adding to the fear born of betrayal and chaos in the public sphere.

From January 2021 to June 2022, as no one could avoid or honestly deny the collusion between media and government during the COVID-19 debacle, news consumers were confronted with a cascade of revelations about the growing distrust in media. Headlines[20] at the political website Axios tell the story of increasing suspicion and even anger at the media and its protector, the establishment:

"Media Trust Hits New Low" (January 2021)
"Conservative Trust in Media has Cratered" (August 2021)
"Distrust in Political, Media, and Business Leaders Sweeps the Globe" (January 2022)
"Americans' Trust in Tech Companies Hits New Low" (April 2022)
"The US Public Thinks Journalists Aren't Doing a Good Job" (June 2022)
"Trust in News Collapses to Historic Low" (July 2022)

And . . .

"Media Confidence in US Matches 2016 Record Low" (October 2023)

Progressive favorites MSNBC and CNN were unmasked during both the Trump presidency and COVID as unserious propagandists for the leftist establishment, even as many in their audiences were swallowed up with the fear that flowed from their agitprop.

Other viewers, however, decided enough was enough, and the ratings began to collapse. After all, being a Democrat doesn't automatically mean you want to be lied to, manipulated, and deliberately made afraid. Grassroots Democrats, the classical liberals we remember being the heart of the party, are also concerned about personal freedom, national security, inflation, illegal immigration, crime, and a better future for their children. The first victims of progressive grifters masquerading as advocates and politicians? Average Americans who happen to be Democrats.

DePauw University professor and media critic Jeffrey McCall told Fox News: "CNN and MSNBC are particularly aggressive in their progressive approaches to news, and only true believers want news solely from an ideological standpoint. There still needs to be some intellectual honesty in the approach to journalism, and audiences are sensing that CNN and MSNBC have become too shrill for measured reporting."[21]

A Titanic Result

The numbers don't lie; millions of Americans want something different than the slanted news stories the left-wing media are feeding them. We also aren't the mindless, drooling infants the liberal media presumes us to be. The years the media spent smearing Donald Trump exposed how deep the bias went. Axios reported on January 21, 2021, just after Biden was inaugurated:

> For first time ever, fewer than half of all Americans have trust in traditional media . . . 56% of Americans agree with the statement that "Journalists and reporters are purposely trying to mislead people by saying things they know are false or gross exaggerations." 58% think that "most news organizations are more concerned with supporting an ideology or political position than with informing the public." When Edelman re-polled Americans after the election, the figures had deteriorated even further, with 57% of Democrats trusting the media and only 18% of Republicans.[22]

The collapse of trust in the media accelerated during Biden's first and second years in the White House. The silver lining of this is that it confirms that millions of Americans clearly see how the liberal media are intellectually bankrupt propagandists. In July 2022, Gallup reported that only "16% of Americans have a great deal/quite a lot of confidence in newspapers," while "11% have some degree of confidence in television news."

In 2023, the mood of Americans about its national news organizations continued its ignominious decline, with respondents confirming what they made clear in 2021—they remain intensely suspicious of the intentions and goals of media. "Half of Americans in a recent survey indicated they believe national news organizations intend to mislead, misinform or persuade the public to adopt a particular point of view through their reporting. The survey . . . goes beyond others that have shown a low level of trust in the media to the startling point where many believe there is an intent to deceive."[23]

How this revulsion is manifesting itself is epic. CNN, which lost massive numbers of viewers as its absurd programming devolved into a steady and pathetic stream of Trump-hatred and an unhinged obsession with attacks on Fox News, got new bosses in 2022. Viewers were abandoning CNN as though it had hit an iceberg and was rapidly taking on water, as it listed to the left. *Forbes* reported:

> [A] review of ratings data compiled by Nielsen shows the internal chaos at the network [CNN] is mirrored by deep declines in viewership across all day parts. . . . Through February 15, CNN . . . a 69% drop from the same period one year ago. Among total viewers . . . a decline of 68% from 2021. . . . MSNBC saw a 62% drop among viewers 25–54 year-over-year, and a 47% decline among all viewers. Fox News Channel was the only cable news network to increase its viewership—up 6% in the key demo and up 2% among total viewers—compared to the same period in 2021.[24]

As they were running out of lifeboats, an epiphany! "CNN's corporate boss David Zaslav wants network for 'Republicans, Democrats' as ratings sink." That's a good sign, and a reminder that choices matter, especially as consumers.

Fake News and Pseudo-Events

When it comes to propagating fear, leftists must do more than determine who is heard and who is not. They also must create events furthering their narrative and the suppressive environment they require and crave.

Historian Daniel Boorstin prophetically warned Americans in his 1962 book *The Image* that the media were replacing what was real with propaganda and what he termed "pseudo-events."[25] This Boorstin classic is an indictment of what he saw as the media creating news instead of reporting it.

Boorstin worried that Americans were becoming inured to fabricated events and accepting the media's increasingly false environment too easily as an attractive, more dramatic replacement of reality. Boorstin's prescient concern and description is widely described today as "fake news." He explains these pseudo-events, in part, as "a happening that possesses the following characteristics:

1. It is not spontaneous, but comes about because someone has planned, planted, or incited it. Typically, it is not a train wreck or an earthquake, but an interview.
2. It is planted primarily (not always exclusively) for the immediate purpose of being reported or reproduced. Therefore, its occurrence is arranged for the convenience of the reporting or reproducing media. Its success is measured by how widely it is reported.... The question, "Is it real?" is less important than, "Is it newsworthy?"[26]

Additionally, the event or assertion must be ambiguous, creating more interest and allowing the readers and viewers to expand on it with their own imaginations. It is also "usually intended to be a self-fulfilling prophecy," with some of the best examples being the fabricated anti-

Trump Russia dossier and the attempted character assassinations of Justice Clarence Thomas and Justice Brett Kavanaugh that we discussed earlier. Outrage porn had been constructed, accusations flew, and the ensuing breathless coverage by the media is what made it all seem real.

Sixty years ago, Boorstin had a perfect grip on the trajectory of the legacy media and their unprincipled inclinations. He wrote that the media would increasingly bring out the best and worst in people. This makes the media a powerful and necessary weapon for those who want power and control over the citizenry.

When we think about media victims like 1996 Atlanta Olympic Park bombing hero Richard Jewell, Justices Thomas and Kavanaugh, Donald Trump, and Nick Sandmann, to name just a few, all of them endured "counterfeit happenings," as Boorstin would put it, inflicted upon them by the media. The media, usually in league with a government agency or propelled by their own liberal agenda, perpetuated completely false or absurd narratives on their targets.

Richard Jewell was falsely accused of being the bomber even though he had actually saved lives by noticing the bomb backpack and moving people to safety. Justices Thomas and Kavanaugh faced uncorroborated and unproven accusations promoted by the media as though unquestionably true. President Trump was painted 24/7 by the media as a Russian agent doing the bidding of President Vladimir Putin. The media smeared teenager Nick Sandmann as a racist bully by using a false narrative about an out-of-context photograph and video. His real crime? Wearing a Trump-supporting MAGA cap while on a field trip with his school.

Pseudo-events, like accusations a judge committed sexual assault, another judge drugged women and participated in a gang rape, a hero security guard was actually a mad bomber, or an American billionaire president was a Russian spy and traitor, succeed in part because they're *dramatic*. Boorstin explains that the elements of counterfeit happenings and pseudo-events are "planned for dissemination, are easier to disseminate and to make vivid. Participants are selected for their newsworthy and dramatic interest. . . . Pseudo-events cost money to create; hence somebody has an interest in disseminating, magnifying, advertising, and extolling them as events worth watching or worth believing."[27]

The "somebody" in our examples is made up of the agents of the establishment itself—the FBI and the Democratic Party, both of which must rely on the media to move their propaganda and "counterfeit happenings."

Considering the danger we are facing with the liberal media throwing its lot in with the corrupt Democratic establishment, Boorstin's warning about the use of propaganda and pseudo-events in totalitarian societies is a valuable touchstone:

> In a totalitarian society, where people are flooded by purposeful lies, the real facts are of course misrepresented, but the representation itself is not ambiguous. The propaganda lie is asserted as if it were true. Its object is to lead people to believe that the truth is simpler, more intelligible, than it really is. "Now the purpose of propaganda," Hitler explained, "is not continually to produce interesting changes for a few blasé little masters, but to convince; that means, to convince the masses. The masses, however, with their inertia, always need a certain time before they are ready even to notice a thing, and they will lend their memories only to the thousandfold repetition of the most simple ideas." But in our society, pseudo-events make simple facts seem more subtle, more ambiguous, and more speculative than they really are. Propaganda oversimplifies experience, pseudo-events overcomplicate it.[28]

It is imperative to understand that every progressive attack on a high-profile person is a message to the average person that if they are willing to destroy the life and reputation of someone, a prominent person with significant resources, then no one is safe. Destroying someone by example is the ultimate mechanism of using fear to crush the will of others. Especially that of the masses of unwashed rubes as we dare to continue to think that we, our opinions, and our dreams matter.

The liberal media regularly attacks the reputations and careers of prominent people who dare to stay true to their classically liberal or conservative values. These people are genuine iconoclasts who refuse to cave to the left's ugly, bizarre, and catastrophic Marxist cultural and political worldview. Ergo, they are to be smashed. In public. With as much vitriol and condemnation as possible. The goal of the leftist media is to leave Americans with one thought, courtesy of their new woke religion cult masters: "There, but for the grace of Marxists and media, go I."

Hitler!

Few journalists could argue with a straight face that the elderly, often-confused, and bumbling Joe "I'm not kidding, folks" Biden—campaigning primarily from his home, ostensibly because of the COVID-19 pandemic—was up to the task of leading America. Instead, the media fearmongers pulled out all the stops to warn of doom and gloom should President Trump be reelected. Trump was portrayed in heavily opinionated news stories as an incompetent, racist, corrupt, criminal, insane, dictatorial sex offender. Outrageously, Trump—the most pro-Israel president in US history, whose daughter Ivanka converted to Judaism when marrying Jared Kushner and whose grandchildren are Jewish—was even absurdly compared in the media to Nazi dictator Adolf Hitler.

A post on Medium was headlined "Thirteen Similarities between Donald Trump and Adolf Hitler."[29] An op-ed in the *Philadelphia Inquirer* was headlined, "Is It Wrong to Compare Trump to Hitler? No."[30] A CNN.com news story was headlined, "Top House Democrats Compare Trump's Rise to Hitler's."[31] These are just a few of the many examples of this slur in the service of media fearmongering.

The campaign to generate fear of Trump worked. A *Wall Street Journal*/NBC News poll in August 2020 found that "58% of registered voters who support Joe Biden in the 2020 election say their vote is more in opposition to President Trump than in support of Biden," Axios reported.[32] The Democrats were still relying on that Hitler! playbook leading up to the 2024 election.

We shouldn't be surprised that most broadcast, online, and print journalists—except for the hosts of opinion shows and writers of columns and editorials, whose job it is to express their opinions—deny they are biased as they work to stoke fear. They would like us to believe they are like Superman, whose secret identity is reporter Clark Kent, and whose motto beginning in 1942 was fighting for "Truth, Justice, and the American Way." As a woke aside, this motto was ridiculously changed to fighting for "Truth, Justice, and a Better Tomorrow" in 2021, pandering in part to the anti-US woke crowd. And they wonder why Americans are tuning out Hollywood.[33]

Fairness and relative objectivity in mainstream news media reports are increasingly rare, as journalists express opinions in the guise of facts ever more frequently. This is because the basic assumptions that most journalists embrace, and that determine what they cover and how they cover it, are the worldview of the left.

Part of the legacy media's process, consciously and subconsciously, has become making sure fear overwhelms reality. Some excuse this as a public service, saying it's "for their own good" to frighten people into what the cosmopolitan set decides is "the right thing," like accepting mask and vaccine mandates. This involves targeting individuals, as we've discussed, but it also requires swamping the environment with narratives promoting fear itself.

There are serious and, yes, frightening events worthy of our *concern* taking place in the world that must be reported by the news media, such as a new virus impacting society, crime, drug abuse, natural disasters, and unvetted illegal immigrants pouring over our border. These discussions and reports add important information to the choices we need to make about our futures. But there's a difference between being informed and naturally concerned about a serious issue and drowning in liquid fear constructed by the liberal media. As social researcher David Altheide explains:

> [T]he constant coupling of crime and other aspects of urban living with fear have produced a unique perspective about our effective environment. While crime is certainly something to be concerned about, as is any potentially dangerous situation, the danger, per se, does not make one fearful, just cautious. Fear is not a thing but a characteristic attributed by someone (e.g. a journalist) to something.[34]

Moreover, beyond conventional reports about discrete events that may elicit concern (and then action), Altheide describes what he terms as media constructing an overall "discourse of fear," constituting a

> [m]ajor public discourse through which numerous problems and issues are framed. A discourse of fear may be defined as the pervasive form of communication, symbolic awareness, and expectation that danger and risk are a central feature of the effective environment of the physical and symbolic environments as people define and experience them in everyday life.[35]

Both climate change and the COVID-19 narratives are perfect examples of manipulating valid news to construct a pervasive message of existential, looming doom. Perpetuating an "expectation of danger and risk" with the primary purpose of establishing fear itself and mass anxiety is a tiny tyrant dream as, they imagine, taking more power as they frighten us out of our desire to live free lives.

An overall political narrative of victimhood and victimizers undermines America's brilliant contribution to humanity, which was the idea that we do not need a common history, race, ethnicity, religion, or other characteristics to become united as a people. Identity politics exists exclusively to divide and set Americans upon each other through a false construct of perpetual victimhood through racism and bigotry. This political correctness strategy has since been massaged into the Diversity, Equity, and Inclusion, a considerably more official-sounding mission to normalize bigotry. Fear is at the center of all the left relies upon, and the mass media provide the mechanism with which victimhood becomes the discourse controlling how we view ourselves and others.

To this point, Altheide notes: "It is not easy to make people afraid. The word fear shows up in a lot of news reports and popular culture. I do not think that this is part of a natural general trend, nor do I think that it is an accident of inconsequential. Fear is the groundwork for the emergence of victimization and the victim identity that is now quite commonplace . . . *the prevalence of fear in public discourse can contribute to stances and reactive social policies that promote state control and surveillance*" [emphasis mine].[36]

Real-life repercussions come with what the liberal media is doing to society. The so-called progressives not only want to remake this nation, they want to punish people who dare to say no. While they can't punish each of us one-by-one, their next-best effort is to terrorize us by proxy using their liberal media cohorts and what they do to others.

Talent on Loan from God

I am a media person. I love the industry. I respect its value and inherent ability to do good, so much so that I am invested in it not being destroyed by a legacy media determined to annihilate dissent and conservative points of view.

My understanding of how threatening free speech was to my comrades on the left really was when I became a radio talk show host at KFI-AM in Los Angeles in 1993. Just a few years prior, I was elected president of the Los Angeles chapter of the National Organization for Women (NOW). Yes, I was a community organizer and pushed that cart for the left.

I was excited by the idea of being able to engage with radio listeners, likely mostly conservatives, because they needed to hear the truth (as the thirty-something Tammy told herself). I thought everyone would be thrilled, but nah. Almost everyone in my life told me not to take the radio job. It would be awful, I was told. Conservative radio talk show hosts, including Rush Limbaugh and Dr. Laura Schlesinger, were broadcast by that station, and I was told I certainly did not want to be associated with *them*.

But I wondered why we wouldn't want to engage with a conservative audience and talk with callers, perhaps influencing them. That was impossible, my fellow liberals said; conservatives were hopeless. And evil. Also Hitler.

Not surprisingly, I took the job anyway, intrigued with the potential and always sure that a good conversation with anyone was worthwhile. Very quickly, I found out why the leftists in my life were so opposed to my joining a conservative radio station as, yes, the token liberal. Speaking with conservatives every day changed me. And meeting Rush Limbaugh changed my life. This is my story about that surprising meeting, first published on social media[37] upon news of his death in February 2021. I remain grateful it has been widely shared by so many others:

> In the 90s, I was a host on a talk radio station in Los Angeles, the same that aired Rush. I was president of LA NOW, & the liberal weekend host when he visited the station. He was so vilified by my then-crowd, I expected a monster. Instead, I met a remarkable, kind and encouraging man.
>
> He was gregarious and generous when we met. He shook my hand and I was shocked that he was nice and genuinely curious about my radio work and activism. I realized I was going to have a fascinating conversation.
>
> There were many events during this time as a radio talk show host that changed me. It was my first job in the medium starting in 1993. My meeting Rush and our conversations made me realize the left had been lying to me about many things.
>
> Rush was not a monster, he wasn't evil, he did not mean people harm, he wasn't a bigot, or any of the other smears lobbed against him by my leftist associates. I liked him very much, and while we disagreed on many things (then) he was nothing as he had been painted.
>
> In my conversations with him we talked about the issues and despite the disagreements, he also took time to give me advice about hosting, style, connecting w the audience, etc. He encouraged me and gave me advice that made a huge difference in my career.
>
> He approached me and everyone else as separate individuals worthy of respect and with a desire to help and inspire. Regardless of the fact that I stood for everything he stood against. It was a generosity of spirit you would never see on the left.

The impact of realizing that I'd been lied to about Rush was significant, but that as a conservative he represented more of what I felt was valuable and important was a revelation. He made it possible to even consider that, which is what made him so dangerous to the left.

During this time as an activist leftist, it was talk radio, the audience, & meeting Rush Limbaugh that was the undeniable trigger making it possible for me to rethink my alliances & eventually leave the leftist establishment. It wasn't just Rush, but I'd also been lied to about conservatives in general, realizing that by speaking with callers every day who were conservative and responding fairly & with curiosity to my arguments on the air. Rush made that medium, and experience, possible.

My leftist associates begged me not to go into talk radio. I eventually realized they were so opposed because of what I would learn. That leftist effort to deny access to ideas and information continues with even more vitriol & punishment for those who dare to challenge leftist lies.

Rush created the potential of the medium, and set the tone for entertainment, analysis, and education. Honest conversations open to everyone is anathema to the left which is why they're obsessed with creating fear & the cancel culture.

The ugliness of the left will be seen throughout today and the days to come in response to the death of Rush, an American titan & defender of conservative values. The left is ugly and horrible but it is exactly their nature and should serve to remind you the importance of our fight.

The good news is, Rush not only changed our lives by helping us understand the imperative of freedom & generosity, but he now serves as an even more essential example for all of us.

Rush may be gone, but now it's up to all of us to continue his commitment to our great nation. Thank you, Sir, for the time you took with an arrogant and smug LA leftist feminist, one of the millions of lives you changed for the better.[38]

This experience was invaluable for me because it crystallized why there was such an obsession on the left with controlling information and speech, while demonizing conservatives.

Ironically, the bigger the liberal bias, the weaker the whole liberal ecosystem becomes. It can spread bigger untruths, but it has to do so to maintain its hegemony. When the predicted doomsday never arrives, you need complete compliance in pretending the prediction was never made, or be so successful with gaslighting and fearmongering that you can convince people to not believe their lying eyes. Hence, journalists are turning inward and demonizing other media, such as Fox News, and even other journalists within liberal news organizations who remain committed to independent and fair journalism.[39]

CHAPTER 9

A Climate of Crisis

The only way to get our society to truly change is to frighten people with the possibility of catastrophe.

—DANIEL BOTKIN[1]

"Your money or your life!" If cornered by an armed robber making that demand, just about all of us would hand over our cash and credit cards. Death, after all, is the ultimate fear. Self-preservation is a powerful motivator.

The left is exploiting our fear not just of our own deaths, but of a nightmarish and absurd scenario it has concocted forecasting the collapse of civilization and death on an unprecedented scale of most of the people, animals, and plants on Earth due to climate change. Imagine Chicken Little's cry that "the sky is falling," but on steroids.

Compounding the problem, many leftist news organizations have proclaimed this climate hysteria to be "settled science" and refuse to even report on alternate views, treating eminent scientists who dissent like ignoramuses who claim the Earth is flat. This illustrates how, for much of America, the belief in impending climate catastrophe is no longer grounded in science but has become a new radical environmentalist theology. Forget about evidence, forget about open debate—just embrace climate alarmism as an immutable article of faith, or risk being denounced as a heretic.

Daniel Botkin, a biologist and ecologist working on the issue of global warming since 1968 and the source of our epigraph for this chapter, knows the importance of following the science, not the political shiny object. Open-minded enough to remain committed to where the evidence takes him, Botkin has moved from a global warming true believer to a climate rationalist.

"I'm not a naysayer. I'm a scientist who believes in the scientific method and in what facts tell us. I have worked for 40 years to try to improve our environment and improve human life as well. I believe we can do this only from a basis in reality, and that is not what I see happening now," Botkin wrote in an opinion piece published by the *Wall Street Journal* in 2007. "Some colleagues who share some of my doubts argue that the only way to get our society to change is to frighten people with the possibility of a catastrophe, and that therefore it is all right and even necessary for scientists to exaggerate."[2]

This suggestion that scientists would propagate what the political elite call "noble lies" isn't fantastical at all. Noble lies are falsehoods meant to facilitate actions that the political establishment has decided are best for everyone or will provide legitimacy to a particular political narrative or social goal. As we discussed, we were all subjected to the impact of this disgusting, patronizing, and dangerous fear-based strategy during the COVID-19 pandemic. Lying for them is second, if not first, nature. Being able to excuse it as a necessary tool to manage the contemptible hoi polloi is simply too good for them to resist.

Paul Krugman, the *New York Times* columnist and recipient of the 2008 Nobel Prize in Economic Sciences, is also the man who hysterically and infamously predicted the 2016 election of Donald Trump to the presidency would condemn the world to a global recession. Instead, before the pandemic, the Trump years lifted 6.6 million people out of poverty, a feat not seen since the 1960s. That's the largest three-year poverty reduction for the start of any presidency since the initial drop in 1964, when the War on Poverty began.[3] So it's not surprising someone as unhinged as Krugman holds the same point of view of leftist activists advocating for the American people to be lied to about serious issues to allow the government to do whatever it wants.

In 2012, on HBO's *Real Time,* hosted by Bill Maher, Krugman famously described how good it would be for authorities to lie to the American people about an invasion from outer space, allowing the government to go on a spending spree. "I actually have a serious proposal, which is that we have to get a bunch of scientists to tell us that we're facing a threatened alien invasion, and in order to be prepared for that alien invasion, we have to do things like build high-speed rail," Krugman said. "And then, once we've recovered, we can say, 'Look, there were no aliens.' But look, I mean, whatever it takes because right now we need somebody to spend, and that somebody has to be the US government."[4]

Krugman's line about "whatever it takes" could be the motto of leftists. Since the end justifies the means in their minds, they believe it's acceptable to lie and create as much fear as possible so the citizenry will drink their toxic cocktail of bigger government, higher taxes, and less freedom. After all, lying about an apocalyptic end and the fear it creates is the point.

Climate change is even better than an alien invasion. It's everywhere. It's impossible to predict. It could make life worse even if we "win." The solutions happen to be all the things progressives have been trying to do since before Al Gore was born. Governments, businesses, and individuals have caved to the pressure of alarmists to support massive, harmful, and enormously costly changes to the way we work and live to avoid what we've been told will be the greatest catastrophe in global history. Many of these changes will destroy jobs, lower standards of living, increase global hunger, and turn the clock backward on human progress. But how can we resist, if mass extinction is the only alternative?

Like all armed robbers, climate alarmists are eager to take our money. For example, the group GlobalGiving, which wants us to—surprise!—give it money, said in 2021 that the estimated cost of ending global climate change ranges "between $300 billion and $50 trillion over the next two decades."[5] Quite a price tag; the upper estimate is about the size of the combined gross national products of the six wealthiest nations in the world: the United States, China, Japan, Germany, the United Kingdom, and France.[6] But hey, we have to do as the alarmists command, or as they repeatedly assure us, we will all—you guessed it—die.

During a Senate Appropriations Committee hearing, the $50 trillion cost of ending climate change came up again when Louisiana senator John Kennedy asked some very simple questions of Biden's Deputy Secretary of Energy David Turk about the progressive goal of the US going "carbon neutral" by 2050: "If we spend $50 trillion to become carbon neutral by 2050 in the United States of America, how much is that going to reduce world temperatures?" Turk seemed stunned that someone wanted to know what the result of all that spending would be. Here's how the exchange went:[7]

> **Turk:** So, first of all, it's a net cost. It's what, um, benefits we're having from getting our act together and reducing all of those costs and climate benefits. . . .
> **Kennedy:** Let me ask you. Maybe I'm not being clear. If we spend $50 trillion to become carbon neutral by 2050 in the United States of America, how much is that going to reduce world temperatures?
> **Turk:** This is a global problem, so we need to reduce our emissions and we need to do everything to, uh . . .
> **Kennedy:** How much if we do our part is it going to reduce global temperatures?
> **Turk:** So, we're thirteen percent of global emissions . . .
> **Kennedy:** You don't know, do you? You don't know, do you?

Turk did not know and finally confessed that it was just a really big feeling that we had to do something. "In my heart of hearts, there is no way the world gets its act together on climate change unless the US leads," he confessed.

Turk's comments confirm that the progressives controlling the Biden administration's Department of Energy are pushing a strategy about which they are clueless and which will have an unknown impact on world temperatures (if any). Instead, we are told it is to serve as encouragement for the rest of the world to do their part (because they're not).

Progressives know that the Chinese Communist Party isn't going to do the right thing if we show them the way by destroying ourselves. But they do know if they're successful in using climate change as a pretext, it will get Marxists closer to their goal of economically kneecapping the United States and ushering in their final "fundamental transformation" of the US into a weak, vulnerable, and irrelevant nation.

Moreover, the massive new government regulations and tax increases that will be needed to fight the war on "climate change" will inevitably help push America down the dangerous road to socialism, just as the left wants. This road will bring tremendous costs both economically and politically. That's because the more government regulates businesses, our economy, and our lives, the less freedom we will have and the less innovative and successful our economy will become. And the more we pay in taxes, the less money we will have to meet our own needs and solve our own problems, forcing us to become more dependent on Big Government to take care of us. Voilà!

This dangerous leftward drift moves us away from the American Dream of individuals building better lives for ourselves and our families through ambition and hard work in a free society. It moves us closer to the Marxist Dream (which is actually a nightmare) and the rule of George Orwell's Big Brother. Viewed in this context, we see that the campaign to fight climate change—change that has been occurring since the Earth was formed—isn't really about climate at all. It is about making Big Government bigger and shrinking the freedoms of the rest of us.

While many climate activists have been convinced they are working to improve our lives, they should keep the old saying in mind that "the road to hell is paved with good intentions."

Fear Paves the Way for Big Government

Think about it—the Marxists and other malignant operatives among us would never be able to convince anyone of anything if the selling point was the hellfire and misery their actual agenda delivers. Ask the people of the former Soviet Union, Cuba, North Korea, Venezuela, and, of course, those unfortunate enough to live in the hellscape delivered by the Chinese Communist Party, how horrifically their roads to hell were paved.

The demand to do as we're told, to not ask any questions, to not contradict, and to instead conform is because all leftist causes are Trojan horses with which to undermine and eventually dismantle the American government and economic system. These demands are made concurrently with doomsday assertions claiming that only our complete compliance and conformity—no matter how absurd of extreme—will provide any chance of survival. Fear again is the key to our submission.

Yes, I'm a partisan for the United States as created and defined by our Founding Fathers. But don't take just my word for what the "climate change" agenda really is. In 2014, the editorial board at *Investor's Business Daily* didn't mince words as they recounted a speech by former Czech president Vaclav Klaus:

> Global warming alarmists "want to change us, they want to change our behavior, our way of life, our values and preferences," according to a man who knows a thing or two about communist regimes, former Czech President Vaclav Klaus.[8] In a speech to Australia's Institute of Public Affairs in 2011, he stressed: "They want to restrict our freedom because they themselves believe they know what is good for us. They are not interested in climate. They misuse the climate in their goal to restrict our freedom. Therefore, what is in danger is freedom, not the climate. . . . They don't care about resources or poverty or pollution. They hate us, the humans. They consider us dangerous and sinful creatures who must be controlled by them. I used to live in a similar world called communism. And I know it led to the worst environmental damage the world has ever experienced."[9]

Empowering Big Government to tax, spend, and regulate on a massive scale beyond anything our nation has ever known will be no easy task. After all, as Americans we cherish our freedom—that's been true since the American Revolution. We want our government to serve the people, unlike in dictatorships, where the people serve the government. Dictatorships have no use for freedom, democracy, or the free enterprise system.

We see the American left echoing these authoritarian views, such as when Democratic senator Elizabeth Warren of Massachusetts and Democratic Socialist senator Bernie Sanders of Vermont (both millionaires) argue for gargantuan tax increases to punish people for hard work and success, and demand overregulation that would cripple our economy and make us more dependent on foreign suppliers for essential products. Yet most Americans don't buy the Warren and Sanders policies—even the left-leaning electorate that votes in Democratic primaries turned its thumb down to Warren and Sanders in their bids for presidential nomination in 2020.

So how does the left get Americans to accept the supersizing of Big Government and pave the way to a socialist utopia? Through fear. And the greater the fear, the better. Not the kind of fear that makes us just a little scared, but the fear that leaves us absolutely terrified.

Nothing sparks nationwide fear like a major crisis. Americans have a long history of giving up some of our freedoms and letting the government grow more powerful when such crises hit. We saw this in the 1930s and 1940s, for example, when the American people mobilized to deal with two very real and overwhelming fears: economic collapse caused by the Great Depression; and the threat of world conquest by Nazi Germany, Fascist Italy, and Imperial Japan during World War II. Americans supported the creation of an alphabet soup of government agencies and massive government spending and expansion to fight the depression. About 16 million served in the military (including over 400,000 who died) in the war against the Axis powers.[10, 11]

On top of this, Americans endured tax rates to fund our involvement in World War II that would bring tears of joy to Warren, Sanders, and other far-left radicals like Representative Alexandria Ocasio-Cortez of New York. The wartime Democratic-controlled Congress approved raising the federal tax on incomes of over $200,000 (about $3.2 million in

2022 dollars) to an astounding 94 percent. Believe it or not, that was less than Democratic president Franklin Delano Roosevelt wanted.

In 1942, shortly after America entered World War II, Roosevelt asked Congress to approve a top tax rate of 100 percent, saying that because America faced "grave national danger," he believed "no American citizen ought to have a net income, after he has paid his taxes, of more than $25,000 a year." Talk about progressive! But members of Congress must have reached the obvious conclusion that if Uncle Sam collected every penny people made over $25,000, a lot of people would make no effort to earn more. Why work longer hours or risk losing money on a business expansion that would create new jobs if there was zero chance of financial reward? Despite big Democratic majorities in both chambers of Congress, Roosevelt's proposed 100 percent rate was never enacted.[12]

Bernie Sanders, born in 1941, likely wasn't tuned in to political news as a baby, but if little Bernie was paying attention, he probably would have cried when he learned of the rejection of the 100 percent tax rate. When he was all grown up and seeking the Democratic presidential nomination in 2019, the proud socialist told the *New York Times*: "I don't think that billionaires should exist," explaining that he intended to raise taxes so high that no one could accumulate so much wealth. His proposal was designed to outflank Senator Warren on the left, after she came out with a wealth tax proposal not *quite* as radical.[13]

Marxists and others consumed with envy tend to believe they have sole possession of the truth and believe they are the ones who should determine what other people can, and cannot, have. Perhaps Bernie was at his beach house, one of three homes he and his wife enjoy, contemplating what sort of people should not exist and what they should or should not have.[14] Some progressive and Marxist activists rake in the cash while those they supposedly care about continue to suffer. But that's part of how envy is industrialized, capitalized, and weaponized by the professional grievance mob.[15]

Not surprisingly, one of the reasons Sanders used to justify his proposal for massive tax increases on Americans was . . . you guessed it . . . fear of climate change. Without a world war or a depression to justify sky-high tax rates, Sanders figured climate fear was his best bet to make

Uncle Sam grow into the Incredible Hulk. He proposed the most expensive climate plan of all Democratic presidential candidates, costing a staggering $16.3 trillion.[16]

By way of comparison, Sanders's plan to wage war on climate change would have cost nearly four times the amount America spent fighting World War II ($296 billion in the 1940s, which comes to about $4.3 trillion in 2020 dollars, the year Sanders campaigned on his proposal).[17]

The Bernie Sanders website actually makes the alarmist comparison between World War II and the battle against climate change, stoking fears of an uninhabitable planet by stating: "The scientific community is telling us in no uncertain terms that we have less than 11 years left to transform our energy system away from fossil fuels to energy efficiency and sustainable energy, if we are going to leave this planet healthy and habitable for ourselves, our children, grandchildren, and future generations. . . . The scope of the challenge ahead of us shares similarities with the crisis faced by President Franklin Delano Roosevelt in the 1940s."[18]

World War II was far from the only crisis in US history that prompted Americans to support giving up some of their freedoms and allowing government and their tax bills to grow. We saw the impact of a crisis again after the September 11, 2001, terrorist attacks on America, prompting the US invasion of Afghanistan, a spike in military enlistments, the creation of the massive Department of Homeland Security, and the growth of government surveillance and other incursions on our individual liberties.

We saw a frightened crisis response again with the advent of the coronavirus pandemic in 2020, with government mandates shutting down private businesses, requiring us to wear masks, canceling worship services and other gatherings, keeping our kids out of school, and in some cases mandating getting vaccinated or losing our jobs. In all these cases, the "states of emergency" and the fear they generated allowed the government to take actions circumventing the normal constitutional process. Politicians delivered political rhetoric, reinforced by media and Big Tech, leading to what can only be described as a mass hysteria, allowing illegal and unconstitutional actions to be implemented. Those who question the narrative, the orthodoxy, or "The Science" are shamed, fired, or banished from the public square. These actions are meant to silence basic questioning and dissent, as well as spread more fear throughout every community.

The Ideal Crisis

From the point of view of the left, climate change is the ideal crisis to create a record level of fear among the population and inject Big Government with a shot of growth hormone. Think back to our opening discussion of the left as a domestic abuser on a mass scale. Do they blame the rest of us for causing all our problems? Absolutely. Do they intend to terrorize us with threats of violence and death? Every misleading headline about increasing natural disasters says yes. Do they isolate us from our friends and family? Yes, by telling us not to travel and by telling us to cut nonbelievers out of our lives. Do they try to manipulate the people we care about into telling us their way is the best way for everyone? It's nonstop. Do they try to restrict our access to financial independence? That's all they do!

But there's more! And there always will be. Forget about cow flatulence being a problem. There's a much bigger issue on the horizon—human *breathing*. As Britney Spears might note, oops, they've done it again! They've moved from condemning us for the things we do right into condemning us for existing. The *New York Post* Editorial Board had a few thoughts:

> Get ready, humanity: The next climate crackdown target looks to have been chosen—breathing! That's right: New research indicates "exhaled human breath can contain small, elevated concentrations of methane (CH4) and nitrous oxide (N2O), both of which contribute to global warming." The research, from the UK Centre for Ecology and Hydrology, reveals we're all climate criminals, just like how it turned out a few years ago that we're all racists.[19]

The *Post* reminds us this isn't at all far-fetched considering the overall agenda of climate extremists: "For huge swathes of the green movement, remember, 'degrowth' is a preferred solution to all climate issues. That means an effective reduction of global living standards via artificial scarcity, which would necessarily entail mass death. So the idea of greens moving to suffocate humans to save the climate isn't that far-fetched."[20]

Great! We should start right away. Them first.

Hollywood celebrities, Democratic politicians, and millionaire business executives who live in mansions and travel in private jets and yachts on luxurious vacations—and ironically, travel the world attending climate-change conferences—are among those telling the rest of us we must make painful sacrifices to avert a climate apocalypse. Never mind that they generate gigantic carbon footprints with their privileged lifestyle.

The rich and famous tell us to live in smaller homes, turn down the heat so we shiver in winter, lower the air-conditioning so we swelter in summer, give up our gasoline-powered cars to ride mass transit or buy expensive electric vehicles, stop eating meat, and make other sacrifices. Never mind that the wealthy climate hypocrites do none of these things. The "little people" need to do as the elite say, not as they do.

On top of this, the climate elitists don't care that hardworking men and women in the oil, natural gas, and coal industries would lose their jobs with the elimination of fossil fuels. Hillary Clinton admitted this about coal miners when she ran for the Democratic presidential nomination in March 2016. "I'm the only candidate which [*sic*] has a policy about how to bring economic opportunity, using clean, renewable energy as a key into coal country. Because we're going to put a lot of coal miners and coal companies out of business," the former first lady, senator, and secretary of state said.[21]

Oops!

Clinton backtracked and said she regretted the comment after it sparked predictable and understandable outrage, including a question at a campaign event in West Virginia by unemployed coal worker Bo Copley, who pointedly asked her, "How can you say you are going to put a lot of coal miners out of jobs and then come here and tell us how you're going to be our friend?"[22] Turns out the only one kept out of a job by the comment was Clinton herself, who lost votes in coal-producing states as a result of sticking her foot in her mouth and—for a change—telling the truth about what she would do if she became president.

Then there are the folks at the Natural Resources Defense Council. Those in charge describe their mission as working "to safeguard the earth—its people, its plants and animals, and the natural systems on which all life depends." Well, that's heady!

One particularly asinine claim by the zealots at the NRDC in the crusade against climate change condemns our use of toilet paper—yes, toilet paper—because of the "long-term climate impact it leaves behind" (so to speak) as a result of chopping trees down to manufacture the product. "Toilet Paper Is Driving the Climate Crisis with Every Flush," the group warned in a headline on its blog in June 2020.[23] What a perfect, intensely personal way to instill even more guilt and self-loathing into people.

But never fear! A solution is at hand (wink wink) to this wasteful problem. Jon Sufrin helpfully provided it in an essay headlined "TP Free: Why I Stopped Using Toilet Paper (and You Should, Too)," published in 2018 by the Canadian newspaper *The Globe and Mail*. To save our planet, Sufrin helpfully explained that "four months ago, I decided to remove toilet paper from my life completely. I now step into the shower after using the toilet and use nothing but water (a miraculous cleaning agent) and my own hand, which I wash afterward with soap."[24]

Lovely. Thanks, but no.

Progressives are deluded enough to think their climate change hype can frighten you into abandoning toilet paper, but they decided something more dramatic would be needed to take your gas stove—the health and safety of children. Their usual incantation is that fossil fuels are evil incarnate and must be abandoned completely if we are to save the planet. So out, damn gas stove, out!

In January 2023, when Biden-appointed Consumer Product Safety Commissioner Richard Trumka Jr. announced that a ban on gas stoves was "on the table,"[25] we suddenly saw a united media narrative declaring that gas stoves were responsible for over 12 percent of childhood asthma.

That's a scary headline that understandably would provoke worry, concern, and fear, and that's the point. The media coverage coinciding with Trumka's statement was prompted by a study asserting that a significant percentage of childhood asthma could be attributed to gas stoves. The problem is, it's not true.

The group behind the study is the Rocky Mountain Institute, a green energy group that describes itself as an entity that "transforms the global energy system to secure a clean, prosperous, zero-carbon future for all."[26] The backlash was swift after the study itself came under scrutiny, leading the RMI to deny that their study made the connection. The *Washington Examiner* reported, "Responding to a request for comment, RMI manager Brady Seals told the *Washington Examiner* in an email . . . that the think tank's study 'does not assume or estimate a causal relationship between childhood asthma and natural gas stoves.' Rather, she said, it 'only reports on a population-level reflection of the relative risk given what we know about exposure to the risk factor.'"[27]

Why the confusion that led to the walk back? Perhaps it was due to how Seals had been promoting the RMI study. At her LinkedIn page, as an example, she wrote: "Our new study is finally out. We found 12.7% of US childhood asthma can be attributed to gas stove use. This is similar to children's asthma risk of being exposed to secondhand smoke. In some states like Illinois, California and New York that number is around 20%. It is clear we must move away from fossil fuel appliances and go all-electric, not only for the climate but for our health,"[28] with a link to the four-page study.[29]

Sounds at least like a causal relationship assumption, no? It's good she clarified, but the gas-stoves-give-kids-asthma cat was out of the bag.

Yet, months after the debunking of the causal link to childhood asthma with gas stoves, as well as a multitude of other studies finding *no connection* between gas stoves and children's health, Chicken Little news and opinion pieces continued to appear.[30]

In the meantime, legacy media and even Democratic senator Chuck Schumer told us that concerns about gas stoves being banned were a "MAGA conspiracy theory."[31] And yet multiple blue states and cities are—wait for it—banning gas stoves. The web magazine *Fast Company* cites ninety-nine US cities and counties having "some form of building decarbonization ordinance in place."[32] Most recently, New York State has banned gas stoves in new residential buildings. New York City already issued a ban for new buildings in 2021. Once again, a "conspiracy" that ended up being true.

Yet of all the fear-induced madness spawned by climate alarmists, the biggest and most breathtakingly idiotic of them all has to be the Green New Deal, introduced in 2019 by Representative Alexandria Ocasio-Cortez and fellow Democrat Senator Ed Markey of Massachusetts. In addition to banning the use of almost all fossil fuels in ten years, the proposal is a far-far left wish list of irrational ideas, including providing universal health care and guaranteed jobs paying wages high enough to support a family for all Americans. The ten-year plan would cost taxpayers anywhere from at least $10 trillion, according to supporters, and up to $93 trillion, according to critics.[33]

The Green New Deal, which died in the Senate, also called for eliminating as many gasoline-powered vehicles "as is technologically feasible," building hundreds or even thousands of renewable energy facilities around the nation, removing all greenhouse gas emissions and pollution from all industries and farms, making every building in the United States energy efficient by 2030, expanding high-speed train service on "a scale where air travel stops becoming necessary" (someone neglected to check with Hawaii for their opinion), and making college free.

"Green New Deal" is a misnomer. It should really be called the "Giant New Disaster," considering that, if implemented, the only thing left would be the ruins of Western civilization. But once again, we stumble upon the point.

Besides blowing a gigantic hole in the federal budget, the plan would destroy millions of American jobs, sending US industries to other countries.[34, 35, 36]

Ocasio-Cortez proposed paying for all this by taxing income above $10 million a year at a 70 percent rate (the top tax rate is currently 37 percent), and by deficit spending and simply printing more money.[37] Really.

Climate alarmism has run rampant for decades and has often been proven wrong over time. In fact, just listing all the exaggerated and inaccurate statements made by climate change alarmists would take up more pages than are in this book. The *New York Post* published a partial list in 2021 of planetary disasters that were wrongly predicted over the past fifty years.[38] The newspaper reported that in 1972, a headline screamed, "UN Environment Protection Boss Warns: 'We Have Ten Years to Stop the Catastrophe.'" Somehow, we have survived. Then in 1982, the *New York Times* breathlessly reported that Mostafa K. Tolba, executive director of the United Nations environmental program, said that if nations continued their prevailing policies by the year 2000, the world would face "an environmental catastrophe which will witness devastation as complete, as irreversible, as any nuclear holocaust."[39] Yeah, no.

In 1989, another UN official predicted disaster would strike in 1999, with "Global disaster, nations wiped off the face of the earth, crop failures."[40] Funny, I don't remember that one happening either. Piling on, the *Guardian* (a British newspaper) reported in 2004 that "a secret report from the Pentagon to President George W. Bush said climate change would 'destroy us.'" One prediction was that Britain would develop a "Siberian" climate by 2020. News flash: it didn't. Another was that the world would be plagued by nuclear war, severe droughts, famine, and rioting. Well, if this was a prediction of the impact of the disastrous Joe Biden presidency, this at least could have been fact-checked as partially true.[41]

Lies, Panic, and Bad Decisions

These hyperbolic assertions have been repudiated not just by the passage of time, but by many reputable experts, including Michael Shellenberger, president of Environmental Progress (an independent nonprofit research organization). A longtime environmental and energy expert who was designated as a "Hero of the Environment" by *Time* magazine for his work to reduce the impact of climate change, Shellenberger is also the author of *Apocalypse Never: Why Environmental Alarmism Hurts Us All*, which *is* rooted in science rather than climate alarmism.

Shellenberger argues that while climate change is real, its harmful impacts have been enormously exaggerated. He points out that carbon dioxide emissions have been declining, and innovations like increased reliance on nuclear power (which emits no carbon dioxide or other greenhouse gases) can prevent the harmful impacts of a warming climate that alarmists claim are heading our way.[42]

In an article in *Forbes* magazine in 2019, Shellenberger wrote that "no credible scientific body has ever said climate change threatens the collapse of civilization, much less the extinction of the human species."[43] He wrote in the same *Forbes* article: "Journalists and activists alike have an obligation to describe environmental problems honestly and accurately, even if they fear doing so will reduce their news value or salience with the public." He also noted that exaggerated fears of climate disaster "have real-world impacts," pointing out that "a group of British psychologists said children are increasingly suffering from anxiety from the frightening discourse around climate change."[44]

Bjørn Lomborg, who has authored three books about climate change and is president of the Copenhagen Consensus Center think tank in Denmark, agrees that the dangers of a slight warming of global temperatures have been greatly exaggerated. He does warn of the grave dangers of such climate alarmism. "A YouGov poll in 2019 found that almost half of the world's population believes climate change will likely end the human race," he wrote in an op-ed published by Britain's Sky News in 2020. "It makes school children ask why they should educate themselves, when they don't have a future anyway. If climate change really could end the world, then perhaps this alarmism might be warranted, but that is simply not the case." He added: "Climate alarm has real consequences. When we panic, we make bad decisions. Over the decades, we have consistently chosen expensive and inefficient climate solutions, costing trillions of dollars, that have had almost no effect."[45]

Lomborg, Shellenberger, and other climate experts who shun alarmism say innovation is the best way to cut our reliance on fossil fuels and move to other energy sources—including solar, wind, hydropower, and nuclear power—that don't emit greenhouse gases.[46, 47, 48] They're right. This climate alarmism prompts us to act irrationally, out of fear and anxiety, spending money on the wrong things, and neglecting more urgent needs, and sometimes doing more harm than good.

One example of irrational action caused by climate alarmism is the idiotic war on fossil fuels. For Marxists, fossil fuels must be targeted because they have driven wars and empires, but perhaps more importantly, personal freedom and genuine human progress.

Fossil fuels play a major role in modern agriculture around the world. Developing nations struggling to feed their populations need to prioritize increasing their food production, so it makes sense for them to move from primitive to modern farming practices, even though tractors and other farm equipment are powered by diesel fuel or gasoline engines that emit greenhouse gases. The mechanization of agriculture has allowed America to replace 22 million horses and mules with about 5 million tractors and enabled a mere 1.4 percent of the US workforce in 2020 to produce enough food for our nation and millions of people around the world. In contrast, in 1900, it took 41 percent of the American workforce working on farms to feed our population.[49, 50]

In addition, a by-product of oil refining, petroleum coke, is used to manufacture ammonia and urea ammonium nitrate used to create nitrogen fertilizers, which increase crop yield.[51] It would make no sense for developing nations to refuse to modernize their farming and, as a result, let their citizens go hungry in the name of fighting climate change. And farmers in America and other developed nations obviously aren't going to turn back the clock and start plowing their fields with horses and mules and stop using modern fertilizers on their crops, triggering food shortages that would bring about mass starvation.

Deadly Consequences

At its most extreme, climate alarmism has deadly consequences. Tragically, a fifty-year-old climate activist set himself on fire on Earth Day in April 2022 in front of the Supreme Court to protest the lack of action to fight climate change. He died of the severe burns he suffered.

Dr. Kritee Kanko, a Zen Buddhist priest and climate scientist at the

Environmental Defense Fund, tweeted afterward: "This guy was my friend. He meditated with our sangha. This act is not suicide. This is a deeply fearless act of compassion to bring attention to climate crisis. We are piecing together info but he had been planning it for at least one year . . . I am so moved."[52] To romanticize and essentially endorse such a horrific act is the height of irresponsibility and highlights the nature of the rhetoric the emotionally vulnerable hear far too often. The suicidal activist had posted a warning of "irreversible" climate change on his Facebook page and placed a fire emoji next to it with his planned date of self-immolation nearly three weeks before killing himself.[53]

Fortunately Dr. Kanko, perhaps recognizing the deleterious effect of the constant climate fear/catastrophizing on well-meaning people, adjusted her sentiment. She told the *New York Times* in an interview "that she was not completely certain of his intentions, but that 'people are being driven to extreme amounts of climate grief and despair' and that 'what I do not want to happen is that young people start thinking about self-immolation.'"[54]

In the midst of the loss of her friend, she did not need to reject her concern for the environment, but recognized the unacceptable extremes to which some people are being driven by the liquid fear dominating "social justice" issues.

Similarly, in 2018, a sixty-year-old lawyer and environmentalist poured gasoline on himself and set himself ablaze in Booklyn's Prospect Park to call attention to global warming and pollution. "My early death by fossil fuel reflects what we are doing to ourselves," he wrote in an email he sent to news organizations immediately before ending his life.[55]

Both of these shocking events are a horrible but predictable result of unrelenting doomsday prophesizing and humanity-loathing by climate alarmists, leftist gadflies, and cynical politicians. They are indictments not of climate change but of the horrific rhetoric used to radicalize compassionate people with prophecies of annihilation. Accusations of human (ergo personal) responsibility for a global cataclysm can push some over an edge.

On Earth Day in 2022, one leftist candidate for Congress tweeted a meme saying, "Nature always wins. Maybe humans are the disease and

COVID is the cure,"[56] prompting at least one reader to suggest being anti-human and/or pro-COVID wasn't exactly the best way to get people to vote for him.

David Graber, a research biologist for the National Park Service, asserts that human beings have become a "cancer" and "plague" on Earth, and to correct that problem, "some of us can only hope for the right virus to come along."[57]

In 2020, Britain's leftist *The Guardian* newspaper featured Les Knight, a man leading a campaign "for the extinction of the human race." In his column, he explains, "We're causing the extinction of hundreds of thousands of other species. With us gone, I believe ecosystems will be restored and there will be enough of everything. . . . If we go extinct, other species will have a chance to recover. I'll never see the day when there are no humans on the planet, but I can imagine what a magnificent world it would be—provided we go soon enough."[58]

The *New York Times* chimed in with its stamp of approval on the idea that the existence of humanity isn't all it's been purported to be by publishing an opinion piece by Todd May, a professor of philosophy at Clemson University, not very subtly titled "Would Human Extinction Be a Tragedy?"[59]

Coy and manipulative, May's answer to the headline is—surprise—nope, not really a tragedy. We're just too awful, you see. "Our species possesses inherent value, but we are devastating the earth and causing unimaginable animal suffering."[60] And after all, how would it be a tragedy if everyone is gone and no one is left to lament our absence? "It may well be, then, that the extinction of humanity would make the world better off and yet would be a tragedy. I don't want to say this for sure, since the issue is quite complex."[61]

Remember my corollary about the left's tactics mirroring domestic violence perpetrators—as you read this—domestic abuse victims are three times more likely to commit suicide than nonvictims.[62] Their abusers inflict so much despair and hopelessness they give up, and the suicidal ideation often originates with their abuser. This is not an accidental similarity when we think about the goals of sociopathic abusive spouses and what we see coming from the far-left fringe.

Nonhostile coverage in the *New York Times* on any issue is viewed as its stamp of approval for the leftist worldwide intelligentsia. And so it is for the obscene idea of suicide as a national duty of humanity. Readers are introduced to thinking that their (and everyone else's) very existence is a stain on nature and all that is good. This disgraceful rhetoric permeating so much of liberal society becomes one more piece of the puzzle explaining why human interaction is increasingly cruel, unforgiving, and violent.

The all-humans-must-die theme is not a new refrain from the left. As with everything rooted in envy, Marxism has finessed the reasons why we would all be better off with huge groups of people gone.

The *Economist*, an unabashedly global liberal news magazine that touts itself as offering "fair-minded, fact-checked coverage of world politics, economics, business, science, culture and more," got an early foothold onto the humans-should-die act. Of all things, its "Christmas Special" section in 1998 vomited up "Sui Genocide,"[63] an essay discussing the ruinous impact of humanity on the planet. The goal was to open the door to the proposed solution to the problem of humans. And the answer is . . . you guessed it . . . suicide.

"It is clear that human history will end; the only mystery is when. It is also clear that if the timing is left to nature (or, if you prefer, to God) and humans hang on until the bloody end, the race's final exit will be ignoble . . ." writes the anonymous seer who authored the article. "It is hard, indeed, to imagine any reason to be against voluntary human extinction. The tricky question is not whether to extinguish, but when."[64]

Moreover, the article romantically describes this ultimate act of personal violence as "far and away, the greatest act of goodness ever contemplated, the ennoblement of a whole species; an act, almost, of angels."[65]

This reviling of human life permeates the left not just on climate extremism, but on every issue it co-opts. Hatred of humanity invites the expectation and acceptance of violence. Culture and society become an orgy of fear, violence, selfishness, guilt, paranoia, and anxiety. The idea that our very existence is the problem presents the perfect storm with which to divide, quell, and even eliminate populations.

After constant hectoring for decades by climate extremists, major newspapers, and magazines legitimizing the fiction that human beings are a scourge, climate extremists then offer up surprise and faux lamentation when a poor soul sets himself on fire to protest climate change. Disgracefully reinforcing their advocacy of the desperate and horrific act, the victims (and they are victims of the left) are lauded as "martyrs," described as providing a "sacrifice," are "fearless," offering "an act of compassion," and "an act of generosity."[66]

None of this is "complex." For the left, it is mission accomplished.

The Need for Fossil Fuels

Despite the lack of a factual basis for climate alarmism, the dire predictions from the alarmists stubbornly persist. While we can prove that disastrous climate change forecasts in the past were indisputably wrong, the new crop of predictions won't be proven equally false until we arrive at those future years. For example, as I noted in chapter 3, Representative Alexandria Ocasio-Cortez crazily predicted in 2019 that the world would end in twelve years if climate change is not addressed. This is nuts, but if Ocasio-Cortez had not later backed away from this claim herself after she was ridiculed, her doomsday scenario would no doubt be treated as gospel by the far left until 2031 arrives.

"Climate Kid" Greta Thunberg, the Swedish girl elevated by the left to the status of world-famous prophet since she began leading climate protests and writing books at the tender age of fifteen, has written: "Around 2030 we will be in a position to set off an irreversible chain reaction beyond human control that will lead to the end of our civilization as we know it."[67] Well, 2030 hasn't arrived yet, so her fans no doubt still believe her alarmist predictions.

"Earth isn't ending in 12 years. . . . Earth, as a whole, will be okay—for at least another few billion years," Sheril Kirshenbaum wrote in *Scientific American* in 2019 in response to Ocasio-Cortez. The executive director of the nonpartisan organization Science Debate, Kirshenbaum wrote in the same article: "Doomsday scenarios may generate clicks and sell advertisements, but they always fail to convey that science is nuanced.

Arbitrary 'time left to apocalypse' predictions are not evidence based, and the story of climate change doesn't fit neatly into brief bullet points competing for your attention in today's saturated media environment. Stoking panic and fear offers a false narrative that can overwhelm readers, leading to inaction and hopelessness."[68] A spot-on analysis.

We are blessed with brains that allow us to assess risk. We need to judge the risks that face us rationally and clearly, and resist giving in to fear that leads us to make bad decisions that bring about more harm than good. The real "inconvenient truth," if I may borrow a phrase from former vice president and continuing climate alarmist Al Gore, is that people around the world today depend on coal, oil, and natural gas in just about every aspect of their lives. Enormous quantities of these energy sources are buried under America's land and coastal waters and could be extracted safely and in an environmentally responsible manner, allowing the US to supply energy to much of the world. Doing this would reduce our trade deficit, create American jobs, and reduce world dependence on oil and natural gas from less desirable sources, such as Russia and certain Middle Eastern countries.

Unfortunately, President Biden so fears the climate alarmists who make up the base of the Democratic Party that he has, in effect, put large "Do Not Disturb" signs on much of our country, refusing to allow fossil fuel extraction in many areas under federal jurisdiction. He even blocked the Keystone XL pipeline, which would have brought over 830,000 barrels of Canadian crude oil to US refineries every day.[69] Some states have imposed further restrictions of their own, such as New York's ban on extracting large oil and natural gas deposits in the state using a technique known as fracking.[70]

Like it or not, fossil fuels are used to power every type of transportation vehicle, to make fertilizer to grow the crops essential to our food supply, and to manufacture plastics that go into thousands of products. Even if you drive an electric car, there's a good chance it's powered by fossil fuels because about 61 percent of the electricity in the US is generated by such fuels, with the remaining 20 percent coming from renewable sources, and 19 percent coming from nuclear power.[71] "We are a fossil-fueled civilization whose technical and scientific advances, quality of life, and prosperity rest on the combustion of huge quantities of fossil carbon," says Vaclav Smil, an environmental scientist and professor emeritus at the University of Manitoba in Canada, "and we cannot simply walk away from this critical determinant of our fortunes in a few decades, never mind years."[72]

Fossil fuels assumed their important role in modern life because they provide efficient, reliable, and portable power. Technological innovation may eventually allow renewables and nuclear power to replace fossil fuels for many uses. But this won't happen overnight. (It may not happen ever.)* It makes no sense to let fear driven by climate fearmongering prompt us to hurriedly abandon fossil fuels at all costs, such as increasing world hunger or crippling our economy. As we do when making other decisions, we need to make a cost-benefit analysis to determine what actions we should take.

The hysterical fear porn the left is peddling to get us to accept the growth of Big Government, higher taxes, new limits on our freedom, and a one-way ticket to a socialist future is something we must refuse to accept. The world will not end because of climate change. But our right to liberty and the pursuit of happiness described so eloquently in the Declaration of Independence—and many of our dreams for better days ahead—will be endangered if fear of climate change overwhelms us. Yet, in reality, this will only happen if we allow the fear merchants to succeed.

---

* The growth of renewables has only slowed the growth of fossil fuels use. Replacement is almost certainly out of the question, as any near-term replacement will be of traditional biofuels (meaning, burning wood to keep warm).

CHAPTER 10

BLM's Toxic Agenda of Fear

They're not going to stop and everyone beware, because they're not going to stop. . . . Everyone should take note of that on both levels. They're not going to let up and they should not and we should not.

—KAMALA HARRIS[1]

This epigraph quotes then-senator Kamala Harris on June 17, 2020, as America was watching the violence of the Black Lives Matter and Antifa riots engulf major cities. It was also just two months before Biden chose her to be his vice presidential running mate. Just five months before the 2020 presidential election, on national television with *Late Show* host Stephen Colbert, and sounding bizarrely like a proud mama, she excitedly told Americans to "beware" and then promised that the obscene violence of the riots was not going to end after the election,[2] a message Antifa adopted just a few months later.[3]

The violence unfolding was explained as a response to the killing of George Floyd, forty-six, by Minneapolis police officer Derek Chauvin on May 25, 2020. The nightmare leading to his murder began when four officers responded to a call from a grocery store clerk who reported a black man had used what appeared to be a counterfeit twenty-dollar bill to make a purchase. Floyd, who was unarmed, was handcuffed by officers and lay face down on the street, not posing a threat.

The four officers were fired, convicted of crimes, and sentenced to prison. The longest sentence—twenty-one years on federal charges and twenty-two and one-half years on state charges, to be served concurrently—went to Chauvin, who was found guilty of murder, manslaughter, and other charges.[4, 5] In addition, Minneapolis paid Floyd's family members $27 million to settle a lawsuit they filed.[6] Thankfully, the justice system held those responsible accountable and served true justice.

What happened in the few weeks following Floyd's death was stunning and historic. Some 4,700 demonstrations were held across the country to protest the police killings of Floyd and other black people. A *New York Times* analysis concluded that the protests were attended by an estimated 15 million to 26 million people. "These figures would make the recent protests the largest movement in the country's history, according to interviews with scholars and crowd-counting experts," the *Times* reported.[7] Protests also took place in countries around the world.[8]

Were these massive protests spontaneous reactions by individuals outraged at the unjustified killing of Floyd? For some who participated, yes. But they were not organic demonstrations. They were organized by a militant group of anti-American Marxists with a nice-sounding name that many Americans had never heard of: the Black Lives Matter organization and subsequent "movement." The goal of the organization, aside from raising as much money as possible, was turning a statistical rarity into a looming, apocalyptic race problem hidden in every corner of American life. In the summer of an election year, it was the perfect example of how the left never lets a good crisis go to waste, and in this case Marxist activists weaponized and exploited the pain and suffering of others to further the leftist agenda of fear and control.[9]

They didn't try to hide who they were—a typical Marxist group with a big side of woke. It was displayed openly on their website until people began to notice. As their identity politics pandering was mocked and criticized, their word-salad mission statement rewrite began in earnest. Fortunately, the *Blaze* reported on the original we're-fabulous-and-everything-for-everyone version in 2020 before it got a makeover: "'We affirm the lives of Black queer and trans folks, disabled folks, undocumented folks, folks with records, women, and all Black lives along the gender spectrum,' the BLM website reads. 'We make space for transgender brothers and sisters to participate and lead. We are self-reflexive and do the work required to dismantle cisgender privilege and uplift Black trans folk, especially Black trans women who continue to be disproportionately impacted by trans-antagonistic violence.'"[10]

The problem too many wouldn't recognize at this early point is the history of Marxist organizers co-opting important issues with the goal of maintaining the pain while scooping up as much money and power in the process as possible. But that realization would begin to emerge soon enough.

As the *New York Times* reported: "One of the reasons there have been protests in so many places in the United States is the backing of organizations like Black Lives Matter (BLM). While the group isn't necessarily directing each protest, it provides materials, guidance and a framework for new activists. . . . Those activists are taking to social media to quickly share protest details to a wide audience."[11]

What exactly is the interest of BLM leadership in stoking civil unrest? They claimed it was justice. However, the actual result has made life worse for black Americans.

When I was a community organizer in the 1990s, I was educated quickly by my leftist mentors that the "issues" were convenient excuses with which to exploit and fundraise. Fear of being called a racist or a sexist, fear of the repercussions for not virtue signaling that one is fully committed to the left's caustic agenda, opens the pocketbooks of many. From major American companies to workers across the economic spectrum, it is the ancient ritual of offering "tribute" to those who would otherwise use their influence to harm you. The left has learned how stoking fear can facilitate a liberally sanctioned version of extortion.

Many of the protests sparked by Floyd's murder were very different from the nonviolent marches led by Dr. Martin Luther King Jr. and other civil rights leaders in the 1960s to protest racial discrimination. While most of the Floyd protesters were peaceful, sizable numbers (including members of the dangerous far-left anarchist Antifa group[12]) broke into and looted stores, including many owned by blacks. They stole merchandise, set stores and cars on fire, and assaulted police and others. It became clear the agenda was really to inflict violence, chaos, and intimidation onto the general public. It was the use of fear during an election season, and the prospect of big money, fueling that fire.

If you are picturing an angry domestic abuser smashing things, making threats, and saying your actions forced them to do this, you are not the only one.

Despite the efforts of the Democratic Party and their lapdogs in the legacy media to convince you otherwise, BLM and the 2020 summer of riots were not a natural, organic uprising of concerned citizens. Mike Gonzalez,[13] one of the premier researchers, analysts, and reporters on Critical Race Theory, identity politics, diversity, multiculturalism, assimilation, and nationalism, as well as foreign policy, exposed the putrid founding history of the BLM machine in an article for the Heritage Foundation. His investigation uncovered information the legacy media will never share. He writes:

> The founders of the BLM movement (especially groups such as the Movement for Black Lives and the Black Lives Matter Global Network Foundation) and the members of the web around them are committed Marxists who, for years, created a vast revolutionary infrastructure in which to meet and strategize. They received ideological direction, strategic support, and emotional encouragement from foreign actors—Venezuela, especially, but also China.[14]

Moreover, Gonzalez tells us, "Garza, Cullors, Opal Tometi (the other BLM founder), and many others who were key in the ideological work behind the riots . . . traveled the world in the years since, and before, to coordinate activities in the numerous fora of the global Marxist left. All of this happened years before George Floyd was to breathe his last in 2020."[15]

Of course, stealing TVs, computers, clothing, and other items from stores is *not* a legitimate act of free speech and assembly protected under the Constitution. Nor are acts of arson and violence. They are crimes, and they created an epidemic of fear across the nation. Some of the biggest protests and worst rioting took place in Minneapolis; New York City; Portland, Oregon (lasting for an incredible one hundred consecutive nights[16]); the nation's capital in Washington; Kenosha, Wisconsin; Philadelphia; Rochester, New York; and Seattle. These are deep blue Democratic-run cities where political leadership was already either frightened of the political power of the far-left Marxist fringe or more than sympathetic to their aims.

In 2020, rioters caused an estimated $1–$2 billion in insured property damage.[17] This was the largest civil disorder loss to the insurance industry in inflation-adjusted dollars since records began being kept in 1950.[18]

Yet even this staggering figure understates the true amount of property damage caused by the riots, because 75 percent of US businesses are underinsured and about 40 percent of small businesses have no insurance, which are not accounted for in the $1–2 billion figure. On top of this, businesses suffered additional losses as a result of being forced to close temporarily, and sometimes permanently, by the riots. Many lost customers who feared venturing into neighborhoods where rioting had taken place, even long after the disturbances ended. Businesses also had to replace stolen or destroyed merchandise, faced higher insurance rates, and experienced lower property values after the riots.[19]

Most tragically of all, some forty-seven people—many of them black—were killed in rioting, and many more, including police officers, were injured, according to the nonprofit Armed Conflict Location and Event Data Project.[20] A report by the organization, which worked with Princeton University to study the protests, said 633 turned into riots, with at least 88 percent of those involving Black Lives Matter activists.[21]

The BLM Effect

No government should tolerate this level of lawlessness and ignore its most important obligation: protecting the safety of its citizens. Americans should not have to live in fear of rioters terrorizing their communities.

After all, the lives of people killed in the rioting mattered just as much as Floyd's. But too many Democratic leaders shirked their duty, giving in to the woke mob and dangerously telling police to hang back and "encourage crowd self-monitoring."[22] How progressive! It was as if the Democrats believed Floyd's murder somehow justified the chaos, anarchy, and deaths in response. Many considered then-senator Kamala Harris's repugnant remarks on *The Late Show*, in the midst of the unfolding anarchy, as a stamp of approval.

Paralyzed by the intense fear of being called racists and losing votes if they stopped rioters from destroying their own cities, some Democratic officials and their legacy media lapdogs regularly attempted to gaslight by characterizing rioters as "protesters" rather than criminals.

One of those killed in the riots that followed Floyd's murder was David Dorn, a seventy-seven-year-old retired St. Louis police captain. He was shot as he tried to stop looting at a friend's pawnshop. Stephan Cannon, twenty-six, was later convicted of first-degree murder, robbery, burglary, and other charges in Dorn's killing, and sentenced to life in prison. Both Dorn and Cannon were black, but Cannon clearly never got the message that black lives matter. Dorn's widow, retired police sergeant Ann Dorn, spoke at the 2020 Republican National Convention in support of President Donald Trump's reelection as she denounced the senseless lawlessness that caused her husband's death. She called for allowing police to do their jobs and protect the public.[23]

In a heart-wrenching op-ed published in 2022 on the Fox News website, Mrs. Dorn wrote:

> David didn't agree with or support Black Lives Matter. He never understood Black Lives Matter, because it never actually did anything to help Black lives. The same year David was killed, over a dozen children were shot in St. Louis, and never once did Black Lives Matter show up. Their lives mattered. Fifty-five businesses were looted or destroyed the night David was murdered, many of them Black-owned. Their livelihoods mattered. My husband was a Black man who selflessly served his community for over 40 years. His life mattered.[24]

While Dorn's murder and the other deaths resulting from the Black Lives Matter riots garnered media coverage, it was tiny compared to the massive coverage devoted to Floyd's murder—especially in the liberal media. The media were right to cover the killing of Floyd, of course, but left-wing news organizations dropped the ball by paying far less attention to the deaths of Dorn and others of all races who died in the riots. Perhaps a more appropriate slogan for those causing such death and destruction would be "Only Black lives that we can betray and exploit matter."

The BLM organizations expertly exploited Floyd's death for their own financial and political gain, masquerading as a civil rights group focused on opposing police misconduct. Remember the activist telling me that you have to rub salt into a wound? That sometimes you have to make a problem worse to make it better? For the left, and Marxists in particular, there is every intention to make things worse, but their monumental fraud is they have no intention of making things better. Maintaining fear, pain, suffering, and victimhood is their mission. The BLM organizations used fear as a weapon to coerce government to adopt and support policies to its liking, including "no bail" policies and defunding the police, despite horrifically negative consequences for urban areas and communities of color in particular. And as we say, that is the point.

Moreover, BLM entities are dedicated to fomenting racial divisions among our population as part of the Marxist obsession to overthrow our capitalist system. It seeks to generate fear of whites among blacks, of blacks among whites, and fear between every other tribe using the scourge of identity politics. It seeks to make Americans fear police by portraying law enforcement officers as dangerous criminals, and demanding that police departments be defunded and abolished. As we are seeing across the country, this is a disastrous strategy for all of us, sending crime,[25] including homicides,[26] skyrocketing and making Americans even more fearful of the growing dangers around them.

Have you ever asked yourself how they benefit from more crime and more fear? When things get bad enough—and when people fear their lives will get even worse—they are willing to accept previously unimaginable, even revolutionary, change. This is how the communist regime came to power in Russia. It is how both Hitler and Mussolini came to power. An America crippled by divisions and crime would be ripe for a radical new government controlling everything. But like how cancer exists just to perpetuate itself, ultimately killing the host, Marxists never really think about the reality of their end-game catastrophes. They feed on the excitement of the destruction, and then become observers of the cataclysm. It's pathological, and no, they don't mean well, nor are they "misguided." They know exactly what they're doing.

In his second appearance in our discussion, the title of this section, "The BLM Effect," is borrowed from an important statement in 2020 from Senator Tom Cotton, in which he details how the "poisonous ideology" of BLM has made American cities more dangerous. He noted, "[in 2020] our nation experienced the largest single-year increase in murder in American history and endured some of the worst riots in a generation. It's no coincidence that this appalling death and destruction surged at the same time as the virulently anti-law-enforcement 'Black Lives Matter' movement became more popular, powerful, and pervasive. The consequences of the 'BLM Effect' continue today."[27]

Cotton points to data from major cities such as New York, Chicago, and Los Angeles, which have seen significant spikes in homicides and other violent crimes in the wake of the protests as politicians reacted by implementing one of the main "demands" by the Marxists running BLM—weakening and defunding the police. "The BLM Effect caused an even more shocking drop in policing, paired with a stunning rise in murder. From last summer to this winter, police in Chicago made 53 percent fewer arrests compared with the same period in 2019. Murder in the city rose by 65 percent," Cotton continues. "In New York, police made 38 percent fewer arrests and murder rose by 58 percent. In Louisville, Ky., police made 35 percent fewer arrests and murder rose by 87 percent. In Minneapolis, Minn., police made 42 percent fewer arrests and murder rose by 64 percent."[28]

He closes by noting the disgraceful irony of the BLM effect, a hallmark of the Marxist and leftist movements in general—that what they claim to be working against is exactly what they propagate. "If, as they claim, racist policy is defined solely by racially disparate outcomes, then their weak-on-crime proposals are in fact breathtakingly racist. When it comes to the morality of the rule of law, we should never take lectures from those who coddle criminals."[29]

Democrat policies have made it harder to recruit and retain police officers in recent years. Budget constraints have also made it more difficult to fund effective law enforcement initiatives. Additionally, the current climate has created a hostile environment, making it tougher to incentivize officers to take risks. Why stick your neck out to stop a crime if BLM is there to chop it off, and local politicians don't have your back? Whether it be ending cash bail and allowing criminals to roam freely, handcuffing the police so they are unable to arrest those who make life a living hell in urban areas, or creating a hostile environment making it impossible for cities to find those willing to serve in law enforcement, Democratic policies are now the handmaiden of the Marxist hellscape.

Who suffers the most? While every American is impacted by the menacing bedlam produced by leftist governance, people of color living in urban areas of major cities continue to be the main victims of Marxist madness.

The Democrats' Marxist controllers are crippling our economy, destroying jobs, and spreading lawlessness to bring us closer to abandoning capitalism. This nightmare is exactly what the Marxist leaders of BLM dream of, and it is a goal shared by others on the far left as well.

Make America Marxist

The BLM movement is in the business of generating fear to rake in tens of millions of dollars while collecting sociocultural clout and power. Like the proverbial ambulance-chasing lawyer or a vulture, it swoops down to benefit from the suffering of others. It is far more concerned with green—as in the color of money—than it is with black lives. It throws gasoline on the fires of racial division to make bad situations worse, because if racial division ended, the movement would go out of business and stop hauling in big bucks, and they would have no chance of achieving their ultimate goal—the deconstruction of American society.

The movement, founded in 2013, consisted primarily of two organizations that work in coalition: the Black Lives Matter Global Network Foundation and the Movement for Black Lives, as well as local chapters. On the BLM website[30] the movement says it was founded by "three radical Black organizers—Alicia Garza, Patrisse Cullors, and Opal Tometi" (who now calls herself Ayo Tometi), and operates in the US, Canada, and Britain. Cullors candidly admitted in a 2015 interview that she and Garza are "trained Marxists." Garza, who has a background in the labor movement, said in 2015: "Black lives can't matter under capitalism. They are like oil and vinegar."[31]

Rather than condemn the violence that marked the riots following the murder of George Floyd, these and other BLM leaders defended the rioters. Cullors said rioters were "expressing righteous rage." Tometi minimized the destruction caused by rioters, saying: "I'm not really concerned about broken glass." Ariel Atkins, an organizer with BLM in Chicago, said items stolen by looters were "reparations" and added that "winning has come through riots . . . I will support the looters . . . Anything they want to take, take it."[32]

The violence associated with BLM did not start in 2020. In April 2021, Vox reported on the work of researcher Travis Campbell, a PhD student in economics at the University of Massachusetts Amherst, and his analysis of 1,600 BLM protests from 2014 to 2019, prior to the murder of George Floyd. His research tracked the protests across the country, "largely in bigger cities, with nearly 350,000 protesters. His main finding is a 15 to 20 percent reduction in lethal use of force by police officers—roughly 300 fewer police homicides—in census places that saw BLM protests. Campbell's research also indicates that these protests correlate with a 10 percent increase in murders in the areas that saw BLM protests. That means from 2014 to 2019, there were somewhere between 1,000 and 6,000 more homicides than would have been expected if places with protests were on the same trend as places that did not have protests." This was *before* including data from the George Floyd riots.[33]

The more we investigate, the more it becomes clear that the 2020 summer of riots was no more organic or natural than anything else the Marxists vomit up as they target our families, our values, and ergo, our country. Republicans benefit from problems with practical solutions. Democrats benefit from problems too big for any solution other than turning everything over to the technocrat elite. That's why crime has to be reframed as a valid response to systemic racism that would be racist to solve with more cops.

What we also know is that Cullors trained for a decade as a radical organizer at the Labor/Community Strategy Center headed by Eric Mann, a former member of the Weather Underground who spent eighteen months in prison after being convicted of assault and battery and disturbing the peace. He has said he now wants to overthrow the American system and achieve world revolution through organizing. He calls his strategy center the "Harvard of Revolutionary graduate schools."[34, 35]

The FBI has labeled the Weather Underground (formerly known as the Weathermen) a terrorist group that sought to start a communist revolution in the US.[36] The group operated from 1969 through 1976 and claimed responsibility for twenty-five bombings, including at the US Capitol, the Pentagon, a police station in New York City, and the office of the California attorney general. In their foundation statement in 1969, the Weathermen said they were seeking "the destruction of U.S. imperialism and the achievement of a classless world: world communism."[37] Not exactly subtle.

To call either the Weather Underground or the BLM machines radical would be an understatement. In addition to advocating for defunding and abolishing police departments, the platform for the Movement for Black Lives calls for "an end to all jails, prisons, immigration detention, youth detention and civil commitment facilities."[38] Really. Instead, the platform says government should: "Invest in making communities stronger and safer through quality, affordable housing, living wage employment, public transportation, education, and health care that includes voluntary harm reduction and patient-driven, community-based mental health and substance abuse treatment."[39]

BLM also calls for decriminalizing drug use and prostitution and "a full and comprehensive reparations package for people, families and communities" harmed by the criminalization of drugs and prostitution. The platform demands that communities "[r]emove police and surveillance from schools" (good news for would-be school shooters) and calls for schools to instead invest in "violence prevention and transformative responses that create a nurturing and positive school climate for all students."

The platform also calls for eliminating all restrictions on convicted criminals that limit their eligibility for jobs, parental rights, housing, education, and civil rights. This could pave the way for pedophiles and rapists to work in child care centers and schools, robbers to work in banks, surgeons convicted of medical malpractice to operate on patients, drunk drivers to get jobs driving school buses, and other nightmare scenarios.[40]

One thing you'll no longer find on the BLM website is a commitment to "disrupt the Western-prescribed nuclear family structure." Apparently this was too transparent and was costing the movement support. However, the page remains archived by the Wayback Machine, a nonprofit initiative that has preserved over 788 billion web pages.[41]

Abolition of the family was a central tenet of communism, specifically called for by Karl Marx and Friedrich Engels in *The Communist Manifesto*. The pair said that under communism, the state would be in charge of educating children rather than their parents, and the "exploitation of children by their parents" would end. Marx and Engels denounced the "bourgeois clap-trap about the family and education, about the hallowed co-relation of parents and child" as "disgusting."[42]

All of this sounds horribly familiar, doesn't it? Parents have been pushing back on the disgusting frenzy by teachers' unions to cleave the relationship between parent and child[43] using reasoning that would make Marx and Engels proud.

The lunatic idea of abolishing the family is as much a disaster today as it was in the early Soviet Union some hundred years ago. Families, after all, have been around throughout history and have been vital to support and educate children in a stable environment, and to give them a sense of moral values. Writing in the *Atlantic* almost a century ago in July 1926, someone identified in her byline only as "A Woman Resident in Russia" wrote: "When the Bolsheviki came into power in 1917 they regarded the family, like every other 'bourgeois' institution, with fierce hatred, and set out with a will to destroy it. . . . A law was passed which made divorce a matter of a few minutes, to be obtained at the request of either partner in a marriage. Chaos was the result. Men took to changing wives with the same zest which they displayed in the consumption of the recently restored forty-per-cent vodka."[44]

The writer went on to quote officials who said men were impregnating wives they stayed married to for only a few weeks or months, taking no responsibility for their children. She said there were 300,000 homeless children in Russia. "It is claimed by many Communists that the break-up of the family is responsible for a large percentage of these children," the writer added.[45]

The abject failure of communism in the Soviet Union and everywhere else it was imposed had no impact on Soviet efforts to spread the destructive policy around the world. After World War II, the Soviets shoved communism down the throats of their Eastern European neighbors with military force, and helped prop up communist regimes in China, Cuba, and elsewhere. The founder of the Soviet Union, Vladimir Lenin, sought to spread communism among black Americans and use them to launch disturbances and eventually a communist revolution in the US. The effort went nowhere, even though the Soviets brought prominent Black Americans to Russia—including poet and author Langston Hughes, and actor and singer Paul Robeson—in a propaganda ploy to portray communism as intolerant of racism.[46] Fast-forward to today, and you'll see that Black Lives Matter movement leaders are doing their best to Make America Marxist, fulfilling Lenin's dream.

The Real Threat to Black Lives: Crime and Criminals

A Heritage Foundation review of FBI crime statistics from 2011 through 2020 found that while black people make up about 14 percent of the US population, they accounted for about 33 percent of reported violent crime victims and about 54 percent of reported homicide victims in the nation.[47] And despite the intense media focus on police killings of black people, far more black people are killed by civilians in the US each year.

For example, in 2022, police fatally shot at least 225 black people (compared with 389 whites, 120 Hispanics, 22 people of other races, and 344 people whose race or ethnicity were unreported), according to data provider Statista.[48] But 12,179 black Americans were killed with guns in 2020, compared with 7,286 white Americans, according to the Center for American Progress. This means that black Americans died in 61 percent of all gun homicides, and were ten times more likely than white Americans to die in gun homicides.[49]

It only follows that anyone who sincerely believes that black lives and the lives of people of all races matter will want to see *more* police funding and *more* officers on the street to better protect law-abiding citizens from gun violence and other crimes. This isn't to deny that some police officers engage in brutality, and injure or kill people of all races, as happened in the murder of George Floyd. Such officers should be fired, charged with crimes, convicted, and imprisoned if found guilty. But there are more than 800,000 federal, state, and local law enforcement officers in the United States.[50] The overwhelming majority never kill anyone over the course of their careers and never even fire their weapons on duty.[51] Violence is rare in the millions of interactions law enforcement officers have with civilians each year.

The question comes up over and over: Why does BLM want us to believe that violence is the norm? Because the goal is to convince people the only solution is massive social engineering, and you need to believe society is collapsing and the old solutions are worse.

This is absurd. We've all seen news reports about pedophile priests, doctors who rape patients, lawyers who swindle clients, pharmacists who are illegal drug dealers, and people in other professions who break the law. When caught, these people are charged with crimes, and convicted whenever there is enough evidence to prove their guilt. But we don't hear calls to defund churches, medical care, the justice system, and pharmacies. For the same reason, the notion of defunding the police because of the misconduct of a relatively few officers benefits no one except criminals, which is exactly why the BLM movement has so enthusiastically promoted this poisonous plan.

The demonization of police officers has several harmful effects that make communities less safe and cause the loss of innocent lives. It discourages many qualified people from becoming police officers, is demoralizing for officers trying to do their jobs, and prompts some officers to quit. It also makes officers reluctant to go after criminals and stop crimes from taking place, for fear of being accused of using excessive force and being prosecuted. And it endangers the safety and lives of police by convincing some people to resist and even attack officers.

Irresponsibly disregarding public safety, Democratic mayors and city councils put funding for their police departments on the chopping block. Then-mayor Bill de Blasio and the New York City Council agreed in June 2020 to cut a staggering $1 billion from the city's $6 billion police operating budget in America's most populous city, but was criticized by Ocasio-Cortez for not cutting even more.[52] Los Angeles cut $150 million from its police budget in November 2020.[53] But that was just the tip of the iceberg. In all, 24 of the 50 largest US cities cut their police budgets in 2021, Bloomberg News reported. Other police budget reductions included an 11.2 percent cut in Seattle, a 33.2 percent cut in Austin, a 14.8 percent cut in Minneapolis, and an 8.8 percent cut in Denver.[54]

These budget cuts weakened the ability of police to protect their communities because they caused manpower shortages. In Austin, for example, callers to the 911 emergency line had to wait on hold for an average of two and a half minutes to speak to someone in late 2022—far longer than the national standard of fifteen seconds or less. Two to three minutes may not sound like a long time, but it becomes a lifetime when you're facing an emergency situation.

An Austin city councilwoman had to wait *twenty-eight minutes* to speak to someone to report an emergency in early 2023. A Texas state law enacted in 2021 required Austin to restore the cuts it made to the police budget, but even with money restored, the police department had a hard time filling vacancies.[55] After all, why would someone want to be a cop in a city where no one has your back?

Minneapolis officials even put a referendum on the ballot in November 2021 asking voters if they wanted to abolish their city's police department, replacing it with "a comprehensive public health approach" to public safety overseen by the mayor and the thirteen City Council members. Some 56 percent of voters rejected the radical move and defeated two City Council members who supported the nutty plan in their reelection bids.

The Associated Press reported that according to a preelection poll: "Black voters were less likely to support the proposed public safety department than white voters and are more concerned that cutting the police force would have a negative effect on public safety."[56] That's understandable. Black people are disproportionately victimized by crime, and so, quite sensibly, are more concerned about having adequate police protection against criminals.

The left thinks, with their true believers in control of legacy media, that they can gaslight people enough to make them disbelieve the reality of their own lives. This news shows that Americans aren't willing to walk off into their left's crime-ridden night. No matter, if they fail on this attempt, they will keep trying. After all, it's not like they're busy developing policies that solve our problems and make our lives better.

Regrets, They Have a Few

Police departments around the country are having a hard time hiring and retaining officers, leaving many with dangerous shortages in their ranks. For example, in New York City, which has the largest police department in the US, about 3,200 officers left their jobs in the first ten months of 2022—the most since 2002. A shortage of officers led Mayor Eric Adams to announce in 2022 that police patrolling the subway system would have to put in ten thousand hours of additional overtime *every day.* That incredible amount of overtime is a strain on both the city budget and on officers, forcing them to work long hours and making their jobs less attractive, prompting some to quit.[57]

In another example, the Memphis Police Department had an authorized strength of 2,500 officers in early 2023 but employed only 1,939 because it was unable to fill many vacancies. The shortage arose even though the department offered every new recruit a $15,000 signing bonus and offered $10,000 to out-of-towners to relocate to Memphis. The department also lifted requirements that recruits have military or police experience, or college credits. And it reduced physical fitness standards at the police training academy. The department even sought state permission to hire people with criminal records to become officers.[58]

And now, five black Memphis police officers charged with second-degree murder[59] in the January 2023 beating death of twenty-nine-year-old Tyre Nichols, a black FedEx worker, had only a few years on the force and were not accompanied by a more experienced supervisor because of a shortage of supervisors.

"They would allow just pretty much anybody to be a police officer," Alvin Davis, a former Memphis police lieutenant in charge of recruiting, told the Associated Press. Davis said many new recruits told him they just joined the department for the paycheck and asked him how soon they could quit and still keep their bonuses. "They don't know a felony from a misdemeanor," he added.[60]

A year after Nichols's death, the *New York Times* reported an update revealing, "Five police officers, all of whom are also Black, were fired and later charged with various state felonies, including second-degree murder, and separately indicted by a grand jury on federal civil rights, conspiracy and obstruction offenses. One officer has since taken a plea agreement, which included pleading guilty to two felony charges in federal court." Four of the officers, however, "have pleaded not guilty to multiple state felonies. Those charges include second-degree murder, aggravated assault, aggravated kidnapping, official misconduct and official oppression."[61] At this writing, a trial in the federal case has been scheduled for September 2024.

The vast majority of police officers, however, are doing the job because they love their community, want to protect their fellow citizens, and don't engage in misconduct. Understandably, they find it hard to deal with hatred directed against them by groups like BLM. "Nobody wants to be the world's villain," Colonel Paul Humphrey, deputy police chief in Louisville, Kentucky, and a black man, told the *New York Times* in February 2023. "When you signed up to do good and people are telling you what you're actually doing is harmful, it does cause you to do some soul searching, and probably you should do some soul searching."[62]

Humphrey and other officers told the newspaper that the long hours, relatively low pay, danger, lack of respect in the community, and the chance of being accused of breaking the law have prompted many officers to leave the force or not join in the first place. The Louisville Police Department had three hundred vacancies it was unable to fill with new officers in early 2023. In past years, hundreds of people applied for the forty-eight spots in each police academy class for new recruits, but a recent class was made up of just fifteen recruits.[63]

Louisville isn't alone in its scramble to maintain its police department. ABC News reported in April 2023, "Police departments across the country are facing a 'vicious cycle' of retirements, resignations, and fewer hires, according to policing experts, leaving the communities they protect with understaffed departments and potentially underqualified officers."[64] The *New York Post* tells us that the NYPD is losing officers at "an alarming rate" with recruitment so low the city "plans to cancel the next five Police Academy classes."[65] Moreover, "the number of cops quitting before they reach the 20 years required to receive their full pensions also skyrocketed from 509 in 2020 to 1,040 so far this year—an alarming 104% increase, the data show," reported the *Post*.

In deep blue Washington, DC, a standard-bearer for defunding the police and supporting BLM, crime has skyrocketed. Reporting on data in November 2023 from the DC Metropolitan Police Department on year-over-year crime statistics, we now know just how bad things have become in our nation's capital. Starting in 2020, the district cut its police budget by millions, and now have four hundred fewer police officers. The result? "Homicides have increased by 34% as of Nov. 28 over the same time in 2022, while robberies are up 68%, motor vehicle theft is up 93% and arson is up 125%. Overall, violent crime is up 40% this year, while all crime is up 27%, the data shows," reported Fox News.[66]

Despite this data confirming that our capital has become a snakepit of crime, woke mayor Muriel Bowser decided to spend over a quarter million dollars on refurbishing the infamous Black Lives Matter street mural the city commissioned in June 2020, during the height of the BLM riots. Fox reports the cost of the touch-up appears to be $271,231, all at taxpayer expense.[67] The painted street slogan is so gigantic, in fact, that it was clearly visible in photos taken by satellites in space. One wonders: if only the murders, robberies, rapes, and assaults inflicted on black lives in DC could also be seen from space, maybe the progressive DC establishment would care about them.

In November 2023, Gallup released polls results announcing, "Personal fear at three-decade high in U.S."[68] This doesn't come as a surprise to all of us living in the real world, but it's important to see the degree to which increasing crime affects basic life decisions. "Forty percent of Americans, the most in three decades, say they would be afraid to walk alone at night within a mile of their home," and limits us from engaging in routine activities, including taking a walk, jogging, or going to the neighborhood park, Gallup tells us. The numbers also indicate that crime is higher in cities and among adult living in homes earning less than $40,000 a year. In other words, the very people whom the Democrats claim to represent and champion.

Not surprisingly, Gallup slips in a suggestion about why crime and fear about it have increased, by noting: "Whether *because of sharp increases in violent crime during the pandemic or media coverage of other crimes* [emphasis mine], Americans' sense of security from crime has been rattled in recent years. That carries over into their attitudes today, reflected in a rise in Americans' fear of walking alone at night in their own area to a three-decade high, and their fear of being the victim of several violent crimes being the highest in trends since 2000."[69]

So it's either the pandemic's fault, or media coverage of crime. Got it. It's so easy, but didn't something else start at the same time as the pandemic? Let us think. . . . Oh yeah, the BLM riots were also happening in the summer of 2020, along with attacking, demonizing, and defunding of police departments across the country. Let's also not mention the "no bail" policies implemented in blue cities across the country creating a revolving door rewarding criminals,[70] and progressive rogue district attorneys going soft on prosecutions.[71]

You know things are bad when San Francisco, one of America's deepest blue cities, even recalled their district attorney over rising crime. Voters overwhelming fired Chesa Boudin, blaming his progressive policies for the chaos, with CBS noting, "Momentum to recall Boudin picked up steam throughout 2021 as hate crimes against Asian Americans in San Francisco increased dramatically and victims blamed Boudin, saying he was siding with criminals. Recall supporters also pointed to car break-ins and viral smash-and-grab robberies at major retail stores, claiming they were becoming common occurrences as consequences of Boudin's policies."[72]

Gallup decided, however, to surmise about why crime and fear of being victimized are skyrocketing, and conveniently ignored a major public and political agenda kneecapping local police while coddling the criminal class across the country. This is not a gaffe or an accident; instead, like other actions of the establishment, it's an attempt to blur and protect the pernicious result of the leftist agenda.

If BLM's mantra of "Defund the Police" didn't have the effect of gutting police departments, the bitterness and hate they promoted certainly did. It's another example of more fear helping to facilitate the crippling agenda of those who do not mean any of us, or this nation, well.

But as we know, many big businesses, entertainers, and politicians fell over each other in the rush to embrace the phrase "Black Lives Matter" as part of their branding to showcase their opposition to racism. The companies included Nike, Twitter, Citigroup, Facebook, Nordstrom, TikTok, YouTube, Starbucks, Ben & Jerry's, Netflix, Nickelodeon, WarnerMedia, and many more.[73] Companies and individuals then flooded the Black Lives Matter Global Network Foundation, the fundraising arm of the movement, with more money than the movement had ever seen—just over $90 million in donations in 2020. Black Lives Matter co-founder Patrisse Cullors happily described this as "White guilt money."[74]

She also landed a production deal with Warner Bros. and a book deal.[75, 76] Yet, just a few months after the news broke that Cullors was triangulating her "activism" with personally lucrative Hollywood projects, *Politico* published an investigative piece[77] revealing discord among the BLM grassroots, which was beginning to realize something was not quite right. "The operations of Black Lives Matter have always been opaque, with thousands of members and dozens of affiliates. Two of its three co-founders are no longer affiliated with the movement—even as they continue to represent Black Lives Matter on TV. Local Black Lives Matter activists say national leaders cut them off from funding and decision-making, leaving them broke and taking the movement in a direction with which they fundamentally disagree," *Politico* reported. Through all of this, Cullors has repeatedly denied any financial impropriety.

Then, in two impressive investigative pieces, *New York Magazine*, the iconic liberal magazine, examined what appeared to be financial shenanigans besetting Cullors and the Black Lives Matter Global Network Foundation. In January 2022, Sean Campbell's piece "BLM Mystery: Where Did the Money Go?"[78] did a deep dive into the organization's "confusing" financial arrangements and the inevitable organizational collapse when authentic activists began to realize something was not right.

Then just three months later the magazine and Campbell followed up with an explosive report exposing the Cullors/BLM purchase of a $6 million mansion in Southern California.[79] Campbell begins by describing a YouTube video from 2021 featuring the three leaders of BLM enjoying a champagne brunch in the garden of what appears to be an expensive home. The women were complaining specifically about the *New York Post*'s mendacity for reporting on Cullors's spending of millions of dollars on real estate.

New York Magazine was doing the unthinkable for legacy liberal media—actually noticing, investigating, and reporting on the disturbing details of a high-profile leftist group claiming to be one thing but being quite another. This is *the* story of the left for generations—co-opting issues of importance to a community (blacks, gays, women), and then exploiting the people and issues for money and power. Campbell's willingness to shine a light on the betrayal so common by leftist "leadership" is laudable.

In the end, after questionable handling of tens of millions of dollars, and bitter infighting between grassroots activists and national leadership, Cullors stepped down. Ultimately, a new board was appointed, and Marc Elias, a Hillary Clinton and Democratic Party operative best known for funding "Christopher Steele's discredited anti-Trump dossier while he served as Hillary Clinton's 2016 campaign general counsel,"[80] was brought on to, as the *New York Post* put it, "sort out the non-profit's questionable finances."[81] Soon after, Elias left that "top spot," along with another "longtime Bill and Hillary Clinton ally" who served on their board.[82]

A director of a policy and watchdog group told the *Washington Examiner* at the time, "'It is important to note the Elias Law Group is a firm with a laser focus on electing Democrats and pushing the progressive agenda. . . . This makes their disappearance from the latest BLM Global Network Foundation filings a pivotal moment, probably foreshadowing the total collapse of what is left of the organization.'"[83]

Over time, the invisible line between the Democratic Party and BLM became a bit more apparent. Having escaped the left as an organizer myself, I have said repeatedly none of this was organic, but organized leftist agitprop. But make no mistake, while the BLM iteration of leftist protest organizing, urban riots, and the ensuing redistribution of wealth is not what it was in 2020, this is just one construct of the type of organized protests and disruption meant to destabilize our nation through fear and violence. It will return. The names and faces may change, but the tactic remains the same: hijack important issues, maintain the pain, and work to destabilize.

CONCLUSION

Breaking the Spell

Life shrinks or expands in proportion to one's courage.

—ANAÏS NIN[1]

The Communist Manifesto opens with the sentence: "A spectre is haunting Europe—the spectre of communism."[2] Today we can say that a different specter (as we spell the word in America) is haunting the minds of people around the world—the specter of fear. This book is a user's guide designed to help you banish the specter of fear that torments so many of us.

Earlier, I described the life-changing moment of conquering fear that gripped me as I ran through Times Square in New York City. Like many of us, I had long coped with fear by evading what frightened me—in this case, a woman who had manipulated me to fear her so she could exercise emotional control over me. My moment in Times Square was like the flip of a switch, moderating my fear, giving me clarity as I came to my senses. It was as though a spell had been broken, and the specter of mind-killing fear vanished. That's when I realized I was in charge and always had been, and I resolved to write this book to help others break the fear spell.

I've been an organizer most of my adult life. My books, columns, and appearances on TV, radio, and podcasts are designed to further my mission of providing information that helps people overcome what the powerful leftists in government and society are doing to manipulate us. My goal is to spread the word as widely as possible that resisting this manipulation is essential to safeguard our personal freedom.

It's safe to say you already know the Marxists and other leftists we fight aren't really interested in policy, programs, or ideas that improve all of our lives. Instead, our self-appointed progressive overlords are driven by blind rage to control and punish those they envy, and to achieve power to mete out that punishment. It's personal, as is the action we need to take to defend ourselves.

Working long hours or at two jobs to keep up with inflation, raising kids, and dealing with unexpected challenges is stressful and understandable priorities for many of us. So is worrying about crime plaguing our communities, terrorist attacks, wars, government dysfunction, incompetent leaders, and propaganda turning our schools into leftist indoctrination centers. As a result, we often don't have the mental or emotional bandwidth to notice just how intensely we're being manipulated. What the liberal establishment also does not want us to know is how easily we can slip those bonds and regain control of our relationship with the reality of daily events, and our own personal value and strength.

Finding that first moment of freedom, *the breaking of the spell*, can be life-changing.

For many of us, the spell was broken due to the shockingly malevolent actions of our government, and so many other Western nations, during COVID. For others, it was the distressing wakeup call we experienced as we watched our own government attempt to undermine Trump's campaign and then his work as a duly-elected president. It is best, however, if we don't have to wait for an existential issue to jar us out of the trance and decide for ourselves it's time to lock out the mind-killers. If we remain in the thrall of gaslighting and lies, it can take generations before we learn the truth about issues,[3] if at all.

Awareness is key to breaking the fear spell. The fact that you chose to read this book is a first, and singularly important, step. You knew "something isn't right" but perhaps couldn't put your finger on it considering the volume of information we're all deluged with every day. Now you've taken action and know why and how certain inexplicable things happen. The government's behavior and agenda during COVID was one of the first times when various agencies and politicians didn't even bother to hide their agenda. They tripped on their contempt for the average person and got far too excited about all the power the "emergency" afforded them over our personal lives.

But that backfired, leading to an awareness through experience for the average person that was frightening but invaluable. They wanted us to be afraid, it dawned on us, making us more pliable, more inclined to take orders without question.

While activism and direct involvement is an effective response to many of our problems, the response to fear itself requires an additional approach. The good news is that confronting and defeating those who weaponize fear to control us can be achieved by anyone. It costs no money and can be done anywhere. I'm outlining here *Five Pacts* you make with yourself, establishing a conscious recognition of who you are, what you stand for, and what is important to you. Knowing and owning these things about ourselves makes us immediately less vulnerable to those who prey on confusion and insecurity.

The Pacts are not about creating new values or spinning up personal morality out of thin air. These actions are aimed at reversing the conscious and unconscious fear the establishment has instilled in us over time from political correctness to the new religion of wokeism.

Many of us have been so conditioned by Marxists through school, society, and politics that living our lives with fear and caution has become an enforced, almost invisible, habit. The left wants to normalize living in fear, but we can stop and reverse that as we start the personal fight by defeating the grotesque efforts to control our minds.

First Pact: Resolve to not allow strangers to control how you think about yourself, your values, and your opinions. Making a decision, a true decision, is a powerful thing. This can be accomplished by *deciding* you are in control of how you view yourself. This is key. Fear makes us question our own sense of reality, and even who we are. Over twenty years ago, I was at one of my first conservative events promoting one of my books. Two women approached me, and in our conversation, one noted that "perhaps we should just admit that liberals do hold the high ground on social issues, and we're just better on the economic ones."

I was stunned. It struck me that the constant hectoring falsely accusing conservatives of bigotry had been internalized by this perfectly nice and unprejudiced woman. The conservative argument for freedom and responsibility *is* the "high ground." I informed her that leftist activists, in fact, don't care about solving issues. By the end of our conversation she had *decided* to stop allowing bullies to control her perception, and to again trust herself. Decision-making in general, and especially about yourself, is a game-changer.

Second Pact: Use the power of decision-making to reinforce your own acceptance of your value, morality, and decency. The simplicity of *deciding* that the values that define us as people of faith, conservatives, classical liberals, or recovered leftists is important and meaningful. This provides a bulwark against those who are intent on gaslighting us into believing we're the problem.

We can *decide* that someone calling us bigots is as meaningless as if they called us cocker spaniels. Bullies shouting their nonsense at us have no moral agency whatsoever. Making this pact with ourselves puts us in the driver's seat when we're confronted with direct or indirect challenges to our intentions, decency, and value as people. Much of this won't even happen to our faces, but the constant rhetoric used by the left demonizing Americans for the color of our skin, the work we do, the principles we believe in, or who we voted for is brought to us through the media and other social contexts. No matter how the gaslighting makes its way to us, we won't be caught off guard, inclined to wonder about an accusation, or be confused if we already *know* that what's being said about us is untrue. We have the power to refuse to be emotionally mugged by disturbed Marxists.

Serious people can engage in debates about the issues and have differences of opinion. But we must recognize that anyone set on engaging in ad hominem attacks is a fraud and should not be taken seriously. The left wants to pull the rug out from under us, making us unsure of our own reality. But the truth is that we are the ones in control by the simple process of *deciding to be in charge of our own minds*.

Remember, these Pacts are meant, at first, to be a pact with yourself. We know about domestic abuse and how victims often end up believing what their tormentors tell them. It's abusive, it induces fear, and it's brainwashing. Actively engaging with thoughts and ideas you presumed you already had a handle on can only become stronger the more you contemplate them.

As I've explained in earlier chapters, fear itself is not the problem—*the issue is how we respond* when faced with a frightening and serious situation. Fear *managed* with deliberate consideration, logic, and reason can be a tool that improves and even saves our lives. What the left wants is for fear to make us unmoored, distracted, and overwhelmed. Leftists want us to react emotionally to fear, allowing it to become a mindless beast wreaking havoc on our minds. Ruminating and catastrophizing fear loops are habitual thought patterns that can be broken more quickly than many of you may realize, with the first step *becoming conscious* of what we're doing and deciding to work on breaking the habit. We can never overcome fear—it's an important natural instinct—so our goal is to manage our response to it, making us more resilient and personally powerful.

Third Pact: Regularly take small actions requiring courage. That act will be different for all of us. Merriam-Webster defines courage as the "mental or moral strength to venture, persevere, and withstand danger, fear, or difficulty."[4] Mental and moral strength facilitates withstanding fear. Who knew? Marxists know, and this is why personal denigration, accusation, and condemnation is at the core of the Marxist mind-killing strategy. The bureaucratic establishment and the Marxists that run it want us to be alone, depressed, guilty, unarmed, afraid, living paycheck to paycheck, and high on edibles. Killing our critical and logical mind and the courage it naturally imbues is Job No. 1 for the disturbed left.

Expanding our comfort zones and building emotional strength improves every aspect of our lives. It also disrupts the habit of acquiescing to fear, both consciously and subconsciously. Deliberately moving outside our comfort zones has tremendous benefits. Afraid of public speaking? Confront it by taking a class requiring doing exactly that. I grew up terrified of bees because my mother was afraid of them. I was determined to overcome it and took an introductory beekeeping class when I was in my thirties. It worked. A simple three-hour experience changed a lifelong fear-based behavior. Courage is like a muscle. The more we use it, the stronger it gets, and gifts us the feeling and reality of being in charge of our emotional life.

Fourth Pact: Take action on your beliefs. Keep in mind, taking action can be incremental and private. One of my favorite actions involved millions of people, all across the country. And yet it was private and anonymous for the people participating, but still packed a punch. I speak of the power and success of the Bud Light boycott in the aftermath of the company's descent into wokeness.[5] The establishment swooped in and insisted transphobic bigots were responsible for the outrage. Yeah, no. In fact, the response had nothing to do with transgenderism per se, but was Americans making a statement about being sick and tired of being lectured by the woke cult 24/7 in every conceivable aspect of our culture. It was a last straw.

This boycott was especially revealing because it was organic. There was no organizing for it or campaigns to convince people to engage with it—it just happened. I contend this was so powerful and important because it showed everyone that despite the left making it dangerous to speak up on issues lest you be canceled, attacked on social media, or even fired from your job, Americans had not surrendered. It was a natural opportunity for people to make a statement rejecting woke culture, and they were able to do it *anonymously.* No matter the obstacles, patriots find a way.

Acting on your values is important, and it does not have to get you on the evening news. Some people do take stands that could affect their job or schooling. The COVID mandates are a good example of people getting kicked out of school or losing their job because they refused to comply. The high school football coach got fired for defying the school's prayer ban. There's the baker whom bullies are constantly suing because he refuses to bake their gay wedding cakes that violate his religious beliefs.

Then there was Jaiden, a twelve-year-old student in Colorado Springs, Colorado, who was kicked out of a class because he had a Gadsden "Don't Tread on Me" flag patch on his backpack.[6] He and his mother went to a meeting with a school administrator who explained to them the flag had "origins in slavery" and was "disruptive." The mom defended her son and gave the administrator an obviously needed history lesson. The mom also recorded the exchange and shared it on social media. She was steady, respectful, and forceful without being upset or aggressive. Throughout, the look on Jaiden's face was priceless. You could see how proud he was of his mom and the fact that, together, they weren't allowing the ignorant to determine their reality. Once the video went viral, the school reversed itself, acknowledged that what happened was a mistake, and allowed Jaiden to keep the flag patch.[7] Funny what happens when the light is turned on, isn't it?

Each of us has a different situation, and adjusting to your circumstance is important. Remember, pick your battles. Our goal is not to ruin our lives but to act within the frame of what will enhance our lives and serve our families, our faith, and our nation. We know that courage is contagious as it exposes how weak and spurious the left's woke agenda really is. The left can only survive when it is not confronted.

Fifth Pact: Gather knowledge, develop skills, develop social support with like-minded individuals, and arm yourself. I'll start with the last one first. I got my first handgun when I was in my twenties. I was a young woman living alone and had been violently mugged in Los Angeles, just a block from my apartment. The assault made me hyperaware of the fact that I had to be responsible for my own safety. I took self-defense classes, began to carry Mace, and while I wouldn't carry a gun, I got one for my home.

But possessing a firearm had another unexpected impact on me, something I would learn Thomas Jefferson had described a hundred years earlier. Owning a firearm and being trained on how to use it gave me a unique "independence to the mind." The Thomas Jefferson Monticello Foundation[8] explains:

> In 1785 Thomas Jefferson wrote to his fifteen-year-old nephew, Peter Carr, regarding what he considered the best form of exercise: ". . . I advise the gun. While this gives a moderate exercise to the body, it gives boldness, enterprize, and independance to the mind.

> Games played with the ball and others of that nature, are too violent for the body and stamp no character on the mind. Let your gun therefore be the constant companion of your walks."[9] [Original spellings maintained]

Beyond the practical comfort of knowing we can effectively defend ourselves if need be, having a physical reminder of our responsibility as gun owners is powerful and reminds us that we are worthy of defense and of independence. America's founders knew this, as eloquently described by Jefferson.

Gathering knowledge is always necessary. Like with this book, the more information you have, the less mysterious events and situations become. Knowing there is a method to the madness of what we're experiencing in itself reduces fear and anxiety. With this book, I hope I have unlocked the door for you to learning about fear and its weaponization, and how to overcome it.. Look through the bibliography for more resources to expand on this issue, and many others.

I've suggested some approaches to develop new skills to help you through what will be a turbulent time in American and world history. Marxists and the worldwide left never stop because they're driven by a pathological obsession to control and punish. War, crime, economic instability, harassment, denigration, racism, bigotry, have always been their favorite weapons. Your job is to always look for new personal skills to strengthen your own mental health and awareness. The less the left has to exploit with each of us, the less fear they can create.

Consider taking classes on issues at the local college. Or join a group supporting the Second Amendment or another cause you believe in, join a bowling league, or start a book group. During COVID, being afraid and even paranoid was promoted by enforced lockdowns. Humans are creatures of habit, and it's difficult to not internalize years of being told going out and being with people might kill you or your grandma. But we are also social creatures and need human interaction, friendship, and encouragement. So make a point to gather, go out, meet people, and create an IRL (in real life) support system rather than living in the virtual world of screens.

In the end, remember as I did, that we are in charge of our minds, and they can only be co-opted or killed when we unconsciously allow it to happen. We have been the targets of techniques to quell populations for millennia, so of course we're affected. The bad news for party apparatchiks, establishment bureaucrats, and Marxist bullies is that compliance and surrender are not American strong suits. They may continue to try to kill our minds, but they will fail.

ACKNOWLEDGMENTS

I had the immense pleasure of meeting iconic American author Ray Bradbury when I was a radio host in Los Angeles in the 1990s. A hero of mine starting in my childhood, I interviewed him and found that he not only was a brilliant man, but funny, charming, and genuinely kind. After that first meeting, I had the special honor to accompany him to some of his appearances, or when one of his new plays would open in Pasadena, California.

Mr. Bradbury was a man who loved writing, and it showed. Ideas flowed constantly from him. I told him his energy and enthusiasm for work was unusual, and his point to me was that you will love your work when you know it's important. If you want your work to help make things better, inspiration, determination, and enthusiasm will follow. Thoughts were powerful, he would tell me, and believing in what the future could be was an important step in making it possible.

We lost Mr. Bradbury in 2012 and while I knew him a short time, his impact on me has been lifelong, and felt especially intensely while writing this book. I remind myself every day about his lessons about gratitude, responsibility, happiness, and the power of ideas and writing. He was right about everything. Thank you, Mr. Bradbury.

Speaking of gratitude, I am especially beholden to my friends for their patience with me during this time. We've all been through a difficult several years politically and otherwise, and their understanding while I was hunkered down writing has been a special and generous gift. I will be spending quite a bit of time making up for missed lunches, dinners, and visits. You all know who you are, and I'll be making sure you also know how much I love and appreciate you.

To the Broadside Books team at HarperCollins: Eric Nelson, Broadside's editorial director and my editor, was so thoughtful and adept at helping me with direction and clarity, while making sure I was being true to my mission. My thanks to Eric, for challenging me when needed, and helping make this book as powerful as possible, and to his associate James Neidhardt, who was a terrific help with bringing everything together. Then there's David Wienir, the assistant general counsel at HarperCollins, who had the assignment of providing the legal overview of the book. He proved that working with a lawyer who is critiquing your writing can actually be an inspiring and encouraging experience. His knowledge of and love for the medium was obvious, as was his professional expertise and respect for the work itself. Having David on the team has made this process even more transformative.

For almost twenty years now I have had the honor of being able to join the conversations and speak my mind on Fox News and Fox Business. I want to issue a special thank-you to everyone at both networks, and to Sean Hannity directly for his support and friendship. I love being a guest on his show and am always excited when I get tapped to fill in for him. It's an amazing and fun experience. The very first show I did on Fox was *Hannity & Colmes* just after the network launched in 1996. I was still a liberal community organizer! It was getting to know Sean that added to my realization that maybe conservatives weren't the bad guys the left had always portrayed them to be. My thanks to Sean and his entire team, including Tiffany Fazio, Alyssa Carey, Stephanie Woloshin, and Robert Samuel, for including me, keeping me prepared, and making everything so easy.

My thanks also to Lauren Petterson at Fox Nation and Fox News for giving so freely of her time and guidance. Lynne Jordal Martin at FoxNews.com is always a joy to work with, and a special salute to Stuart Varney on Fox Business with his eponymous *Varney & Co.*, and his team, for their generosity with my regular Friday spot on his show to pontificate on the political and business news of the day. And they make it fun!

I'd like to share a special acknowledgment of some wonderful people for their kindness and support: Glenn Beck, Ruby Bruce, James Jay Carafano, Vince Coglianese, Kira Davis, Harris Faulkner, Steve Forbes, Newt and Callista Gingrich, Mollie Hemingway, Steve Hilton, Charlie Hurt, Caitlyn Jenner, David Limbaugh, Andrew McCarthy, Deroy Murdock, Charles Payne, Johnny Phillips, David Trulio, President Donald Trump, and Jonathan Turley; and Pam Smith, Bob Carlstrom, Andy Mangione, and the entire team at my column home, AMAC.us. It's a pleasure and honor to know all of you.

And to you, the American people, who continue to make this nation the best place on Earth because freedom, and the power of the individual, have always mattered and always will. While there will be ups and downs, we will survive and continue to thrive because of your commitment to the values that make this country great, and the future possible. Thank you for including me on your journey.

NOTES

Introduction: Something's Not Right

1. Barnadette Hogan, Carl Campanile, and Bruce Golding, "Cuomo Nursing Home Order Did Cause More Deaths, Should've Been Reversed Sooner: Task Force," *New York Post*, June 15, 2021, https://nypost.com/2021/06/15/cuomo-nursing-home-order-caused-more-deaths-task-force/.
2. Luis Ferré-Sadurní and Amy Julia Harris, "Does Cuomo Share Blame for 6,200 Virus Deaths in N.Y. Nursing Homes?" *New York Times*, July 8, 2020, https://www.nytimes.com/2020/07/08/nyregion/nursing-homes-deaths-coronavirus.html.
3. Rob Frehse, "New York Health Department under Cuomo Administration Undercounted Nursing Home Deaths by about 4,100, Audit Shows," CNN, March 16, 2022, https://www.cnn.com/2022/03/16/us/new-york-nursing-home-covid-19-deaths-undercount/index.html.
4. Philip Wegman, "House GOP: Dems' COVID Policy for Nursing Homes Was Deadly," Center Square, June 16, 2020, https://www.thecentersquare.com/national/article_c69aca98-b01c-11ea-86e1-9b3c5fb279a8.html.
5. Cassidy Morrison, "Five Governors Besides Cuomo Who Sent COVID-19-Positive Patients into Nursing Homes," *Washington Examiner*, March 1, 2021, https://www.washingtonexaminer.com/news/five-governors-cuomo-covid-19-positive-patients-nursing-homes.
6. Andrew Mark Miller, "Professor Blasted after Calling for 'Amnesty' to Forgive Coronavirus Lockdown Supporters: 'Hell No,'" Fox News, November 5, 2022, https://www.foxnews.com/us/professor-blasted-after-calling-for-amnesty-to-forgive-coronavirus-lockdown-supporters-hell-no.
7. William Claiborne, "Witnesses Allege Abuse by Simpson," *Washington Post*, January 12, 1995, https://www.washingtonpost.com/archive/politics/1995/01/12/witnesses-allege-abuse-by-simpson/706c89c6-9f5f-4ef2-8d47-bbed4d7ce296/.

8. Michale Brendan Dougherty, "Anthony Fauci: I Am the Science," *National Review*, November 29, 2021, https://www.nationalreview.com/2021/11/anthony-fauci-i-am-the-science/.
9. Lisa Aronson Fontes, PhD, "The Mind Control Tactics of Domestic Abusers: Abusers Control Their Partners by Making Them Feel Disoriented and Afraid," *Psychology Today*, May 27, 2021, https://www.psychologytoday.com/us/blog/invisible-chains/202105/the-mind-control-tactics-domestic-abusers.
10. Alexandra Steigrad, "Fox News Reporter Trey Yingst Visibly Shaken as He Shares Gruesome Details of Hamas Terrorist's Israel Massacre Confession," *New York Post*, October 23, 2023, https://nypost.com/2023/10/23/media/fox-news-war-reporter-limits-grisly-details-of-hamas-terrorists-confession-about-israel-massacre/.
11. Nomi Kaltmann and Gabe Friedman, "Sydney Government Apologizes for Pro-Palestine Protest That Had 'Gas the Jews' Chants," *Times of Israel*, October 13, 2023, https://www.timesofisrael.com/sydney-government-apologizes-for-pro-palestine-protest-that-had-gas-the-jews-chants/.
12. David Marcus, "Pro-Hamas Protests Force Jewish Students to Hide. How Can America Let This Happen Again?" Fox News, October 27, 2023, https://www.foxnews.com/opinion/pro-hamas-protests-force-jewish-students-hide-america-happen.
13. Aaron Bandler, "'Everyone Was Screaming': Tulane Jewish Students Assaulted at Pro-Palestinian Rally," *Jewish Journal*, October 26, 2023, https://jewishjournal.com/news/united-states/364469/everyone-was-screaming-tulane-jewish-students-assaulted-at-pro-palestinian-rally/.
14. Jerusalem Post Staff, "Pro-Palestinian Demonstrators Batter Pro-Israel Activist Helping Old Man in Skokie," *Jerusalem Post*, October 24, 2023, https://www.jpost.com/diaspora/antisemitism/article-769934.
15. Noah Rothman, "The Insane Logic of 'Whiteness,'" *Commentary*, January 18, 2021, https://www.commentary.org/noah-rothman/the-insane-logic-of-whiteness/.
16. Dave Huber, "Critical Race Theory, 'Whiteness' Reach New Absurd and Inane Heights," College Fix, March 18, 2021, https://www.thecollegefix.com/critical-race-theory-whiteness-reach-new-absurd-inane-heights/.
17. Mark Moore, "Traditional Values like Patriotism, Religion and Community Have Plunged Dramatically among Americans: Poll," *New York Post*, March 27, 2023, https://nypost.com/2023/03/27/values-like-patriotism-religion-falling-out-of-favor-among-americans-poll/.
18. Editorial Board, "America Has a Free Speech Problem," *New York Times*, March 18, 2022, https://www.nytimes.com/2022/03/18/opinion/cancel-culture-free-speech-poll.html.

19. Emily Ekins, "Most Americans Are Scared Stiff to Talk Politics. Why?" Cato Institute, August 6, 2020, https://www.cato.org/commentary/most-americans-are-scared-stiff-talk-politics-why.
20. Dr. Martin Luther King Jr., "I Have a Dream" (speech), August 28, 1963, in "Read Martin Luther King Jr.'s 'I Have a Dream' Speech in Its Entirety," NPR, January 16, 2023, https://www.npr.org/2010/01/18/122701268/i-have-a-dream-speech-in-its-entirety.
21. C. S. Lewis, "On Living in an Atomic Age," in *Present Concerns: Journalistic Essays*, ed. Walter Hooper (New York: HarperOne, 2017), 69–75, Kindle.

Chapter 1: The Terrible, Obscure Bioweapon

1. Edmund Burke, "A Philosophical Inquiry into the Origins of Our Ideas of the Sublime and the Beautiful," *British Literature, 1640–1780: An Anthology*, 4th ed., ed. Robert DeMaria (Oxford: Blackwell, 2016), 998–1002.
2. "President Roosevelt's Inaugural Address" (speech), March 4, 1933, PBS, https://www.pbs.org/newshour/spc/character/links/roosevelt_speech.html.
3. Evita Duffy-Alfonso, "Poll: Two-Thirds of Americans Think Corporate Wokeness Has Gone Too Far," *Federalist*, March 5, 2021, https://thefederalist.com/2021/03/05/poll-two-thirds-of-americans-think-corporate-wokeness-has-gone-too-far/.
4. Thomas B. Edsall, "Is Wokeness 'Kryptonite for Democrats'?" *New York Times*, May 26, 2021, https://www.nytimes.com/2021/05/26/opinion/democrats-republicans-wokeness-cancel-culture.html.
5. Chris Cillizza, "Why 'Wokeness' Is the Biggest Threat to Democrats in the 2022 Election," CNN, July 12, 2021, https://www.cnn.com/2021/07/12/politics/woke-green-new-deal-defund-the-police/index.html.
6. Alexandra Pollard, "Gaslight: How a Harrowing Ingrid Bergman Film Inspired 2022's Word of the Year," *Independent*, November 29, 2022, https://www.independent.co.uk/arts-entertainment/films/features/gaslighting-ingrid-bergman-film-merriam-webster-b2235486.html.
7. The 1944 film is a remake of a 1940 version, which was an adaptation of a 1938 play. For a discussion about the films, their genesis, and other details, including the 1944 version being the film debut of an eighteen-year-old Angela Lansbury, see: J. Hoberman, "Why 'Gaslight' Hasn't Lost Its Glow," *New York Times*, August 21, 2019, https://www.nytimes.com/2019/08/21/arts/gaslight-movie-afterlife.html.
8. Rikki Schlott, "Five Professors Tell Why They Were Canceled, and Why They Fought Back," *New York Post*, April 30, 2022, https://nypost.com/2022/04/30/professors-on-how-they-were-canceled-why-they-fought-back/.

9. Grégoire Sauvage, "How Black Lives Matter Put Slave Reparations Back on the Agenda," France 24, April 18, 2021, https://www.france24.com/en/americas/20210418-how-black-lives-matter-put-slave-reparations-back-on-the-agenda.
10. Susan Ellingwood, "What Is Critical Race Theory, and Why Is Everyone Talking about It?" *Columbia News,* July 1, 2021, https://news.columbia.edu/news/what-critical-race-theory-and-why-everyone-talking-about-it-0.
11. Christopher F. Rufo, "Critical Race Theory: What It Is and How to Fight It," *Imprimis* 50, no. 3 (March 2021), https://imprimis.hillsdale.edu/critical-race-theory-fight/.
12. Gerald F. Seib, "In Crisis, Opportunity for Obama," *Wall Street Journal*, November 21, 2008, https://www.wsj.com/articles/SB122721278056345271.
13. Maia Szalavitz, "How Terror Hijacks the Brain," *Time*, April 16, 2013, https://healthland.time.com/2013/04/16/how-terror-hijacks-the-brain/.
14. Joseph E. LeDoux, "Coming to Terms with Fear," *Proceedings of the National Academy of Sciences* 111, no. 8 (February 2014): 2871–78, https://doi.org/10.1073/pnas.1400335111.
15. Szalavitz.
16. Ibid.
17. Ibid.
18. Corey Robin, *Fear: The History of a Political Idea* (New York: Oxford University Press, 2004); Sergio Starkstein, *A Conceptual and Therapeutic Analysis of Fear* (Cham, Switzerland: Palgrave Macmillan, 2018).
19. Raymond Taras, *Fear and the Making of Foreign Policy: Europe and Beyond* (Edinburgh: Edinburgh University Press, 2015), 5.
20. John P. McCormick, "Machiavelli's *The Prince* at 500: The Fate of Politics in the Modern World," *Social Research* 81, no. 1 (Spring 2014): xxiv.
21. Starkstein, 126.
22. Taras, 5.
23. Starkstein, 130–31.
24. Starkstein notes this is the case "given that this emotion may be analysed from the different perspectives of philosophy, theology, psychology, sociology, psychiatry, the neurosciences, the history of emotions and lexical uses" (5–6).
25. *Oxford English Dictionary*, 3rd ed., s.v. "fear, n.," 2a.
26. Robin, 4.
27. Edmund Burke, *A Philosophical Enquiry into the Origin of Our Ideas of the Sublime and the Beautiful*, in *The Works of the Right Hon. Edmund Burke*, vol. 1 (London: Holdsworth and Ball, 1834), 38, https://archive.org/details/worksrighthoned00burkgoog/page/n135/mode/2up.

28. Robin, 4.
29. Ibid.
30. Ibid., 2.
31. Tammy Bruce, *The Death of Right and Wrong* (New York: Crown Forum, 2004), 2–7.
32. Tammy Bruce, *The New Thought Police* (New York: Three Rivers Press, 2001), 99.

Chapter 2: Hiding Your Wrongthink

1. "Marie Curie: Facts about the Pioneering Chemist," History, updated February 22, 2021, https://www.history.com/news/marie-curie-facts.
2. George Orwell, *1984* (New York: Harcourt Brace, 1956).
3. Steven Blakemore, "Language and Ideology in Orwell's 1984," *Social Theory and Practice* 10, no. 3 (Fall 1984): 349–56.
4. For more extensive analysis see Roger Kimball, *Tenured Radicals: How Politics Has Corrupted Our Higher Education* (New York: HarperCollins, 1990); Dinesh D'Souza, *Illiberal Education: The Politics of Race and Sex on Campus* (New York: Free Press, 1991); and of course the classic from Allan Bloom, *The Closing of the American Mind* (New York: Simon & Schuster, 1987). All provide early warnings, perspective, and background on where our culture is today.
5. "Rosemary's Baby," Internet Movie Database, https://www.imdb.com/title/tt0063522/.
6. Christopher F. Rufo, "What Critical Race Theory Is Really About," Manhattan Institute, May 6, 2021, https://manhattan.institute/article/what-critical-race-theory-is-really-about.
7. Ibid.
8. Bruce, 2001.
9. Bruce, 2003.
10. Frank Ellis, "Political Correctness and the Ideological Struggle: From Lenin and Mao to Marcuse and Foucault," *Journal of Social, Political, and Economic Studies* 27, no. 4 (Winter 2002): 409–10.
11. Ibid., 410.
12. L. D. Burnett, "'Politically Correct': A History (Part I)," Society for U.S. Intellectual History (blog), February 7, 2015, https://s-usih.org/2015/02/politically-correct-a-history-part-i/.
13. James L. Gibson and Joseph L. Sutherland, "Keeping Your Mouth Shut: Spiraling Self-Censorship in the United States," *Political Science Quarterly* 138, no. 3 (Fall 2023): 361–76, https://academic.oup.com/psq/article/138/3/361/7192889.
14. Editorial Board, "America Has a Free Speech Problem."

15. Ibid.
16. Emily Ekins, "Poll: 62% of Americans Say They Have Political Views They're Afraid to Share," Cato Institute, July 22, 2020, https://www.cato.org/survey-reports/poll-62-americans-say-they-have-political-views-theyre-afraid-share.
17. FIRE, "2024 College Free Speech Rankings," full report, https://5666503.fs1.hubspotusercontent-na1.net/hubfs/5666503/CFSR%202024_final.pdf.
18. Emma Camp, "Two-Thirds of College Students Think Shouting Down a Public Speaker Can Be Acceptable," *Reason*, September 6, 2023, https://reason.com/2023/09/06/two-thirds-of-college-students-think-shouting-down-a-public-speaker-can-be-acceptable/.
19. Martin Luther King Jr., "Martin Luther King, Jr. and Nonviolence," in *Let Nobody Turn Us Around: Voices on Resistance, Reform, and Renewal: An African American Anthology*, ed. Manning Marable and Leith Mullings (Washington, DC: Rowman & Littlefield, 2003), 377–82.
20. Mike Gonzalez, "Multiculturalism and the Fight for America's National Identity," Heritage Foundation, November 23, 2016, https://www.heritage.org/civil-society/report/multiculturalism-and-the-fight-americas-national-identity.
21. Roger Burbach, "The (Un)defining of Postmodern Marxism," in *Globalization and Postmodern Politics* (London: Pluto Press, 2001), 82, 88–89.
22. Ibid.
23. Ernst Cassirer, "The Technique of the Modern Political Myths," in *The Myth of the State* (New Haven, CT: Yale University Press, 1946), 282, referenced in Jason Stanley, *How Fascism Works* (New York: Random House, 2018), 78.
24. Editorial Board, "The Standford Guide to Acceptable Words," *Wall Street Journal*, December 19, 2022, https://www.wsj.com/articles/the-stanford-guide-to-acceptable-words-elimination-of-harmful-language-initiative-11671489552.
25. Olivia Land, "Stanford Releases Guide against 'Harmful Language'—Including the Word 'American,'" *New York Post*, December 20, 2022, https://nypost.com/2022/12/20/stanford-releases-guide-against-harmful-language-including-term-american/.
26. Michael Nietzel, "Stanford University Backs Away from Its Harmful Language List," *Forbes*, January 8, 2023, https://www.forbes.com/sites/michaeltnietzel/2023/01/08/stanford-university-backs-away-from-its-harmful-language-list/?sh=13634baf62df.
27. Ibid.
28. Susan D'Agostino, "Amid Backlash, Stanford Pulls 'Harmful Language' List," *Inside Higher Education*, January 10, 2023, https://www

.insidehighered.com/news/2023/01/11/amid-backlash-stanford-removes-harmful-language-list.

29. Ibid.
30. Ibid.
31. Nietze, "Stanford University Backs Away."
32. Priscilla Ki Sun Hwang, "Words and Phrases You May Want to Think Twice about Using," CBC News, November 29, 2021, https://www.cbc.ca/news/canada/ottawa/words-and-phrases-commonly-used-offensive-english-language-1.6252274.
33. Snopes Staff and Barbara Mikkelson, "Did the Word 'Picnic' Originate with Lynchings?" Snopes, January 21, 2001, https://www.snopes.com/fact-check/picnic-origin/.
34. "Fact Check: The Word Picnic Does Not Originate from Racist Lynchings," Reuters, July 13, 2020, https://www.reuters.com/article/uk-factcheck-picnic-origin-lynchings-idUSKCN24E21V/.
35. Robin J. Ely, Debra Meyerson, and Martin N. Davidson, "Rethinking Political Correctness," *Harvard Business Review*, September 2006, https://hbr.org/2006/09/rethinking-political-correctness.
36. Gabriel S. Mendlow, "Why Is It Wrong to Punish Thought?" *Yale Law Journal* 127, no. 8 (June 2018): 2342.
37. Lucas Swaine, "Freedom of Thought as a Basic Liberty," *Political Theory* 46, no. 3 (June 2018): 407.
38. C. G. Jung, *The Undiscovered Self: The Dilemma of the Individual in Modern Society* (New York: New American Library, 2006), 12.

Chapter 3: The Fear Industrial Complex

1. Winston S. Churchill, *Europe Unite: Speeches 1947 and 1948* (London: Cassell, 1950), 347.
2. Greg Piper, "Treasury Department Tacitly Endorses Debanking Opponents of Transgender Hormones for Kids," *Just the News*, March 14, 2024, https://justthenews.com/government/federal-agencies/treasury-tacitly-endorses-debanking-opponents-transgender-hormones-kids.
3. John Hayward, "Hillary Clinton: You're Not Just 'Deplorable,' but 'Irredeemable' and Not Part of America," Breitbart News, September 13, 2016, https://www.breitbart.com/politics/2016/09/13/irredeemable-clinton-deplorable/.
4. Jon Miltimore and Dan Sanchez, "The New York Times Reported 'the Mainstreaming of Marxism in US Colleges' 30 Years Ago. Today, We See the Results," Foundation for Economic Education, September 10, 2020, https://fee.org/articles/the-new-york-times-reported-the-mainstreaming-of-marxism-in-us-colleges-30-years-ago-today-we-see-the-results/.

5. Ibid.
6. *Oxford English Dictionary*, s.v. "envy, n.," 1a and 3a. Accessed March 2022, https://doi.org/10.1093/OED/2928468204.
7. John Rawls, *A Theory of Justice* (Cambridge, MA: Harvard University Press, 1999), 124.
8. Anne Hendershott, *The Politics of Envy* (Manchester, NH: Crisis, 2020), 6–7.
9. Aristotle, *Rhetoric*, Book II, Ch. 10, Sec. 1, in Greek & Roman Materials, from Perseus Digital Library, ed. Gregory R. Crane, https://www.perseus.tufts.edu/hopper/text?doc=Perseus%3Atext%3A1999.01.0060%3Abook%3D2%3Achapter%3D10.
10. Hendershott, 12.
11. Joseph Epstein, *Envy* (New York: Oxford University Press, 2003), 7.
12. Ibid., 15.
13. Proverbs 14:30 (New American Standard Bible).
14. Zygmunt Bauman, *Liquid Fear* (Cambridge, UK: Polity Press, 2006).
15. Gavin de Becker, *The Gift of Fear* (New York: Little, Brown, 1997), 318.
16. Ibid., 319.
17. Dr. Rachael Sharman, "Paralysed with Fear: Why Do We Freeze When Frightened?" The Conversation, June 13, 2016, https://theconversation.com/paralysed-with-fear-why-do-we-freeze-when-frightened-60543.
18. Thierry Steimer, PhD, "The Biology of Fear- and Anxiety-Related Behaviors," *Dialogues in Clinical Neuroscience* 4, no. 3 (September 2002): 231–49, National Library of Medicine, https://www.ncbi.nlm.nih.gov/pmc/articles/PMC3181681/.
19. Nicola Davis, "Antarctica Was Warm Enough for Rainforest Near South Pole 90M Years Ago," *Guardian*, April 1, 2020, https://www.theguardian.com/world/2020/apr/01/antarctic.
20. Patrick Pester and Kim Ann Zimmerman, "Pleistocene Epoch: The Last Ice Age," LiveScience, February 28, 2022, https://www.livescience.com/40311-pleistocene-epoch.html.
21. "Nostradamus," History Channel, updated May 14, 2020, https://www.history.com/topics/paranormal/nostradamus.
22. John Bowden, "Ocasio-Cortez: 'World Will End in 12 Years' If Climate Change Not Addressed," *Hill*, January 22, 2019, https://thehill.com/policy/energy-environment/426353-ocasio-cortez-the-world-will-end-in-12-years-if-we-dont-address/.
23. Lukas Mikelionis, "AOC Says Only a 'Sea Sponge' Would Believe Her '12 Years' Doomsday Remark, but Most Dems Bought It," Fox News, May 23, 2019, https://www.foxnews.com/politics/ocasio-cortez-doomsday-claim-world-end-poll-shows-67-percent-of-dems.

24. Ibid.
25. de Becker, *The Gift of Fear*, 326.
26. Frank Furedi, *How Fear Works: Culture of Fear in the Twenty-First Century* (New York: Bloomsbury Continuum, 2019), 25.
27. Ibid.
28. Bauman, 1.

Chapter 4: Indoctrination Centers

1. President Ronald Reagan, "Remarks to the National Catholic Education Association in Chicago, Illinois," April 15, 1982, Ronald Reagan Presidential Foundation & Institute, https://www.reaganfoundation.org/ronald-reagan/reagan-quotes-speeches/remarks-to-the-national-catholic-educational-association/.
2. Jack Schneider and Jennifer Berkshire, "Parents Claim They Have the Right to Shape Their Kids' School Curriculum. They Don't," *Washington Post*, October 21, 2021, https://www.washingtonpost.com/outlook/parents-rights-protests-kids/2021/10/21/5cf4920a-31d4-11ec-9241-aad8e48f01ff_story.html.
3. Ibid.
4. Ibid.
5. Philip Short, *Pol Pot: Anatomy of a Nightmare* (New York: Henry Holt, 2006), 346, Kindle.
6. Ibid., 325.
7. Rachel Sharp, "Parents of Kids at New England Private Schools Launch Campaign to Fight 'Indoctrination' of Students with 'Woke' ideas [. . .]" *Daily Mail*, July 12, 2021, https://www.dailymail.co.uk/news/article-9780361/Parents-kids-New-England-private-schools-fight-indoctrination-students-woke-ideas.html.
8. Jason Rantz, "Under Threat of Woke Curricula, Parents Are Fighting Back," *Newsweek*, April 20, 2022, https://www.newsweek.com/under-threat-woke-curricula-parents-are-fighting-back-opinion-1699080.
9. "The Constitution of the United States: A Transcription," National Archives, https://www.archives.gov/founding-docs/constitution-transcript.
10. "Persistent Fear and Anxiety Can Affect Young Children's Learning and Development: Working Paper 9," National Scientifc Council on the Developing Child, Harvard University, Cambridge, MA, February 2010, https://developingchild.harvard.edu/resources/persistent-fear-and-anxiety-can-affect-young-childrens-learning-and-development/.
11. "Immigrants in the United States," American Immigration Council, September 21, 2021, https://www.americanimmigrationcouncil.org/research/immigrants-in-the-united-states.

12. Ron E. Hassner, "From Which River to Which Sea?" *Wall Street Journal*, December 5, 2023, https://www.wsj.com/articles/from-which-river-to-which-sea-anti-israel-protests-college-student-ignorance-a682463b.
13. Talia Kaplan, "Anti-Semitism on College Campuses on the Rise, Report Finds," *New York Post*, September 9, 2021, https://nypost.com/2021/09/09/anti-semitism-on-college-campuses-on-the-rise-report-finds/.
14. Tabia Lee, "I Was a DEI Director—DEI Drives Campus Antisemitism," *New York Post*, October 18, 2023, https://nypost.com/2023/10/18/i-was-a-dei-director-dei-drives-campus-antisemitism/.
15. Ibid.
16. Shawn Fleetwood, "Terry McAuliffe Says Parents Shouldn't Be Telling Schools What to Teach Their Kids," *Federalist*, September 29, 2021, https://thefederalist.com/2021/09/29/terry-mcauliffe-says-parents-shouldnt-be-telling-schools-what-to-teach-their-kids/.
17. Eva McKend and Dan Merica, "Virginia Republicans Seize on Parental Rights and Schools Fight in Final Weeks of Campaign," CNN, October 7, 2021, https://www.cnn.com/2021/10/07/politics/glenn-youngkin-parental-rights-education-strategy/index.html.
18. "About NEA: Purpose and Power in Community," National Education Association, https://www.nea.org/about-nea.
19. Bradford Betz, "Teachers Union Tweet Claims Educators Know 'Better than Anyone' What Kids Need to 'Learn and Thrive,'" Fox News, November 13, 2022, https://www.foxnews.com/us/teachers-union-tweet-claims-know-better-than-anyone-what-kids-need-learn-thrive.
20. "China Sending Children of Exiled Uighur Parents to Orphanages, Says Amnesty," BBC, March 19, 2021, https://www.bbc.com/news/world-asia-china-56454609.
21. Sarah El Deeb, Anastasiia Shvets, and Elizaveta Tilna, "How Moscow Grabs Ukrainian Kids and Makes Them Russians," Associated Press, October 13, 2022, https://apnews.com/article/ukrainian-children-russia-7493cb22c9086c6293c1ac7986d85ef6.
22. "American Indian Boarding School," *Britannica*, https://www.britannica.com/topic/American-Indian-boarding-school.
23. Hassan Kanu, "U.S. Confronts 'Cultural Genocide' in Native American Boarding School Probe," Reuters, May 18, 2022, https://www.reuters.com/legal/government/us-confronts-cultural-genocide-native-american-boarding-school-probe-2022-05-18/.
24. Erin Blakemore, "A Century of Trauma at U.S. Boarding Schools for Native American Children," *National Geographic*, July 9, 2021, https://

www.nationalgeographic.com/history/article/a-century-of-trauma-at-boarding-schools-for-native-american-children-in-the-united-states.

25. Kendall Tietz, "National School Board Association Calls On the Biden Admin to Police Parents Using Domestic Terror Laws," Daily Caller, September 30, 2021, https://dailycaller.com/2021/09/30/national-school-board-association-biden-admin-police-parents-terror-laws/.
26. "Garland Says Authorities Will Target School Board Threats," NBC News, October 5, 2021, https://www.nbcnews.com/politics/justice-department/garland-says-authorities-will-target-school-board-threats-n1280774.
27. See https://defendinged.org/.
28. Peter Hasson, "Education Secretary Cardona Solicited NSBA Letter Comparing Protesting Parents to Domestic Terrorists: Email," Fox News, January 11, 2022, https://www.foxnews.com/politics/education-secretary-cardona-solicited-nsba-letter-comparing-parents-domestic-terrorists-email.
29. Ibid.
30. Patrick Reilly, "NSBA Head Knew about AG's Controversial School Board Memo, Emails Show," *New York Post*, February 14, 2022, https://nypost.com/2022/02/14/nsba-head-chip-slaven-knew-about-ags-controversial-school-board-memo-emails-show/.
31. Editorial Board, "About Those Domestic-Terrorist Parents," *Wall Street Journal*, October 26, 2021, https://www.wsj.com/articles/about-those-domestic-terrorists-national-school-boards-association-merrick-garland-memo-fbi-11635285900.
32. Hannah Grossman, "Garland Says Incendiary Memo Directing FBI to Use Counterterrorism Tools on Parents Never Rescinded," Fox News, September 21, 2023, https://www.foxnews.com/media/garland-says-incendiary-memo-directing-fbi-use-counterterrorism-tools-parents-never-rescinded.
33. Jeremiah Poff, "FBI Opened Multiple Investigations into Protesting Parents, GOP Lawmakers Say," *Washington Examiner*, May 12, 2022.
34. Margaret Mead, *Coming of Age in Samoa* (New York: William Morrow, 1928), 246, https://archive.org/details/comingofageinsam00mead/page/n7/mode/2up.
35. Dana Kennedy, "Mount Holyoke Grad Deprogrammed from Women-Only Woke Culture," *New York Post*, November 26, 2022, https://nypost.com/2022/11/26/mount-holyoke-grad-deprogrammed-from-women-only-woke-culture/.
36. Ibid.
37. Ibid.
38. Marc A. Thiessen, "Opinion: The Poetic Justice in Eric Swalwell's Relationship with a Chinese Spy," *Washington Post*, December 10, 2020,

https://www.washingtonpost.com/opinions/2020/12/10/poetic-justice-eric-swalwells-relationship-with-chinese-spy/.

39. Eric Swalwell Twitter account, November 9, 2022, https://twitter.com/RepSwalwell/status/1590545381641060352.
40. Jonathan Turley, "'Please Tell Me What I'm Missing Here': Eric Swalwell's Curious Case against Parental Rights," JonathanTurley.org, November 13, 2022, https://jonathanturley.org/2022/11/13/please-tell-me-what-im-missing-here-swalwell-appears-to-embrace-medical-and-legal-malpractice-in-opposing-parental-rights/.
41. Jon Levine, "Elite $60K-a-Year NYC Schools Forcing Woke Indoctrination on Parents, Too," *New York Post*, October 22, 2022, https://nypost.com/2022/10/22/elite-nyc-prep-schools-aim-woke-indoctrination-at-parents-too.
42. James Lynch, "Mike Pompeo Says Randi Weingarten Is More Dangerous than Kim Jong Un or Xi Jinping," Daily Caller, November 22, 2022, https://dailycaller.com/2022/11/22/mike-pompeo-randi-weingarten-more-dangerous-kim-jong-un-xi-jinping/.
43. Steven Greenhouse, "Teachers' Union Head Accuses Pompeo of Stoking Hate with 'Filth' Comments," *Guardian*, November 23, 2022, https://www.theguardian.com/us-news/2022/nov/23/teachers-union-randi-weingarten-pompeo.
44. "Failing Grade: Literacy in America," *The Policy Circle*, August 30, 2022, https://www.thepolicycircle.org/brief/literacy/.
45. Talia Kaplan, "'Woke' NYC School Curriculum Prompts Dad to Move Daughter to Florida," Fox News, April 26, 2021, https://www.foxnews.com/us/woke-nyc-school-curriculum-father-move-florida.
46. Dana Kennedy, "Inside the Growing Underground Network of Parents Fighting 'Anti-Racism' in NYC Schools," *New York Post*, April 24, 2021, https://nypost.com/2021/04/24/how-parents-are-fighting-critical-race-theory-in-nyc-schools/.
47. Ibid.
48. Sharp, "Parents of Kids at New England Private Schools."
49. Zoe Christen Jones, "Florida Governor Ron DeSantis Signs 'Parental Rights in Education' Bill into Law—Known by Critics as 'Don't Say Gay' Bill," CBS News, March 28, 2022, https://www.cbsnews.com/news/florida-desantis-dont-say-gay-bill-signed-parental-rights-in-education/.
50. See https://parentalrights.org/news/.

Chapter 5: Destroying Individualism

1. "Civil Disobedience: Thoreau in Jail," Libertarianism.org, https://www.libertarianism.org/publications/essays/civil-disobedience-thoreau-jail.

2. "March on Washington for Jobs and Freedom," National Park Service, August 4, 2020, https://www.nps.gov/articles/march-on-washington.htm.
3. Dr. Martin Luther King Jr., "I Have a Dream."
4. Rep. Dan Bishop's Twitter thread with details about the woke and equity inclusions in the 2022 Congressional Omnibus spending bill. See https://threadreaderapp.com/thread/1605253710753501186.html.
5. Asra Nomani, "The War on Merit Takes a Bizarre Turn: Why Are Administrators at a Top-Ranked Public High School Hiding National Merit Awards from Students and Families?" *City Journal*, December 21, 2022, https://www.city-journal.org/war-on-merit-takes-bizarre-turn. For video of Fairfax County Public Schools Superintendent Michelle Reid speaking about her desire for 'equal outcomes' for all students, see: https://www.youtube.com/watch?v=ujpcvIsMZBU.
6. See https://southcountyms.fcps.edu/academics/grading-policy.
7. Nomani, "The War on Merit."
8. Ibid.
9. Nick Minock, "Fairfax County Parents Call for Accountability after National Merit Award Scandal," ABC 7News, December 30, 2022, https://wjla.com/news/local/thomas-jefferson-high-school-delay-notifying-students-national-merit-awards-ann-bonitatibus-brandon-kosatka-tj-fairfax-county-fcps-parents-angry-top-ranked-northern-virginia-scadal-education-scholarship-college-admissions-demand-firing-investigation.
10. Ibid.
11. See the FCPS full statement: "Statement on Thomas Jefferson High School for Science and Technology Delay in Sharing National Merit Scholarship Corporation Recognitions," December 30, 2022, https://www.fcps.edu/news/statement-thomas-jefferson-high-school-science-and-technology-delay-sharing-national-merit.
12. Danielle Wallace, "Virginia AG Expands Probe after More than a Dozen Schools Withheld Merit Awards during 'Equity' Push," Fox News, January 17, 2023, https://www.foxnews.com/us/virginia-ag-expands-probe-more-than-dozen-schools-withheld-merit-awards-equity-push.
13. Ibid.
14. Sarah Mervosh and Ashley Wu, "Math Scores Fell in Nearly Every State, and Reading Dipped on National Exam," *New York Times*, October 24, 2022, https://www.nytimes.com/2022/10/24/us/math-reading-scores-pandemic.html.
15. Erica L. Green and Dana Goldstein, "Reading Scores on National Exam Decline in Half the States," *New York Times*, updated December 5, 2019, https://www.nytimes.com/2019/10/30/us/reading-scores-national-exam.html.
16. "PISA 2018 Worldwide Ranking—Average Score of Mathematics,

Science and Reading," FactsMap, https://factsmaps.com/pisa-2018-worldwide-ranking-average-score-of-mathematics-science-reading/.

17. "Programme for International Student Assessment (PISA) Results from PISA 2018," Organisation for Economic Co-operation and Development, https://www.oecd.org/pisa/publications/PISA2018_CN_USA.pdf.
18. Catrin Wigfall, "District Admin Growth 10x Greater than Student, Teacher, Growth," American Experiment, November 22, 2023, https://www.americanexperiment.org/district-admin-growth-10x-greater-than-student-teacher-growth/.
19. Sami Edge, "Oregon Again Says Students Don't Need to Prove Mastery of Reading, Writing or Math to Graduate, Citing Harm to Students of Color," *The Oregonian*, October 19, 2023, https://www.oregonlive.com/education/2023/10/oregon-again-says-students-dont-need-to-prove-mastery-of-reading-writing-or-math-to-graduate-citing-harm-to-students-of-color.html&subscribed=auth0%7C65f674342ab350666124f5a7.
20. Baker A. Mitchell Jr., "Why Johnny Still Can't Read," *National Review*, October 10, 2020, https://www.nationalreview.com/2020/10/public-schools-passing-students-who-cant-read/.
21. Doug Lederman, "Graduated but Not Literate," *Inside Higher Education*, December 15, 2005, https://www.insidehighered.com/news/2005/12/16/graduated-not-literate.
22. "New Study on the Literacy of College Students Finds Some Are Graduating with Only Basic Skills," American Institutes for Research, January 19, 2006, https://www.air.org/news/press-release/new-study-literacy-college-students-finds-some-are-graduating-only-basic-skills.
23. Ibid.
24. Martha C. White, "The Real Reason New College Grads Can't Get Hired," *Time*, November 10, 2013, https://business.time.com/2013/11/10/the-real-reason-new-college-grads-cant-get-hired/.
25. Meghan Marrin, "Why Business Leaders Think College Grads Aren't Ready to Work," Poets & Quants, August 10, 2023, https://poetsandquantsforundergrads.com/news/meghans-why-business-leaders-think-40-of-college-grads-are-not-ready-to-work/.
26. "Medical Schools That Don't Require the MCAT: What You Should Know," Inspira Advantage, August 9, 2022, https://www.inspiraadvantage.com/blog/medical-schools-that-dont-require-the-mcat-what-you-should-know.
27. Ilana Kowarski, "What the MCAT Test Is Like and How to Prepare," *U.S. News & World Report*, June 21, 2022, https://www.usnews.com/education/best-graduate-schools/top-medical-schools/articles/what-is-the-mcat-test-like-and-how-do-you-prepare-for-it.

28. Heather Mac Donald, "The Corruption of Medicine," *City Journal*, Summer 2022, https://www.city-journal.org/the-corruption-of-medicine.
29. Editorial Board, "Medical Education Goes Woke," *Wall Street Journal*, July 26, 2022, https://www.wsj.com/articles/medical-training-goes-woke-association-of-american-medical-colleges-doctors-11658871789.
30. Ibid.
31. See American Medical Association at https://www.ama-assn.org/.
32. "AMA Releases Plan Dedicated to Embedding Racial Justice and Advancing Health Equity," press release, American Medical Association, May 11, 2021, https://www.ama-assn.org/press-center/press-releases/ama-releases-plan-dedicated-embedding-racial-justice-and-advancing.
33. Ibid.
34. Sam Dorman, "American Medical Association Criticizes 'Equality as a Process' and 'Myth of Meritocracy' in New Equity Plan," Fox News, May 13, 2021, https://www.foxnews.com/us/american-medical-association-equity-plan.
35. "About Us," Do No Harm, https://donoharmmedicine.org/about/.
36. Dr. Stanley Goldfarb and Laura L. Morgan, "Top Med School Putting Wokeism ahead of Giving America Good Doctors," *New York Post*, September 2, 2022, https://nypost.com/2022/09/02/top-med-schools-putting-wokeism-ahead-of-giving-america-good-doctors/.
37. See https://donoharmmedicine.org/.
38. Goldfarb and Morgan, "Top Med School."
39. Jack Crowe, "UPenn Med School Leaders Turn on Former Dean over 'Racist' Affirmative-Action Criticism," *National Review*, June 1, 2022, https://www.nationalreview.com/news/upenn-med-school-leaders-turn-on-former-dean-over-racist-affirmative-action-criticism/.
40. Eric L. Gottlieb, "UpToDate Has a Racism Problem. Its Name Is Dr. Stanley Goldfarb," STAT, October 17, 2022, https://www.statnews.com/2022/10/17/uptodate-racism-problem-stanley-goldfarb/.
41. Brian Flood, "Doctor Blames 'Cancel Culture' on Losing Key Gig after Speaking Out against Liberal Ideology in Healthcare," Fox News, November 1, 2022, https://www.foxnews.com/media/doctor-blames-cancel-culture-losing-key-gig-speaking-out-against-liberal-ideology-healthcare.
42. Mac Donald, "The Corruption."
43. Ibid.
44. Kyle Morris, "Biden Administration Guidance Prioritizes Race in Administering COVID Drugs," Fox News, January 8, 2022, https://www.foxnews.com/politics/biden-administration-guidance-prioritizes-race-administering-covid-drugs.

45. Ibid.
46. Bram Wispelwey and Michelle Morse, "An Antiracist Agenda for Healthcare," *Boston Review*, March 17, 2021, https://www.bostonreview.net/articles/michelle-morsebram-wispelwey-what-we-owe-patients-case-medical-reparations/.
47. Sam Dorman, "NYC Chief Medical Officer Calls for Racial Preferences in Medical Care, Criticizes 'Colorblind' Practices," Fox News, March 29, 2021, https://www.foxnews.com/us/nyc-doctor-racial-preference-minorities-medical-care.

Chapter 6: The Bureaucratic Tyranny of Fear

1. Bertrand Russell, *An Outline of Intellectual Rubbish* (Girard, KS: Haldeman-Julius, 1943), https://www.scribd.com/document/184984359/An-Outline-of-Intellectual-Rubbish-1943.
2. Zeke Miller, "Hillary Clinton Says Half of Donald Trump's Supporters Are in 'Basket of Deplorables,'" *Time*, September 10, 2016, https://time.com/4486437/hillary-clinton-donald-trump-basket-of-deplorables/.
3. Adam Kelsey, "Behind Hillary Clinton's Basket of Deplorables Line," ABC News, September 13, 2016, https://abcnews.go.com/Politics/hillary-clintons-basket-deplorables-line/story?id=42069200.
4. Dan Merica and Sophie Tatum, "Clinton Expresses Regret for Saying 'Half' of Trump Supporters Are 'Deplorables,'" CNN, September 12, 2016, https://www.cnn.com/2016/09/09/politics/hillary-clinton-donald-trump-basket-of-deplorables/index.html.
5. Christopher Cadelago and Olivia Olander, "Biden Calls Trump's Philosophy 'Semi-Fascism,'" *Politico*, August 25, 2022, https://politi.co/3AJWC4V.
6. Douglas Murray, "Biden Calling Half the Country 'Fascist' Is a Cynical Political Ploy," *New York Post*, September 1, 2022, https://nypost.com/2022/09/01/biden-calling-half-the-country-fascist-is-a-cynical-political-ploy.
7. Steven Nelson, "If You Don't Agree with Majority, You Are 'Extreme': White House's Jean-Pierre," *New York Post*, September 1, 2022, https://nypost.com/2022/09/01/white-house-insists-bidens-speech-is-not-political.
8. Alexandra Hutzler, "Biden Attacks Trump and MAGA Republicans as Threat to American Democracy," ABC News, September 1, 2022, https://abcn.ws/3KzkQlL.
9. Julia Manchester, "Majority of Americans View Biden's Anti-MAGA Speech as Divisive: Poll," *Hill*, September 13, 2022, https://thehill.com/homenews/administration/3640627-majority-of-americans-view-bidens-anti-maga-speech-as-divisive-poll/.
10. Lee Brown, "Democrats Melt Down after CNN Hosts Criticize Biden

Speech," *New York Post*, September 2, 2022, https://nypost.com/2022/09/02/democrats-melt-down-after-cnn-hosts-criticize-biden-speech.

11. Alana Wise, "Biden Celebrates 'Triumph' of Democracy in Inaugural Address," NPR, January 20, 2021, https://www.npr.org/sections/inauguration-day-live-updates/2021/01/20/958793060/biden-celebrates-triumph-of-democracy-in-inaugural-address.
12. Susan Ferrechio, "Clinton Campaign Helped Create the Trump-Russia Conspiracy Theory, Durham Report Shows," *Washington Times*, May 20, 2023, https://www.washingtontimes.com/news/2023/may/20/durham-report-spotlights-how-clinton-campaign-help.
13. Ibid.
14. Ibid.
15. Steven Nelson, "Spy Chief Releases Docs on Claim Hillary Clinton Cooked Up Russia Scandal," *New York Post*, October 6, 2020, https://nypost.com/2020/10/06/spy-chief-releases-docs-on-claim-hillary-clinton-cooked-up-russia-scandal/.
16. Lauren Hirsch, "Can Elon Musk Make the Math Work on Owning Twitter? It's Dicey," *New York Times*, October 30, 2022, https://www.nytimes.com/2022/10/30/technology/elon-musk-twitter-debt.html.
17. Christopher Hutton, "Twitter Files: Tech Giant Was in 'Constant and Pervasive' Contact with FBI," *Washington Examiner*, December 16, 2022.
18. Jonathan Turley, "Congress Is Set to Expose What May Be the Largest Censorship System in U.S. History," *Hill*, February 4, 2023, https://thehill.com/opinion/judiciary/3843751-congress-is-set-to-expose-what-may-be-the-largest-censorship-system-in-u-s-history/.
19. Jacob Sullum, "The 5th Circuit Agrees That Federal Officials Unconstitutionally 'Coerced' or 'Encouraged' Online Censorship," *Reason*, September 11, 2023, https://reason.com/2023/09/11/the-5th-circuit-agrees-that-federal-officials-unconstitutionally-coerced-or-encouraged-online-censorship/.
20. Jose Cardenas, "Trump's Unheralded Border Success," *New York Post*, November 7, 2019, https://nypost.com/2019/11/07/trumps-unheralded-border-success/.
21. Ken Bredemeier, "Biden Signs Executive Orders Reversing Trump Immigration Policies," VOA, February 2, 2021, https://www.voanews.com/a/usa_biden-signs-executive-orders-reversing-trump-immigration-policies/6201520.html.
22. "Border Patrol Chiefs: Biden's Border Crisis Is 'Overwhelming,'" House Committee on Oversight and Accountability, February 7, 2023, https://oversight.house.gov/release/border-patrol-chiefs-bidens-border-crisis-is-overwhelming/.

23. Adam Shaw, Bill Melugin, and Griff Jenkins, "Southern Border Hit by Record Number of Migrant Encounters in a Single Day as Thousands Flood into Texas," Fox News, December 19, 2023, https://www.foxnews.com/politics/southern-border-record-number-migrant-encounters-single-day-thousands-flood-into-texas.
24. Bethany Blankley, "Illegal Border Crossers Total over 10 Million since Biden Inauguration," *Washington Examiner*, October 30, 2023, https://www.washingtonexaminer.com/news/illegal-border-crossers-total-over-10-million-since-biden-inauguration.
25. John Gramlich, "Migrant Encounters at the U.S.-Mexico Border Hit a Record High at the End of 2023," Pew Research Center, February 15, 2024, https://pewrsr.ch/42JsW4w.
26. Adam Shaw, Bill Melugin, Griff Jenkins, "Chinese Illegal Immigration on Pace to Break Records at US Southern Border," February 20, 2024, https://www.foxnews.com/politics/chinese-illegal-immigration-pace-break-records-us-southern-border.
27. Karen Townsend, "Illegal Immigrants Cross Northern Border at Record Levels," Hot Air, February 13, 2024, https://hotair.com/karen-townsend/2024/02/13/illegal-immigrants-cross-northern-border-at-record-levels-n3782833.
28. Bethany Blankley, "Officials Say Border Crisis Tied to Break-Ins Orchestrated by Columbians [*sic*], Chileans," *Washington Examiner*, December 22, 2023, https://www.washingtonexaminer.com/news/officials-say-border-crisis-tied-to-break-ins-orchestrated-by-columbians-chileans.
29. Senator Marco Rubio, "Biden's Open Border Is Bankrolling Organized Crime, Cartels," Fox News, May 25, 2023, https://www.foxnews.com/opinion/bidens-open-border-bankrolling-organized-crime-cartels.
30. Robert Hart, "Opioid Crisis Worse Now than Ever: Drug Overdose Deaths Spike Amid Fentanyl Surge," *Forbes,* May 3, 2023, https://www.forbes.com/sites/roberthart/2023/05/03/opioid-crisis-worse-now-than-ever-drug-overdose-deaths-spike-amid-fentanyl-surge/.
31. See National Center for Drug Abuse Statistics for additional research and details: https://drugabusestatistics.org/drug-overdose-deaths/.
32. Dr. Deborah Birx, *Silent Invasion* (New York: Harper, 2022).
33. Michael Senger, "Deborah Birx's Guide to Destroying a Country from Within," Brownstone Institute, July 14, 2022, https://brownstone.org/articles/deborah-birxs-guide-to-destroying-a-country-from-within/.
34. Jeffrey Tucker, "Dr. Birx Praises Herself While Revealing Ignorance, Treachery, and Deceit," Brownstone Institute, July 16, 2022, https://brownstone.org/articles/dr-birx-praises-herself-while-revealing-ignorance-treachery-and-deceit/.

35. Libby Emmons, "Dr. Deborah Birx Admits Being Deceitful When Recommending Covid Strategies to Trump," *Post Millennial*, July 17, 2022, https://thepostmillennial.com/dr-deborah-birx-admits-being-deceitful-when-recommending-covid-strategies-to-trump.
36. Birx.
37. Emmons, "Dr. Deborah Birx Admits."
38. "Dr. Deborah Birx: White House Virus Expert Quits over Holiday Travel," BBC, December 25, 2020, https://www.bbc.com/news/world-us-canada-55419954.
39. Ibid.
40. Lee Brown, "Deborah Birx Says She Took Thanksgiving Trip after Parents 'Stopped Eating,'" *New York Post*, December 23, 2020, https://nypost.com/2020/12/23/dr-birx-trip-came-after-parents-stopped-eating-and-drinking/.
41. "Dr. Deborah Birx," BBC.
42. Megan K. Stack, "Dr. Fauci Could Have Said a Lot More," *New York Times*, March 29, 2023, https://www.nytimes.com/2023/03/28/opinion/covid-lab-leak-theory-disinformation.html.
43. Michael G. Gordon and Warren P. Strobel, *Wall Street Journal*, "Lab Leak Most-Likely Origin of Covid-19 Pandemic, Energy Department Now Says," February 26, 2023, https://www.wsj.com/articles/covid-origin-china-lab-leak-807b7b0a.
44. Greg Wehner, "Fauci's Ex-Boss Now Says COVID-19 Lab Leak Theory Was Credible, Despite Previous Claims It Was a Distraction," Fox News, January 15, 2024, https://www.foxnews.com/politics/faucis-ex-boss-says-covid-lab-leak-theory-credible-despite-claims-distraction.
45. Michael Dorgan, "Fauci Admits Social Distancing Not Based on Science, 'Sort of Just Appeared,'" January 11, 2024, Fox News, https://www.foxnews.com/health/fauci-admits-social-distancing-not-based-science-sort-just-appeared.
46. "Wenstrup Releases Statement Following Dr. Fauci's Two-Day Testimony," House Committee of Oversight and Accountability, January 10, 2024, https://oversight.house.gov/release/wenstrup-releases-statement-following-dr-faucis-two-day-testimony/.
47. David Wallace-Wells, "Dr. Anthony Fauci Looks Back: Something Clearly Went Wrong," *New York Times Magazine*, April 24, 2023, https://www.nytimes.com/interactive/2023/04/24/magazine/dr-fauci-pandemic.html.
48. Jon Haworth and Emily Shapiro, "Fauci Sets Record Straight on Masks after Presidential Debate," ABC News, September 30, 2020, https://abcnews.go.com/Health/live-updates/coronavirus/fauci-sets-record-straight-on-masks-after-presidential-debate-73340738?id=73333438.

49. See https://x.com/kevinnbass/status/1749575650334130325?s=20.
50. Aundrea Cline-Thomas, "Timeline: How New York's Bail Reform Law Came to Be," CBS News, March 29, 2022, https://www.cbsnews.com/newyork/live-updates/new-york-bail-reform-timeline/.
51. Larry Celona, M'Niyah Lynn, and Tina Moore, "Major Crime Skyrockets 37% in NYC, NYPD Data Shows," *New York Post*, July 18, 2022, https://nypost.com/2022/07/18/major-crime-skyrockets-37-in-nyc-nypd-data-shows/.
52. Craig McCarthy and Nolan Hicks, "Major Crime in NYC Continues to Climb under Mayor Eric Adams—While NYPD Response Times Slow: Report," *New York Post*, September 15, 2023, https://nypost.com/2023/09/15/major-crime-in-nyc-continues-to-climb-under-mayor-eric-adams-while-nypd-response-times-slow-report/.
53. Paul Bedard, "As Crime Surges, 'Defund' Morphs to 'Defend' the Police," *Washington Examiner*, November 29, 2023, https://www.washingtonexaminer.com/news/washington-secrets/as-crime-surges-defund-morphs-to-defend-the-police.
54. Adam Shaw, "Gorsuch Gives Scathing Overview of COVID-Era: 'Fear and the Desire for Safety Are Powerful Forces,'" Fox News, May 20, 2023, https://www.foxnews.com/politics/gorsuch-gives-scathing-overview-covid-era-fear-desire-safety-powerful-forces.
55. Aristotle, Rhetoric, Book II, Part 5, trans. W. Rhys Roberts, Massachusetts Institute of Technology, http://classics.mit.edu/Aristotle/rhetoric.2.ii.html.
56. Lockdown Files Team, "Matt Hancock's Plan to 'Frighten the Pants Off Everyone' about Covid," *Telegraph*, March 4, 2023, https://www.telegraph.co.uk/news/2023/03/04/project-fear-covid-lockdown-files-matt-hancock-whatsapp/.
57. Ibid.
58. Rob Pattinson and Harry Cole, "Matt Hancock's Secret AFFAIR with Aide Exposed after Office Snogs during Covid," *Sun*, June 25, 2021, https://www.thesun.co.uk/news/15388014/matt-hancock-secret-affair-with-aide.
59. Emma Harrison, "Matt Hancock Quits as Health Secretary after Breaking Social Distance Guidance," BBC, June 27, 2021, https://www.bbc.com/news/uk-57625508.
60. Gordon Rayner, "Use of Fear to Control Behaviour in Covid Crisis Was 'Totalitarian,' Admit Scientists," *Telegraph*, May 14, 2021, https://www.telegraph.co.uk/news/2021/05/14/scientists-admit-totalitarian-use-fear-control-behaviour-covid/.
61. Ibid.
62. Ibid.
63. See https://covid19.public-inquiry.uk/.

64. David Pugliese, "Forged Letter Warning about Wolves on the Loose Part of Canadian Forces Propaganda Campaign That Went Awry," *National Post*, October 14, 2020, https://nationalpost.com/news/national/defence-watch/forged-letter-warning-about-wolves-on-the-loose-part-of-canadian-forces-propaganda-campaign-that-went-awry.
65. Ben Makuch, "Military Incompetence Unleashed a Wolf Psyop on Unsuspecting Canadians," *Vice*, October 16, 2020, https://www.vice.com/en/article/m7aqgp/military-incompetence-unleashed-a-wolf-psyop-on-unsuspecting-canadians.
66. Pugliese.
67. Karl Marx, "Critique of the Gotha Program," 1875, https://www.marxists.org/archive/marx/works/1875/gotha/ch01.htm.

Chapter 7: Propaganda and Witch Trials

1. Clarence Thomas, *My Grandfather's Son* (New York: Harper Perennial, 2008), 269.
2. Ibid, 248.
3. Matthew Choi, "Timeline: How an Allegation against Kavanaugh Came to Light and Shook Washington," *Politico*, September 19, 2018, https://www.politico.com/story/2018/09/19/kavanaugh-allegation-timeline-829983.
4. Senator Ron Johnson, "An American Coup Attempt," *Wall Street Journal*, October 8, 2020, https://www.wsj.com/articles/an-american-coup-attempt-11602181261.
5. Alana Abramson, "James Comey Had a Friend Leak His Memo about President Trump," *Time*, June 8, 2017, https://time.com/4811044/james-comey-testimony-media-leaks/.
6. Thomas, 269–70.
7. Tom Elliott, "Why the Racist Left Smears Clarence Thomas as an 'Angry Black Man,'" *Federalist*, July 5, 2022, https://thefederalist.com/2022/07/05/why-the-racist-left-smears-clarence-thomas-as-an-angry-black-man/.
8. Jess Blumberg, "A Brief History of the Salem Witch Trials," *Smithsonian Magazine*, October 23, 2007, https://www.smithsonianmag.com/history/a-brief-history-of-the-salem-witch-trials-175162489/.
9. Haley Sweetland Reynolds, "How Christine Blasey Ford's Testimony Changed America," *Time*, October 4, 2018, https://time.com/5415027/christine-blasey-ford-testimony/.
10. Megan Keller, "Dem Senator Says 'We're Not in a Court of Law' When Asked about Presumption of Innocence for Kavanaugh," *Hill*, September 24, 2018, https://thehill.com/homenews/senate/408100-dem-sen-says-were-not-in-a-court-of-law-when-asked-about-presumption-of/.

11. Valerie Richardson, "Chris Coons: Burden of Proof Lies with Brett Kavanaugh to Prove His Innocence," *Washington Times*, September 25, 2018, https://www.washingtontimes.com/news/2018/sep/25/chris-coons-burden-proof-lies-brett-kavanaugh-prov/.
12. Mairead McArdle, "Kavanaugh Accuser Admits She Fabricated Allegations as a 'Ploy' for 'Attention,'" *National Review*, November 3, 2018, https://www.nationalreview.com/news/kavanaugh-accuser-admits-she-fabricated-allegations/.
13. Jessica Kegu, "Brett Kavanaugh Accuser Deborah Ramirez 'Willing to Testify,' Attorney Says," CBS News, September 26, 2018, https://www.cbsnews.com/news/brett-kavanaugh-second-accuser-deborah-ramirez-lawyer/.
14. Amy Taxin, "Michael Avenatti Sentenced to 14 Years in California Fraud Case," PBS, December 5, 2022, https://www.pbs.org/newshour/politics/michael-avenatti-sentenced-to-14-years-in-california-fraud-case.
15. See https://www.grassley.senate.gov/news/news-releases/swetnick-avenatti-referred-criminal-investigation.
16. See https://www.grassley.senate.gov/search?as_sitesearch=&client=grassley&num=15&numgm=3&q=swetnick.
17. Theodor Reik, *The Compulsion to Confess* (New York: Farrar, Straus & Cudahy, 1959).
18. Mollie Hemingway, "Blasey Ford Attorney Admits Abortion Support 'Motivated' Anti-Kavanaugh Accusations," *Federalist*, September 4, 2019, https://thefederalist.com/2019/09/04/blasey-ford-attorney-admits-abortion-supported-motivated-anti-kavanaugh-accusations/.
19. Jessica Chasmar, "Alleged Kavanaugh Assassination Attempt Latest Instance of Violence, Intimidation Toward Pro-lifers," Fox News, June 9, 2022, https://www.foxnews.com/politics/kavanaugh-assassination-attempt-violence-intimidation-pro-lifers.
20. Adam Sabes, "Brett Kavanaugh Attempted Murder Suspect Nicholas Roske Pleads Not Guilty," June 22, 2022, https://www.foxnews.com/politics/brett-kavanaugh-attempted-murder-suspect-nicholas-roske-pleads-not-guilty.
21. Patrick Reilly, "Feds Indict California Man Found with Gun near Kavanaugh's Home," *New York Post*, June 15, 2022, https://nypost.com/2022/06/15/feds-indict-california-man-nicholas-john-roske-found-with-gun-near-kavanaughs-home/.
22. Nikolas Lanum, "Media, Democratic Rhetoric toward Kavanaugh, Supreme Court under Scrutiny after Assassination Attempt," Fox News, June 10, 2022, https://www.foxnews.com/media/media-democratic-rhetoric-kavanaugh-supreme-court.

23. Gregg Jarrett, "Hillary Clinton Was the Mastermind behind the Trump-Russia Collusion Hoax and May Never Face Justice," Fox News, February 15, 2022, https://www.foxnews.com/opinion/hillary-clinton-trump-russia-collusion-hoax-justice-gregg-jarrett.
24. Gregg Jarrett, "Trump-Russia 'Collusion' Was Always a Hoax—and Dirtiest Political Trick in Modern US History," Fox News, March 25, 2019, https://www.foxnews.com/opinion/gregg-jarrett-trump-russia-collusion-was-always-a-hoax-and-dirtiest-political-trick-in-modern-us-history.
25. Ibid.
26. Tom Cotton, "Tom Cotton: Send in the Troops," *New York Times*, June 3, 2020, https://www.nytimes.com/2020/06/03/opinion/tom-cotton-protests-military.html.
27. Ibid.
28. Rishika Dugyala, "NYT Opinion Editor Resigns after Outrage over Tom Cotton Op-Ed," *Politico*, June 6, 2020, https://www.politico.com/news/2020/06/07/nyt-opinion-bennet-resigns-cotton-op-ed-306317.
29. David Rutz, "Former New York Times Editor Blasts Newspaper over Tom Cotton Op-ed Fiasco: 'Threw Me in the Garbage,'" Fox News, October 18, 2022, https://www.foxnews.com/media/former-new-york-times-editor-blasts-newspaper-tom-cotton-op-ed-fiasco-threw-garbage.
30. Bari Weiss's Twitter thread, June 4, 2020, https://twitter.com/bariweiss/status/1268628680797978625.
31. Bari Weiss, "Resignation Letter," BariWeiss.com, June 2020, https://www.bariweiss.com/resignation-letter.
32. Ibid.
33. Sara Fischer, "Exclusive: Bari Weiss Reveals Business Plan for Buzzy New Media Startup," Axios, December 13, 2022, https://www.axios.com/2022/12/13/bari-weiss-business-plan-free-press.
34. Joseph A. Wulfsohn, "NY Times Editorial Board Member Who Opposed Tom Cotton Op-Ed Now Supports Hochul Sending Troops to NYC," Fox News, March 7, 2024, https://www.foxnews.com/media/ny-times-editorial-board-member-opposed-tom-cotton-op-ed-supports-hochul-sending-troops-nyc.
35. See RealClearPolling, https://www.realclearpolling.com/polls/state-of-the-union/direction-of-country.
36. Jonathan Allen, "New York to Deploy 750 National Guard Soldiers to Check Bags on Subway," Reuters, March 8, 2024, https://www.reuters.com/world/us/new-york-deploy-750-national-guard-soldiers-check-bags-subway-2024-03-06/.
37. Mara Gay, "The National Guard Might Make Subway Riders Feel Safer,"

New York Times, March 6, 2024, https://www.nytimes.com/live/2024/03/05/opinion/thepoint/nyc-subway-crime-national-guard?smid=url-share.

38. Zachary Faria, "The Hypocrisy of Hochul's National Guard Theatre Is Shameless," *Washington Examiner*, March 7, 2024, https://www.washingtonexaminer.com/opinion/beltway-confidential/2908621/the-hypocrisy-of-hochuls-national-guard-theater-is-shameless/.
39. Georgia Worrell, Rich Calder, "Gov. Kathy Hochul Claims National Guard Subway Plan 'Working as Expected,' Even after Man Shot with Own Gun on Train," *New York Post*, March 16, 2024, https://nypost.com/2024/03/16/us-news/hochul-national-guard-subway-plan-working-as-we-expected/.
40. David Mastio, "USA Today Demoted Me for a Tweet—Because Its Woke Newsrooms Are Out of Touch with Readers," *New York Post*, June 23, 2022, https://nypost.com/2022/06/23/usa-today-demoted-me-for-a-tweet-because-the-companys-woke-newsrooms-are-out-of-touch-with-readers/.
41. Andy Meek, "Fox News Channel Has Now Spent 20 Years in the #1 Spot on the Cable News Rankings," *Forbes*, February 1, 2022, https://www.forbes.com/sites/andymeek/2022/02/01/fox-news-channel-has-now-spent-20-years-in-the-1-spot-on-the-cable-news-rankings/.
42. Brian Flood, "Fox News Channel Crushes Cable Competition in 2023, Finishes as Most-Watched Network for the 8th Straight Year," Fox News, December 14, 2023, https://www.foxnews.com/media/fox-news-channel-crushes-competition-2023-finishes-most-watched-network-eighth-straight-year.
43. Mark Joyella, "Fox News Channel Makes History: 22 Consecutive Years at Number One," *Forbes*, January 30, 2024, https://www.forbes.com/sites/markjoyella/2024/01/30/fox-news-channel-makes-history-as-it-marks-22-consecutive-years-at-number-one/.
44. Lexi Lonas, "More Democrats Watch Fox News during Prime Time than CNN: Data," *Hill*, November 4, 2021, https://thehill.com/homenews/media/580171-more-democrats-watch-fox-news-during-primetime-than-cnndata/.
45. Caleb Howe, "Fox News Beats Cable and Broadcast Rivals as News Source Voters 'Most Often Turn To'—NYT/Sienna Poll," Mediaite, December 21, 2023, https://www.mediaite.com/news/fox-news-beats-cable-and-broadcast-rivals-as-news-source-voters-most-often-turn-to-nyt-sienna-poll/.

Chapter 8: Manipulating Reality

1. John F. Kennedy, "Remarks on the 20th Anniversary of the Voice of America," Papers of John F. Kennedy, Presidential Papers, President's Office Files, February 26, 1962, https://www.jfklibrary.org/asset-viewer/archives/JFKPOF/037/JFKPOF-037-02.

2. Ibid.
3. "Soviet Influence at WWII Voice of America," Cold War Radio Museum, December 2, 2019, https://www.coldwarradiomuseum.com/communist-mata-hari-at-wwii-voice-of-america/.
4. Ted Lipien, "Beware of Government Propaganda Experts," VOA80, June 10, 2022, https://www.voa80.com/2022/06/10/beware-of-government-propaganda-experts/.
5. Ibid.
6. Edward R. Murrow, "A Report on Senator Joseph R. McCarthy," *See It Now*, CBS TV, March 9, 1954, http://www.plosin.com/beatbegins/archive/Murrow540309.htm.
7. "Aug. 31, 1920: News Radio Makes News," *Wired*, August 21, 2018, https://www.wired.com/2010/08/0831first-radio-news-broadcast/.
8. "Herb Morrison: Hindenburg Disaster 1937," National Archives, https://www.archives.gov/exhibits/eyewitness/html.php?section=5.
9. David Shedden, "Today in Media History: Hindenburg Explodes and a Reporter Cries Out, 'Oh, the Humanity,'" Poynter Institute, May 6, 2015, https://www.poynter.org/reporting-editing/2015/today-in-media-history-hindenburg-explodes-and-a-reporter-cries-out-oh-the-humanity/.
10. Cary O'Dell, "Crash of the *Hindenburg* (Herbert Morrison, reporting) (May 6, 1937)," Library of Congress, 2002, https://www.loc.gov/static/programs/national-recording-preservation-board/documents/Hindenburg.pdf.
11. "Orson Welles's 'War of the Worlds' Radio Play Is Broadcast," History Channel, https://www.history.com/this-day-in-history/welles-scares-nation.
12. Peter Tonguette, "The Fake News of Orson Welles," *Humanities* 39, no. 4 (Fall 2018), https://www.neh.gov/article/fake-news-orson-welles-war-worlds-80.
13. Ibid.
14. Khaleda Rahman, "Black Lives Matter Chicago Organizer Defends Looting: 'That's Reparations,'" *Newsweek*, August 12, 2020, https://www.newsweek.com/black-lives-matter-chicago-defends-looting-reparations-1524502.
15. Tim Haines, "MSNBC's Ali Velshi Downplays Riot in Front of Burning Building: 'Mostly a Protest,' 'Not Generally Speaking Unruly,'" RealClearPolitics, May 28, 2020, https://www.realclearpolitics.com/video/2020/05/28/msnbcs_ali_velshi_downplays_riot_in_front_of_burning_building_mostly_a_protest_not_generally_speaking_unruly.html.
16. Christine Rosen, "Mostly Peaceful: The Birth of an Excuse," *Commentary*, October 2020, https://www.commentary.org/articles/christine-rosen/media-excuse-destructive-violent-riots/.
17. William Glaberson, "Increasingly, Reporters Say They're Democrats," *New*

York Times, November 18, 1992, https://www.nytimes.com/1992/11/18/us/increasingly-reporters-say-they-re-democrats.html.

18. Editorial Board, "Pretty Much All of Journalism Now Leans Left, Study Shows," *Investors Business Daily*, November 16, 2018, https://www.investors.com/politics/editorials/media-bias-left-study/.
19. Isaac Schorr, "Study Finds That Just 3.4% of American Journalists Are Republicans," *Mediaite*, December 27, 2023, https://www.mediaite.com/news/study-finds-that-just-3-4-of-american-journalists-are-republicans/.
20. Axios "media trust" headline search, retrieved at https://www.axios.com/results?q=media%20trust.
21. Brian Flood, "CNN, MSNBC's Ratings Collapse Due to 'Serious Credibility Problem' Covering Biden, Experts Say," Fox News, June 29, 2021, https://www.foxnews.com/media/cnn-msnbc-serious-credibility-problem.
22. Feliz Salmon, "Media Trust Hits New Low," Axios, January 21, 2021, https://www.axios.com/2021/01/21/media-trust-crisis.
23. David Bauder and the Associated Press, "Trust in Media Is So Low That Half of Americans Now Believe That News Organizations Deliberately Mislead," *Fortune*, February 15, 2023, https://fortune.com/2023/02/15/trust-in-media-low-misinform-mislead-biased-republicans-democrats-poll-gallup/.
24. Mark Joyella, "CNN's Ratings Collapse: Prime Time Down Nearly 70% in Key Demo," *Forbes*, February 21, 2022, https://www.forbes.com/sites/markjoyella/2022/02/21/cnns-ratings-collapse-prime-time-down-nearly-70-in-key-demo/.
25. Daniel J. Boorstin, *The Image: A Guide to Pseudo-Events in America*, 50th Anniversary Edition (New York: Vintage Books, 1992).
26. Ibid., 19.
27. Ibid., 39.
28. Ibid., 35.
29. Thomas David Kehoe, "Thirteen Similarities between Donald Trump and Adolf Hitler," Medium, September 18, 2020, https://tdkehoe.medium.com/thirteen-similarities-between-donald-trump-and-adolf-hitler-3a97a8055dde.
30. David Lee Preston, "Is It Wrong to Compare Trump to Hitler? No," *Philadelphia Inquirer*, January 27, 2021, https://www.inquirer.com/opinion/commentary/trump-hitler-insurrection-autocracy-holocaust-january-6-20210127.html.
31. Devan Cole, "Top House Democrats Compare Trump's Rise to Hitler's," CNN, March 20, 2019, https://www.cnn.com/2019/03/20/politics/james-clyburn-trump-hitler-comparison/index.html.

32. Fadel Allassan, "Poll: 58% of Biden Voters Say Vote Is More 'Against' Trump than 'For' Biden," Axios, August 16, 2020, https://www.axios.com/2020/08/16/biden-trump-poll-against.
33. Adam B. Vary, "Superman Changes Motto to 'Truth, Justice and a Better Tomorrow,' Says DC Chief," *Variety*, October 16, 2021, https://variety.com/2021/film/news/superman-new-motto-dc-fandome-1235090712/.
34. David L. Altheide, *Creating Fear: News and the Construction of Crisis* (New York: Aldine De Gruyter, 2002), 63.
35. Ibid., 60.
36. Ibid., 59–60.
37. See https://threadreaderapp.com/thread/1362128126273347586.html.
38. Tammy Bruce, "How Rush Limbaugh Helped Me Rethink Being a Leftist," RealClearPolitics, February 18, 2021, https://www.realclearpolitics.com/2021/02/18/how_rush_limbaugh_helped_me_rethink_being_a_leftist_536335.html.
39. Judith Miller, "Rise and Fall of New York Times Writer Bari Weiss—a Victim of Far-Left Intolerance," Fox News, July 15, 2020, https://www.foxnews.com/opinion/new-york-times-bari-weiss-judith-miller.

Chapter 9: A Climate of Crisis

1. Daniel Botkin, "Global Warming Delusions," *Wall Street Journal*, October 17, 2007, https://www.wsj.com/articles/SB119258265537661384.
2. Ibid.
3. Andy Pudzer, "The Startling News about Trump's Economy That Mainstream Media Ignored," Fox Business, September 28, 2022, https://www.foxbusiness.com/economy/trump-economy-mainstream-media-andy-puzder.
4. Noel Sheppard, "Krugman: Scientists Should Falsely Predict Alien Invasion So Government Will Spend More Money," Newsbusters, May 26, 2012, https://newsbusters.org/blogs/nb/noel-sheppard/2012/05/26/Krugman-scientists-should-falsely-predict-alien-invasion-so.
5. Sami Adler, "How Much Would It Cost to End Climate Change," Global Giving, March 1, 2021, https://www.globalgiving.org/learn/cost-to-end-climate-change/.
6. "GNP/GNI by Country 2022," *World Population Review*, 2022, https://worldpopulationreview.com/country-rankings/gnp-by-country.
7. Brandon Gillespie, "Kennedy Stumps Biden Official on $50 Trillion Cost to Fight Climate Change: 'You Don't Know, Do You?'" Fox News, May 6, 2023, https://www.foxnews.com/politics/kennedy-stumps-biden-official-fifty-trillion-price-tag-climate-change.
8. Editorial Board, "Global Warming: A Back Door to Socialism—and

Now Even the UN Admits It," *Investor's Business Daily*, January 16, 2014, https://www.investors.com/politics/editorials/climate-change-a-back-door-to-communism-and-the-united-nations-admits-it/.

9. Ibid.
10. Asher Kohen, "It's Amazing Just How Many Americans Served in World War II," Timeline, May 8, 2016, https://timeline.com/its-amazing-just-how-many-americans-served-in-world-war-ii-18d197a685ca.
11. "World War II Casualties by Country 2022," *World Population Review*, https://worldpopulationreview.com/country-rankings/world-war-two-casualties-by-country.
12. Jeff Haden, "How Would You Feel about a 94% Tax Rate?" CBS News, December 7, 2011, https://www.cbsnews.com/news/how-would-you-feel-about-a-94-tax-rate/.
13. Thomas Kaplan, "Bernie Sanders Proposes a Wealth Tax: 'I Don't Think That Billionaires Should Exist,'" *New York Times*, September 24, 2019, updated July 16, 2020, https://www.nytimes.com/2019/09/24/us/politics/bernie-sanders-wealth-tax.html.
14. Martin Gould, "Take a Peek at 'Best Known Millionaire Socialist' Bernie Sanders' Three Homes—One in D.C.," *Daily Mail*, February 20, 2020, https://www.dailymail.co.uk/news/article-8025835/Take-peak-best-known-millionaire-socialist-Bernie-Sanders-three-homes.html.
15. "A Voyeur's Guide to the Homes of Washington's Rich and Famous," *Washingtonian*, October 9, 2016, https://www.washingtonian.com/2016/10/09/voyeurs-guide-homes-washingtons-rich-famous/.
16. Umar Irfan, "5 Things to Know about Bernie Sanders's Aggressive Climate Strategy," Vox, February 19, 2020, https://www.vox.com/2020/2/19/21142923/bernie-sanders-climate-change-policy-plan-2020.
17. Stephen Daggett, "Costs of Major U.S. Wars," Congressional Research Service, June 29, 2010, https://sgp.fas.org/crs/natsec/RS22926.pdf.
18. "The Green New Deal," Bernie Sanders, https://berniesanders.com/issues/green-new-deal/.
19. Post Editorial Board, "Climate Fanatics Now Target BREATHING—Proving How Much They Hate Humanity," *New York Post*, December 21, 2023, https://nypost.com/2023/12/21/opinion/climate-fanatics-target-breathing-proof-they-hate-humanity/.
20. Ibid.
21. David A. Graham, "Gaffe Track: Hillary's Employment Plan for Coal Miners," *Atlantic*, March 14, 2016, https://www.theatlantic.com/politics/archive/2016/03/gaffe-track-hillarys-employment-plan-for-coal-miners/624681/.

22. Martina Stewart, "Emotional Unemployed W.Va. Coal Worker Confronts Hillary Clinton over Comment about Putting Coal 'Out of Business,'" *Washington Post*, May 3, 2016, https://www.washingtonpost.com/news/morning-mix/wp/2016/05/03/unemployed-w-va-coal-worker-confronts-clinton-over-comment-about-putting-coal-out-of-business/.
23. Jennifer Skene, "Toilet Paper Is Driving the Climate Crisis with Every Flush," Natural Resources Defense Council Expert Blog, June 24, 2020, https://www.nrdc.org/experts/jennifer-skene/toilet-paper-driving-climate-crisis-every-flush.
24. Jon Sufrin, "TP Free: Why I Stopped Using Toilet Paper (and You Should, Too)," *Globe and Mail*, April 1, 2018, https://www.theglobeandmail.com/life/first-person/article-tp-free-why-i-stopped-using-toilet-paper-and-you-should-too/.
25. Ari Natter, "A US Government Agency Will Move to Regulate Gas Stoves as New Research Links Them to Childhood Asthma. 'This Is a Hidden Hazard,' Said an Official," Bloomberg, January 9, 2023, https://www.bloomberg.com/news/articles/2023-01-09/us-safety-agency-to-consider-ban-on-gas-stoves-amid-health-fears.
26. "Get to Know Us," RMI, https://rmi.org/about/.
27. Breanne Deppisch, "What to Know about the Study behind the Push to Ban Gas Stoves," *Washington Examiner*, January 11, 2023, https://www.washingtonexaminer.com/news/209154/what-to-know-about-the-study-behind-the-push-to-ban-gas-stoves/.
28. Brady Seals, Manager at RMI, LinkedIn, posted January 4, 2023, retrieved February 2024, https://www.linkedin.com/posts/bradyanneseals_population-attributable-fraction-of-gas-stoves-activity-7016406994584567808-A6B0/.
29. See https://www.mdpi.com/1660-4601/20/1/75.
30. See Google search result: https://www.google.com/search?q=gas+stoves+12.7%25+asthma+children.
31. Thomas Catenacci, "Schumer Roasted for Saying 'Nobody Is Taking Away Your Gas Stove' Just Months before NY Banned Gas Stoves," Fox News, May 4, 2023, https://www.foxnews.com/politics/schumer-roasted-saying-nobody-taking-away-your-gas-stove-months-before-ny-banned.
32. Adele Peters, "The Government Is Coming for Gas Stoves, It's Just Not the Federal Government," *Fast Company*, January 4, 2023, https://www.fastcompany.com/90834734/gas-stoves-cities-states-ban.
33. Janet Nguyen, "Why It's Hard to Put a Price Tag on Plans like the Green New Deal," Marketplace, October 8, 2020, https://www.marketplace.org/2020/10/08/why-its-hard-to-put-a-price-tag-on-plans-like-the-green-new-deal/.
34. Justin Haskins, "Democrats' 'Green New Deal' Is a Crazy New Deal That

Would Be a Disaster for Us All," Fox News, February 7, 2019, https://www.foxnews.com/opinion/democrats-green-new-deal-is-a-crazy-new-deal-that-would-be-a-disaster-for-us-all.

35. Eleanor Cummins, "What the Green New Deal Could Mean for Our Homes and Communities," *Architectural Digest*, October 29, 2020, https://www.architecturaldigest.com/story/what-green-new-deal-means-for-you.
36. Danielle Kurtzleben, "Rep. Alexandria Ocasio-Cortez Releases Green New Deal Outline," NPR, February 7, 2019, https://www.npr.org/2019/02/07/691997301/rep-alexandria-ocasio-cortez-releases-green-new-deal-outline.
37. Glenn Kessler, "Ocasio-Cortez's 70-Percent Tax Rate: Not So Radical," *Washington Post,* January 31, 2019, https://www.washingtonpost.com/politics/2019/01/31/ocasio-cortezs-percent-tax-rate-not-so-radical/.
38. Editorial Board, "50 Years of Predictions That the Climate Apocalypse Is Nigh," *New York Post*, November 12, 2021, https://nypost.com/2021/11/12/50-years-of-predictions-that-the-climate-apocalypse-is-nigh/.
39. Ibid.
40. Ibid.
41. Ibid.
42. Michael Shellenberger, *Apocalypse Never: Why Environmental Alarmism Hurts Us All* (New York: Harper, 2020).
43. Michael Shellenberger, "Why Apocalyptic Claims about Climate Changes Are Wrong," *Forbes*, November 25, 2019, https://www.forbes.com/sites/michaelshellenberger/2019/11/25/why-everything-they-say-about-climate-change-is-wrong/?sh=9e9bb4c12d6a.
44. Ibid.
45. Bjørn Lomborg, "Bjorn Lomborg: 'Climate Alarm' Is as Big a Threat as Climate Change—It Leads to Anxious Lives and Bad Policies," Sky News, September 10, 2020, https://news.sky.com/story/bjorn-lomborg-climate-alarm-is-a-bigger-threat-than-climate-change-it-leads-to-anxious-lives-and-bad-policies-12067383.
46. Ibid.
47. Richard Harris, "Putting a Financial Spin on Global Warming," NPR, June 24, 2009, https://www.npr.org/2009/06/24/105834436/putting-a-financial-spin-on-global-warming.
48. Ted Nordhaus and Michael Shellenberger, "Allay or Adapt? The Real Climate Change Debates Is about Technology," *Scientific American*, October 2, 2014, https://www.scientificamerican.com/article/allay-or-adapt-the-real-climate-change-debate-is-about-technology/.

49. "Ag and Food Sectors and the Economy," US Department of Agriculture Economic Research Service, February 24, 2022, https://www.ers.usda.gov/data-products/ag-and-food-statistics-charting-the-essentials/ag-and-food-sectors-and-the-economy/.
50. Carolyn Dimitri, Anne Effland, and Neilson Conklin, "The 20th Century Transformation of U.S. Agriculture and Farm Policy," US Department of Agriculture Economic Research Service, June 2005, https://www.ers.usda.gov/webdocs/publications/44197/13566_eib3_1_.pdf.
51. Robert Hoshowsky, "Putting Oil Industry By-Products to Work," *Resource in Focus*, August 2020, https://resourceinfocus.com/2020/08/the-future-of-fertilizer/.
52. See https://twitter.com/KriteeKanko/status/1518102124713938948.
53. Chris Cameron, "Climate Activist Dies after Setting Himself on Fire at Supreme Court," *New York Times*, April 24, 2022, https://www.nytimes.com/2022/04/24/us/politics/climate-activist-self-immolation-supreme-court.html.
54. Ibid.
55. Annie Correal, "What Drove a Man to Set Himself on Fire in Brooklyn," *New York Times*, May 28, 2018, https://www.nytimes.com/2018/05/28/nyregion/david-buckel-fire-prospect-park-fossil-fuels.html.
56. Paul Bois, "Climate Activists Hail Man Who Burned Himself Alive on SCOTUS Steps," Breitbart News, April 24, 2022, https://www.breitbart.com/politics/2022/04/24/self-sacrifice-climate-activists-hail-man-burned-himself-alive-supreme-court-steps/.
57. Alex Epstein, "A Humanist Approach to Environmental Issues," *Forbes*, January 29, 2015, https://www.forbes.com/sites/alexepstein/2015/01/29/a-humanist-approach-to-environmental-issues/?sh=2b429a18607e.
58. Les Knight, "I Campaign for the Extinction of the Human Race," *Guardian*, January 10, 2020, https://www.theguardian.com/lifeandstyle/2020/jan/10/i-campaign-for-the-extinction-of-the-human-race-les-knight.
59. Todd May, "Would Human Extinction Be a Tragedy?" *New York Times*, December 17, 2018, https://www.nytimes.com/2018/12/17/opinion/human-extinction-climate-change.html.
60. Ibid.
61. Ibid.
62. Denis Campbell, "Women Who Suffer Domestic Abuse Three Times as Likely to Attempt Suicide," *Guardian*, February 22, 2023, https://www.theguardian.com/society/2023/feb/22/women-who-suffer-domestic-abuse-three-times-as-likely-to-attempt-suicide.
63. "Sui Genocide," *Economist*, December 17, 1998, https://www.economist.com/christmas-specials/1998/12/17/sui-genocide.

64. Ibid.
65. Ibid.
66. Bois, "Climate Activists."
67. Michael Shellenberger, "Why Apocalyptic Claims about Climate Changes Are Wrong," *Forbes*, November 25, 2019, https://www.forbes.com/sites/michaelshellenberger/2019/11/25/why-everything-they-say-about-climate-change-is-wrong/?sh=9e9bb4c12d6a.
68. Sheril Kirshenbaum, "No, Climate Change Will Not End the World in 12 Years," *Scientific American*, August 13, 2019, https://blogs.scientificamerican.com/observations/no-climate-change-will-not-end-the-world-in-12-years/.
69. Brady Dennis and Steven Mufson, "Keystone XL Pipeline Developer Pulls Plug on Controversial Project," *Washington Post*, June 9, 2021, https://www.washingtonpost.com/climate-environment/2021/06/09/keystone-pipeline-dead/.
70. Claudia Tenney, "New York Leads America off a Renewable-Energy Cliff," *Wall Street Journal*, May 11, 2022, https://www.wsj.com/articles/new-york-leads-america-off-an-energy-cliff-natural-gas-fossil-fuels-pipelines-shale-11652296744.
71. "What Is U.S. Electricity Generation by Energy Source?" US Department of Energy, Energy Information Administration, February 2022, https://www.eia.gov/tools/faqs/faq.php?id=427&t=3.
72. Charles Lane, "A Scientist's Inconvenient Truth about Decarbonizing Our Economy," *Washington Post*, May 25, 2022, https://www.washingtonpost.com/opinions/2022/05/25/inconvenient-truths-about-decarbonizing-economy/.

Chapter 10: BLM's Toxic Agenda of Fear

1. "Harris on BLM Riots: 'Beware, They're Not Gonna Stop,'" YouTube, June 2020, https://pjmedia.com/news-and-politics/matt-margolis/2021/01/07/kamala-harris-called-riots-a-movement-last-summer-said-they-should-not-stop-n1310640.
2. Thomas Barrabi, "Flashback: Kamala Harris Said Nationwide Protests Are 'Not Going to Stop,'" Fox News, September 24, 2020, https://www.foxnews.com/politics/flashback-kamala-harris-nationwide-protests-not-going-to-stop.
3. Mia Cathell, "Antifa Terrorize Portland Residents, Business Owners on Election Night: 'Whoever They Vote For, We Are Ungovernable,'" *Post Millennial*, November 4, 2020, https://thepostmillennial.com/antifa-terrorize-portland-residents-business-owners-on-election-night-whoever-they-vote-for-we-are-ungovernable.
4. Jeffrey C. Kummer and Nicholas Boge-Burroughs, "Last 2 Officers In-

volved in George Floyd's Death Are Sentenced to Prison," *New York Times*, July 27, 2022, https://www.nytimes.com/2022/07/27/us/george-floyd-j-alexander-kueng.html.

5. Jay Senter and Shaila Dewan, "Killer of George Floyd Sentenced to 21 Years for Violating Civil Rights," *New York Times*, July 7, 2022, https://www.nytimes.com/2022/07/07/us/derek-chauvin-george-floyd-sentence.html.
6. Rachel Treisman, "Minneapolis Reaches $27 Million Settlement with Family of George Floyd," NPR, March 12, 2021, https://www.npr.org/2021/03/12/976525200/minneapolis-reaches-27-million-settlement-with-family-of-george-floyd.
7. Larry Buchanan, Quoctrung Bui, and Jugal Patel, "Black Lives Matter May Be the Largest Movement in U.S. History," *New York Times*, July 3, 2020, https://www.nytimes.com/interactive/2020/07/03/us/george-floyd-protests-crowd-size.html.
8. Zamira Rahim and Rob Picheta, "Thousands around the World Protest George Floyd's Death in Global Display of Solidarity," CNN, June 1, 2020, https://www.cnn.com/2020/06/01/world/george-floyd-global-protests-intl/index.html.
9. Emma Colton, "Rahm Emanuel Reprises 'Never Let a Crisis Go to Waste' Catchphrase amid Coronavirus Pandemic," *Washington Examiner*, March 24, 2020, https://www.washingtonexaminer.com/news/rahm-emanuel-reprises-never-let-a-crisis-go-to-waste-catchphrase-amid-coronavirus-pandemic.
10. Paul Sacca, "Black Lives Matter Founder Admits Org's Creators Are 'Trained Marxists,' BLM's Goal Is to 'Get Trump Out,'" The Blaze, June 20, 2020, https://www.theblaze.com/news/black-lives-matter-founder-marxist-trump.
11. Buchanan, Bui, and Patel, "Black Lives Matter May Be the Largest Movement in U.S. History."
12. Jason Rantz, "Violent Antifa Turn to New Tactic, Embrace Violent Insurgency," *Newsweek*, May 3, 2021, https://www.newsweek.com/violent-antifa-turn-new-tactic-embrace-violent-insurgency-opinion-1587975.
13. "Mike Gonzalez," Heritage Foundation, https://www.heritage.org/staff/mike-gonzalez.
14. Mike Gonzalez, "Congress Should Investigate the Black Lives Matter Riots," Heritage Foundation, January 3, 2023, https://www.heritage.org/progressivism/commentary/congress-should-investigate-the-black-lives-matter-riots.
15. Ibid.
16. Gillian Flaccus, "Portland's Grim Reality: 100 Days of Protests, Many

Violent," Associated Press, September 4, 2020, https://apnews.com/article/virus-outbreak-ap-top-news-race-and-ethnicity-id-state-wire-or-state-wire-b57315d97dd2146c4a89b4636faa7b70.

17. Stephanie Pagones, "Protests, Riots That Gripped America in 2020," Fox News, December 29, 2020, https://www.foxnews.com/us/protests-riots-nationwide-america-2020.
18. Jennifer A. Kingson, "Costliest U.S. Civil Disorders," Axios, September 16, 2020, https://www.axios.com/2020/09/16/riots-cost-property-damage.
19. Brad Polumbo, "George Floyd Riots Caused Record-Setting $2 Billion in Damage, New Report Says. Here's Why the True Cost Is Even Higher," Foundation for Economic Education, September 16, 2020, https://fee.org/articles/george-floyd-riots-caused-record-setting-2-billion-in-damage-new-report-says-here-s-why-the-true-cost-is-even-higher/.
20. Joy Pullmann, "Study: Up to 95 Percent of 2020 U.S. Riots Are Linked to Black Lives Matter," *Federalist*, September 16, 2020, https://thefederalist.com/2020/09/16/study-up-to-95-percent-of-2020-u-s-riots-are-linked-to-black-lives-matter/.
21. Ibid.
22. Andy Ngo, "Why Portland Police Stand By Passively When Leftists Riot," *Newsweek*, February 29, 2020, https://www.newsweek.com/why-portland-police-stand-passively-when-leftists-riot-1489799.
23. Katie Kull, "Man Sentenced to Life for Killing Retired St. Louis Police Capt. David Dorn," *St. Louis Post-Dispatch*, October 5, 2022, https://www.stltoday.com/news/local/crime-and-courts/man-sentenced-to-life-for-killing-retired-st-louis-police-capt-david-dorn/article_86456436-9538-5da9-9785-a01ef6fd3278.html.
24. Ann Dorn, "My Husband Capt. David Dorn Was Murdered in 2020 Riots. His Killer Had Help Dividing America," Fox News, August 23, 2022, https://www.foxnews.com/opinion/husband-dorn-murdered-riots-killer-help-dividing-america.
25. Representatives Steve Scalise and Randy Feenstra, "This Is What Democrats' Soft-on-Crime Insanity Does to American Families," Fox News, February 25, 2023, https://www.foxnews.com/opinion/this-is-what-democrats-soft-crime-insanity-does-american-families.
26. Emma Colton, "BLM Silent When Confronted with Data Showing Massive 2020 Spike in Black Murder Victims," Fox News, April 19, 2022, https://www.foxnews.com/us/black-lives-matter-silent-2020-black-murder-spike-experts-blm-defund-contributed.
27. Tom Cotton, "The BLM Effect," *National Review*, July 29, 2021, https://www.nationalreview.com/2021/07/the-blm-effect/.
28. Ibid.

29. Ibid.
30. See https://blacklivesmatter.com/.
31. Black Lives Matter website, "Herstory," https://blacklivesmatter.com/herstory/.
32. Daniel Greenfield, "Black Livers Matter Leaders Support Violent Riots and Looting, Biden Won't Condemn Them," *Israel National News*, October 3, 2020, https://www.israelnationalnews.com/news/288292.
33. Jerusalem Demas, "The Effects of Black Lives Matter Protests," Vox, April 9, 2021, https://www.vox.com/22360290/black-lives-matter-protest-crime-ferguson-effects-murder.
34. "Alicia Garza," Influence Watch, 2023, https://www.influencewatch.org/person/alicia-garza/.
35. Mike Gonzalez, "To Destroy America," *City Journal*, September 1, 2020, https://www.city-journal.org/marxist-revolutionaries-black-lives-matter.
36. "Weather Underground Bombings," Federal Bureau of Investigation, https://www.fbi.gov/history/famous-cases/weather-underground-bombings.
37. "Weather Underground," Counter Extremism Project, 2023, https://www.counterextremism.com/supremacy/weather-underground.
38. M4BL Policy Platform, https://m4bl.org/policy-platforms/end-jails-prisons-detention/.
39. Policy Platform, "End the War on Black Communities," Movement for Black Lives, 2023, https://m4bl.org/policy-platforms/end-the-war-on-black-communities/.
40. Policy Platform, "Vision for Black Lives," Movement for Black Lives, 2023, https://m4bl.org/policy-platforms/.
41. "What We Believe," archived page on the Black Lives Matter website, https://web.archive.org/web/20200408020723/https://blacklivesmatter.com/what-we-believe/.
42. Karl Marx and Friedrich Engels, "Chapter II: Proletarians and Communists," in *The Communist Manifesto*, 1848, https://www.marxists.org/archive/marx/works/1848/communist-manifesto/ch02.htm.
43. Tammy Bruce, "It's for the Children," AMAC, September 6, 2023, https://amac.us/newsline/education/its-for-the-children/.
44. A Woman Resident of Russia, "The Russian Effort to Abolish Marriage," *Atlantic*, July 1926, https://www.theatlantic.com/magazine/archive/1926/07/the-russian-effort-to-abolish-marriage/306295/.
45. Ibid.
46. Jennifer Wilson, "When the Harlem Renaissance Went to Communist Moscow," *New York Times*, August 21, 2017, https://www.nytimes.com/2017/08/21/opinion/when-the-harlem-renaissance-went-to-communist-moscow.html.

47. GianCarlo Canaparo and Abby Kassal, "Who Suffers the Most from Crime Wave?" Heritage Foundation, April 12, 2022, https://www.heritage.org/crime-and-justice/commentary/who-suffers-the-most-crime-wave.
48. Marissa Edmund, "Number of People Shot to Death by the Police in the United States from 2017 to 2023, by Race," Statista, January 2023, https://www.statista.com/statistics/585152/people-shot-to-death-by-us-police-by-race/.
49. "Gun Violence Disproportionately and Overwhelmingly Hurts Communities of Color," Center for American Progress, June 30, 2022, https://www.americanprogress.org/article/gun-violence-disproportionately-and-overwhelmingly-hurts-communities-of-color/.
50. "Law Enforcement Facts," National Law Enforcement Officers Memorial Fund, 2023, https://nleomf.org/memorial/facts-figures/law-enforcement-facts/.
51. Tim Stelloh, "Most Officers Never Fire Their Guns. But Some Kill Multiple People—and Are Still on the Job," NBC News, April 22, 2021, https://www.nbcnews.com/news/us-news/most-officers-never-fire-their-guns-some-kill-multiple-people-n1264795.
52. Dana Rubenstein and Jeffery C. Mays: "Nearly $1 Billion Is Shifted from Police in Budget That Pleases No One," *New York Times*, June 30, 2020, updated August 10, 2020, https://www.nytimes.com/2020/06/30/nyregion/nypd-budget.html.
53. "LAPD Budget to Be Cut by $150 Million; Decision Triggered by Widespread Protests," City News Service, November 7, 2020, https://www.nbclosangeles.com/news/local/lapd-budget-to-be-cut-by-150-million-decision-triggered-by-widespread-protests/2456578/.
54. Fola Akinnibi, Sarah Holder, and Christopher Cannon, "Cities Say They Want to Defund the Police. Their Budgets Say Otherwise," Bloomberg, January 12, 2021, https://www.bloomberg.com/graphics/2021-city-budget-police-funding/.
55. Paul Best, "Austin Police, 911 Staffing Levels Questioned after Street Racers Take Over Major Intersection, Injure Cop," Fox News, February 19, 2023, https://www.foxnews.com/us/austin-police-911-staffing-levels-questioned-street-racers-take-major-intersection-injure-cop.
56. "Minneapolis Voters Reject Plan to Overhaul City Policing," Minnesota Public Radio, November 2, 2021, https://www.mprnews.org/story/2021/11/02/minneapolis-police-ballot-vote.
57. James Barron, "Why Police Officers Are Leaving: Low Pay, Overwork and High Costs," *New York Times*, December 14, 2022, https://www.nytimes.com/2022/12/14/nyregion/nypd-pay-work-costs.html.
58. Bernard Condon, Jim Mustian, and Adrian Sainz, "Amid Soaring Crime,

Memphis Cops Lowered the Bar for Hiring," Associated Press, February 7, 2023, https://apnews.com/article/law-enforcement-tyre-nichols-memphis-crime-93033874b99a4893c6c996fd56676795.

59. Jonathan Frankling and Russell Lewis, "5 Memphis Ex-Police Are Charged with Murder and Jailed over the Death of Tyre Nichols," NPR, January 26, 2023, https://www.npr.org/2023/01/26/1151721800/memphis-officers-charged-tyre-nichols-murder.
60. Associated Press, "Tyre Nichols Case Highlights US Police Recruiting and Retention Crisis," *Guardian*, February 8, 2023, https://www.theguardian.com/us-news/2023/feb/08/police-tyre-nichols-memphis-recruitment-retention.
61. Emily Cochrane and Rick Rojas, "The Questions That Remain a Year After Tyre Nichol's Death," *New York Times*, February 14, 2024, https://www.nytimes.com/article/tyre-nichols-memphis-police-dead.html.
62. Jamie Thompson, "Nobody Wants to Be the World's Villain," *New York Times*, February 28, 2023, https://www.nytimes.com/2023/02/28/magazine/louisville-police-department.html.
63. Ibid.
64. Peter Charalambous, "'Vicious Cycle': Inside the Police Recruiting Crunch with Resignations on the Rise," ABC News, April 6, 2023, https://abcnews.go.com/US/police-departments-face-vicious-cycle-challenges-retaining-recruiting/story?id=98363458.
65. Tina Moore and Dean Balsamini, "NYPD Cops Leave Force in Alarming Rate—over 2,500 Turned In Badges So Far in 2023," *New York Post*, November 25, 2023, https://nypost.com/2023/11/25/metro/2516-nypd-cops-head-for-exits-so-far-in-2023-pension-data/.
66. Joe Schoffstall, "Dem-Run City Drops Six Figures to Repaint BLM Street Mural as Crime Skyrockets," Fox News, November 29, 2023, https://www.foxnews.com/politics/dem-run-city-drops-six-figures-repaint-blm-street-mural-crime-skyrockets.
67. Ibid.
68. Lydia Saad, "Personal Safety Fears at Three-Decade High in U.S.," Gallup, November 16, 2023, https://news.gallup.com/poll/544415/personal-safety-fears-three-decade-high.aspx.
69. Ibid.
70. Editorial Board, "NY's Leaders Just Ignore Post's Proof That No-Bail Feeds Soaring Crime," *New York Post*, July 31, 2022, https://nypost.com/2022/07/31/nys-leaders-just-ignore-posts-proof-that-no-bail-feeds-soaring-crime/.
71. Zack Smith and Charles Stimson, "It's Not Just Rising Crime: Rogue Prosecutors Are a Huge Problem," Heritage Foundation, February 7, 2022,

https://www.heritage.org/crime-and-justice/commentary/its-not-just-rising-crime-rogue-prosecutors-are-huge-problem.

72. Musadiq Bidar, "San Francisco Votes Overwhelmingly to Recall Progressive DA Chesa Boudin," CBS News, June 8, 2022, https://www.cbsnews.com/news/chesa-boudin-san-francisco-da-recalled/.
73. Tiffany Hsu, "Corporate Voices Get Behind 'Black Lives Matter' Cause," *New York Times*, updated June 10, 2020, retrieved at https://www.nytimes.com/2020/05/31/business/media/companies-marketing-black-lives-matter-george-floyd.html.
74. Joe Schoffstall, "BLM Co-Founder Patrisse Cullors Says Group Flooded with 'White guilt money,'" Fox News, May 16, 2022, retrieved at https://www.foxnews.com/politics/blm-patrisse-cullors-group-flooded-white-guilt-money.
75. Jon Brown, "'Trained Marxist' BLM Co-Founder Patrisse Cullors Inks Warner Bros. TV Deal," Daily Wire, October 19, 2020, retrieved at https://www.dailywire.com/news/trained-marxist-blm-co-founder-patrisse-cullors-inks-warner-bros-tv-deal.
76. Warner Todd Huston, "Ex-BLM Leader Patrisse Cullors Preps Warner Bros. Projects Focused on Slavery Reparations," Breitbart, January 30, 2022, retrieved at https://www.breitbart.com/entertainment/2022/01/30/ex-blm-leader-patrisse-cullors-preps-warner-bros-projects-focused-on-reparations/.
77. Maya King, "Black Lives Matter Power Grab Sets off Internal Revolt," Politico, December 10, 2020, retrieved at https://www.politico.com/news/2020/12/10/black-lives-matter-organization-biden-444097.
78. Sean Campbell, "BLM Mystery: Where Did the Money Go?," *New York Magazine*, January 31, 2022, retrieved at https://nymag.com/intelligencer/2022/01/black-lives-matter-finances.html.
79. Sean Campbell, "Black Lives Matter Secretly Bought a $6 Million House," *New York Magazine*, April 4, 2022, retrieved at https://nymag.com/intelligencer/2022/04/black-lives-matter-6-million-dollar-house.html.
80. Andrew Kerr and Jerry Dunleavy, "Clintonworld Steps Away from Black Lives Matter on Eve of Financial Disclosure," *Washington Examiner*, May 13, 2022, https://www.washingtonexaminer.com/news/1074475/clintonworld-steps-away-from-black-lives-matter-on-eve-of-financial-disclosure/.
81. Isabel Vincent, "BLM Hires Clinton Aide Who Paid for Steele Dossier to Sort Shady Finances," *New York Post*, February 17, 2022, https://nypost.com/2022/02/17/blm-hires-clinton-aide-marc-elias-who-paid-for-steele-dossier/.
82. Jonathan Turley, "New Financial Controversies Rock BLM as Marc

Elias Reportedly Ends 'Key Role' with the Group," JonathanTurley .org, May 18, 2022, https://jonathanturley.org/2022/05/18/new-financial -controversies-rock-blm-as-marc-elias-reportedly-leaves-board/.

83. Kerr and Dunleavy, "Clintonworld Steps Away."

Conclusion: Breaking the Spell

1. Anaïs Nin, *The Diary of Anaïs Nin, 1939–1944*, ed. Gunther Stuhlmann, vol. 3, (New York: Harcourt, Brace & World, 1969), 125.
2. Karl Marx and Friedrich Engels, "The Communist Manifesto," 1848, https://www.marxists.org/archive/marx/works/1848/communist-manifesto /ch01.htm.
3. Lisa Marshall, "Skeletal Remains Debunk Myth Surrounding 1918 Spanish Flu Pandemic," October 9, 2023, https://phys.org/news/2023 -10-skeletal-debunk-myth-flu-pandemic.html.
4. Merriam-Webster, s.v. "courage," https://www.merriam-webster.com /dictionary/courage.
5. James Bickerton, "How Bud Light Sales Are Faring Six Months since Devastating Boycott," *Newsweek*, September 30, 2023, https://www .newsweek.com/how-bud-light-sales-are-faring-six-months-since -devastating-boycott-1831111.
6. Gabriel Hays, "12-Year-Old Boy Booted from Class over Gadsden Flag Patch on Backpack: 'Origins with Slavery,'" Fox News, August 29, 2023, https://www.foxnews.com/media/12-year-old-boy-booted-class-gadsden -flag-patch-backpack-origins-slavery.
7. Yaron Steinbuch and Ronny Reyes, "Middle Schooler Allowed to Display 'Don't Tread on Me' Patch after Mom Accuses School of Violating His First Amendment Rights," *New York Post*, August 30, 2023, https:// nypost.com/2023/08/30/mom-of-student-kicked-out-over-flag-claims-it -violated-his-first-amendment-rights/.
8. See https://www.monticello.org/.
9. Thomas Jefferson Monticello Foundation, "Firearms," https://www .monticello.org/research-education/thomas-jefferson-encyclopedia/firearms/.

BIBLIOGRAPHY

Altheide, David L. *Creating Fear: News and the Construction of Crisis.* New Brunswick, NJ: Aldine Transaction, 2015.

Arendt, Hannah. *The Origins of Totalitarianism.* New York, NY: Harcourt Brace Jovanovich, 1973.

Aristotle. *Aristotle's Art of Rhetoric.* Translated by Robert C. Bartlett. Chicago, IL: University of Chicago Press, 2021.

Bauman, Zygmunt. *Liquid Fear.* Cambridge, UK: Polity Press, 2006.

Beck, Glenn, and Justin Haskins. *The Great Reset: Joe Biden and the Rise of 21st Century Fascism.* Brentwood, TN: Forefront Books, 2022.

Birx, Deborah L. *Silent Invasion: The Untold Story of the Trump Administration, Covid-19, and Preventing the Next Pandemic Before It's Too Late.* New York, NY: Harper, 2022.

Bloom, Allan. *The Closing of the American Mind: How Higher Education Has Failed Democracy and Impoverished the Souls of Today's Students.* New York, NY: Simon & Schuster, 2012.

Boorstin, Daniel J. *The Image: A Guide to Pseudo-Events in America.* New York, NY: Knopf Doubleday Publishing Group, 2012.

Bradbury, Ray. *Fahrenheit 451: The Temperature at Which Book Paper Catches Fire and Burns.* New York, NY: Simon & Schuster, 2012.

Bruce, Tammy. *The Death of Right and Wrong: Exposing the Left's Assault on Our Culture and Values.* New York, NY: Three River Press / Crown, 2003.

Bruce, Tammy. *The New Thought Police: Inside the Left's Assault on Free Speech and Free Minds.* New York, NY: Prima / Random House, 2001.

Burke, Edmund. *A Philosophical Enquiry into the Origin of Our Ideas of the Sublime and Beautiful.* Mineola, NY: Dover Publications, 2008.

Cassirer, Ernst. *The Myth of the State*. New Haven, CT: Yale University Press, 2013.

de Becker, Gavin. *Fear Less: Real Truth about Risk, Safety, and Security in a Time of Terrorism*. New York, NY: Little, Brown & Co., 2002.

de Becker, Gavin. *The Gift of Fear: Survival Signals That Protect Us from Violence*. New York, NY: Little, Brown and Company, 1997.

Dodsworth, Laura. *State of Fear: How the UK Government Weaponised Fear during the COVID-19 Pandemic*. London, UK: Pinter & Martin, 2021.

Eller, Jonathan R., ed. *Remembrance: Selected Correspondence of Ray Bradbury*. New York, NY: Simon & Schuster, 2023. Kindle edition.

Epstein, Joseph. *Envy*. New York, NY: Oxford University Press, 2003.

Ferraro, Kenneth F. *Fear of Crime: Interpreting Victimization Risk*. Albany, NY: State University of New York Press, 1995.

Forward, Susan, and Donna Frazier. *Emotional Blackmail: When the People in Your Life Use Fear, Obligation, and Guilt to Manipulate You*. New York, NY: Harper, 2019.

Furedi, Frank. *How Fear Works: Culture of Fear in the Twenty-First Century*. New York, NY: Bloomsbury Continuum, 2019.

Furedi, Frank. *Politics of Fear beyond Left and Right*. London, UK: Bloomsbury Continuum, 2006.

Gardner, Dan. *The Science of Fear: Why We Fear the Things We Shouldn't—and Put Ourselves in Greater Danger*. New York, NY: Dutton, 2008.

Goldberg, Jonah. *Liberal Fascism: The Secret History of the American Left from Mussolini to the Politics of Change*. New York, NY: Forum, 2009.

Gonzalez, Mike. *BLM: The Making of a New Marxist Revolution*. New York, NY: Encounter Books, 2021.

Gonzalez, Mike. *The Plot to Change America: How Identity Politics Is Dividing the Land of the Free*. New York, NY: Encounter Books, 2022. Kindle edition.

Hegseth, Pete. *Battle for the American Mind: Uprooting a Century of Miseducation*. New York, NY: Broadside Books, 2022.

Hemingway, Mollie Ziegler, and Carrie Severino. *Justice on Trial: The Kavanaugh Confirmation and the Future of the Supreme Court*. Washington, DC: Regnery Publishing, 2020.

Hemingway, Mollie Ziegler. *Rigged: How the Media, Big Tech, and the Democrats Seized Our Elections*. Washington, DC: Regnery Publishing / Salem Media Group, 2021.

Hendershott, Anne B. *The Politics of Envy*. Manchester, NH: Crisis Publications, 2020.

Herbert, Frank. *Dune*. Vol. 1. 15 vols. New York, NY: Penguin Books, 2016.

Horowitz, David. *I Can't Breathe: How a Racial Hoax Is Killing America*. Washington, DC: Regnery Publishing, 2021.

Horowitz, David. *Radical Son: A Generational Odyssey*. New York, NY: Simon & Schuster, 1998.

Houck, Davis W. *FDR and Fear Itself: The First Inaugural Address*. College Station, TX: Texas A & M University Press, 2002.

Huxley, Aldous. *Brave New World*. New York, NY: Everyman's Library, 2013.

Jarrett, Gregg. *The Russia Hoax: The Illicit Scheme to Clear Hillary Clinton and Frame Donald Trump*. New York, NY: Broadside Books, 2019.

Jarrett, Gregg. *Witch Hunt: The Story of the Greatest Mass Delusion in American Political History*. New York, NY: Broadside Books, 2019.

Kimball, Roger. *Tenured Radicals: How Politics Has Corrupted Our Higher Education*. Chicago, IL: Ivan R. Dee, 2008.

Kolk, Bessel van der. *The Body Keeps the Score: Brain, Mind, and Body in the Healing of Trauma*. New York, NY: Penguin Books, 2015.

Lasch, Christopher. *The Culture of Narcissism American Life in an Age of Diminishing Expectations*. New York, NY: W. W. Norton & Company, 2018.

Lasch, Christopher. *The Revolt of the Elites and the Betrayal of Democracy*. New York, NY: W. W. Norton & Company, 1996. Kindle edition.

Levin, Mark R. *American Marxism*. New York, NY: Threshold Editions, 2023.

Lewis, C. S., and Walter Hooper. *Present Concerns: Journalistic Essays*. New York, NY: HarperOne, 2017. Kindle edition.

Lomborg, Bjørn. *False Alarm: How Climate Change Panic Costs Us Trillions, Hurts the Poor, and Fails to Fix the Planet*. New York, NY: Basic Books, 2021.

Marable, Manning, and Leith Mullings, eds. *Let Nobody Turn Us Around: Voices of Resistance, Reform, and Renewal: An African American Anthology*. New York, NY: Rowman & Littlefield, 2000.

Marsh, Abigail. *The Fear Factor: How One Emotion Connects Altruists, Psychopaths, and Everyone In-Between*. New York, NY: Basic Books, 2017.

Marx, Karl, and Friedrich Engels. *The Communist Manifesto*. San Diego, CA: Booklover's Library Classics, 2021.

Maté, Gabor. *The Myth of Normal: Trauma, Illness, and Healing in a Toxic Culture*. New York, NY: Avery / Penguin Random House, 2022.

McWhorter, John H. *The Language Hoax*. New York, NY: Oxford University Press, 2016.

Mullis, Kary. *Dancing Naked in the Mind Field*. New York, NY: Vintage Books, 2000.

Murray, Douglas. *The Madness of Crowds: Gender, Race and Identity*. New York, NY: Bloomsbury Continuum, 2021.

Nin, Anaïs. *The Diary of Anaïs Nin*. Edited by Gunther Stuhlmann. Vol. 3. 7 vols. New York, NY: Harcourt Brace Jovanovich, 1969.

Orwell, George, and George Packer. *All Art Is Propaganda*. Boston, MA: Mariner Books, 2021.

Orwell, George. *1984*. Boston, MA: Houghton Mifflin Harcourt, 2021.

Orwell, George. *Animal Farm*. New York, NY: Signet Classic, 1996.

Orwell, George. *Fascism and Democracy*. New York, NY: Penguin Books, 2020.

Orwell, George. *George Orwell: Volume 1: An Age Like This, 1920–1940*. Edited by Ian Angus and Sonia Orwell. Boston, MA: Cavid R. Godine, 2000.

Orwell, George. *Politics and the English Language: And Other Essays*. London, UK: Benediction Classics, 2009.

Peck, M. Scott. *People of the Lie: The Hope for Healing Human Evil*. New York, NY: Simon and Schuster, 1998.

Pieper, Josef. *Abuse of Language, Abuse of Power*. Translated by Lothar Krauth. San Francisco, CA: Ignatius Press, 1992.

Ramaswamy, Vivek. *Woke, Inc: Inside Corporate America's Social Justice Scam*. New York, NY: Center Street, 2021.

Rawls, John. *A Theory of Justice (Revised)*. Cambridge, MA: Belknap Press / Harvard University Press, 1999.

Reik, Theodore. *The Compulsion to Confess: On the Psychoanalysis of Crime and of Punishment*. New York, NY: Farrar, Straus & Cudahy, 1959.

Robin, Corey. *Fear: The History of a Political Idea*. New York, NY: Oxford University Press, 2004.

Sarkis, Stephanie. *Gaslighting: Recognize Manipulative and Emotionally Abusive People—and Break Free*. New York, NY: Da Capo / Hachette, 2021. Kindle edition.

Schulman, Sarah. *Conflict Is Not Abuse: Overstating Harm, Community Responsibility, and the Duty of Repair*. Vancouver, BC, Canada: Arsenal Pulp Press, 2021.

Schweizer, Peter. *Red-Handed: How America's Most Powerful People Help China Win*. New York, NY: Harper, 2022.

Shellenberger, Michael. *Apocalypse Never: Why Environmental Alarmism Hurts Us All*. New York, NY: Harper, 2020.

Short, Philip. *Pol Pot: Anatomy of a Nightmare*. New York, NY: Henry Holt, 2006. Kindle edition.

Stanley, Jason. *How Fascism Works: The Politics of Us and Them*. New York, NY: Random House, 2020.

Starkstein, Sergio E. *A Conceptual and Therapeutic Analysis of Fear*. Cham, Switzerland: Palgrave Macmillan, 2018.

Stein, Alexandra. *Terror, Love and Brainwashing: Attachment in Cults and Totalitarian Systems*. New York, NY: Routledge, 2021.

Stern, Robin. *The Gaslight Effect: How to Spot and Survive the Hidden Manipulations Other People Use to Control Your Life*. New York, NY: Harmony Books, 2018. Kindle edition.

Taras, Raymond C. *Fear and the Making of Foreign Policy: Europe and Beyond*. Edinburgh, Scotland: Edinburgh University Press, 2015.

Thomas, Clarence, and Mark Paoletta. *Created Equal: Clarence Thomas in His Own Words*. Edited by Michael Pack. Washington, , DC: Regnery Publishing, 2024. Kindle edition.

Thomas, Clarence. *My Grandfather's Son: A Memoir*. New York, NY: Harper Perennial, 2008.

Virilio, Paul. *The Administration of Fear*. Cambridge, MA: Semiotext(e) / MIT Press, 2012.

INDEX

ABOUT THE AUTHOR

Tammy Bruce, an independent conservative, is the *New York Times* bestselling author of *The Death of Right and Wrong*, and is a podcast host, columnist, speaker, and Fox News Contributor. After a history in the 1990s of being a leftist community organizer, she now works to make sure her that experience is used to expose and help defeat the leftist agenda. *Fear Itself* is her fourth book.

In 2005 she joined Fox News as a political contributor. In addition to providing commentary and political analysis on a variety of the network's shows, she frequently serves as a guest host for various programs. Ms. Bruce's column appears weekly at AMAC.us, and she has been profiled, and her editorials and commentaries on significant social issues have been published, in a wide variety of magazines and newspapers including the *New York Times*, the *Los Angeles Times*, *USA Today*, the *Washington Times*, the *Guardian*, the *San Francisco Chronicle*, *Esquire*, and the *Advocate*, among others.

In addition to her weekly column, Ms. Bruce also speaks to a variety of groups nationwide, including college, business, and civic organizations about a range of topics, including her most requested commentary, "Contrary to Popular Belief: How Conservative Ideals Empower Women, Gays, and Blacks." In 2022, she was the recipient of Log Cabin Republicans' Spirit of Lincoln award, which honors "individuals who exemplify a commitment to enhancing personal freedom, encouraging individual responsibility, and ensuring equality under the law for all Americans."

A native of Los Angeles, Ms. Bruce holds a bachelor's degree in political science from the University of Southern California, from which she graduated cum laude. Ms. Bruce notes her interest in politics and individual liberty was sparked during her childhood, in part because of the work of authors Ray Bradbury and George Orwell, both of whom remain her favorite writers. Ms. Bruce lives in New York and is routinely bossed around by Ruby, her mini Australian shepherd.